IMPERIAL CADDY

IMPERIAL CADDY

THE RISE OF DAN QUAYLE IN AMERICA AND THE DECLINE AND FALL OF PRACTICALLY EVERYTHING ELSE

—

JOE QUEENAN

HYPERION

NEW YORK

Portions of the following works are used here by permission:

Cat's Cradle © 1964 Kurt Vonnegut

Imperial Masquerade © 1990 Lewis Lapham

Nixon Agonistes © 1969, 1970 Garry Wills

Book design by Margaret Wagner

Library of Congress Cataloging-in-Publication Data

Queenan, Joe.
    Imperial caddy : the rise of Dan Quayle in America and the decline
and fall of practically everything else / Joe Queenan.—1st ed.
        p.   cm.
    ISBN 1-56282-939-4
    1. Quayle, Dan, 1947-   —Humor.   2. Vice-presidents—United
States—Humor.   3. United States—Politics and government—1989-
—Humor.   I. Title.
E840.8.Q28Q44   1992
973.928'092—dc20   92-25271
                                                                 CIP

FIRST EDITION

10   9   8   7   6   5   4   3   2   1

TO FRANCESCA

ACKNOWLEDGMENTS

I would like to thank my editor, Patricia Mulcahy; my agents, Joe and Janis Vallely; and my friend Christopher Leo Taylor for their help in producing this book. Thanks also to Garry Trudeau for the Beatles material in Chapter 4, and to John Brodie and Bob Mack for the Lee Atwater material, which also appears in Chapter 4. Finally, thanks to my sister Eileen, a single mother, who thinks politicians should be seen but not heard.

CONTENTS

Contents

IMPERIAL CADDY

I

THE MEANING OF QUAYLE

So tonight, I am one humble Hoosier, whose efforts to devote part
of his life to public service have led him here.

—DAN QUAYLE, during his acceptance speech,
August 18, 1988

The American vice presidency is an inherently bizarre institution, whose
closest historical parallel is the "cage" system that prevailed under the
Turkish sultanate a few hundred years ago. In this system, the reigning
sultan's immediate successor—be it brother, son, cousin—was kept
under house arrest in the imperial court until the sultan died, thus
ensuring that the next-in-line could not head an insurrection. Upon the
sultan's death, the cage door was unlocked and the prisoner immediately became the most powerful man in the empire.

This was a strange way to prepare royalty for assuming their imperial duties, particularly in those instances where the heirs apparent
spent three decades in the cage and emerged from them utterly insane.
But, on balance, it was probably only slightly stranger than anointing
a little-known senator from Indiana as the second most powerful man
on the planet, and then telling him to spend eight years at funerals in
Ecuador and hospital-wing openings in Oak Park, Illinois, trying as
hard as possible not to make a fool of himself.

Dan Quayle is a figure of utter mirth in this society, the nightly butt
of cruel jokes by Jay Leno, David Letterman, and many other humor-
ists, some of them spectacularly gifted, some less so. Polls assure us that
a substantial portion of the American population is dismayed by the

thought of a Quayle presidency, an impression that was reinforced when George Bush experienced his mysterious breathing problems in 1991, and then fainted while visiting Japan in January 1992.

For the past four years, we have all been regaled with tales about Quayle's unenviable military record, his wife's esoteric religious practices, his foibles on the fairways, his underdeveloped appreciation of foreign cultures, his father's extremist political beliefs. He is, we are assured again and again, no John Kennedy (though, as time goes by, it is becoming apparent that John Kennedy himself was no John Kennedy). The overriding questions that any serious biographer would seek to answer is: How did a person like this ever get himself elected vice president, and what does his position a heartbeat away from the presidency say about the future of our fragile democracy?

These, however, are not the questions that I will be seeking to answer. The questions that I will be seeking to answer are:

1. If Dan Quayle becomes president tomorrow, is there any way I can hedge my portfolio to avoid a total bloodbath?
2. If not, would I be better off in stocks or bonds when the market meltdown occurs?
3. If Dan Quayle is likely to become the next president of the United States, either because Bush dies or he is elected on his own merits in 1996, should I be investing in Dan Quayle autographs, Dan Quayle anatomically correct dolls, or Dan Quayle campaign buttons? What kinds of prices should I be paying? Which dealers are the best?

I do not mean to imply that these are the only questions under consideration. The burning issue of whether Quayle is as awkward, unsophisticated, and generally dim as he is made out to be by the media has never been effectively resolved; the press, which is contemptuous of Quayle's intellect, and envious of the good fortune that has smiled on him throughout most of his career, looks down on him, adopting the same sneering attitude that it manifested toward Ronald Reagan: Never mind the votes in the Electoral College; this guy is a moron. Still, not even conservative Republicans are eager to defend the vice president against his detractors, and no one has ever voiced the opinion that Dan Quayle would make a supremely desirable chief executive. This is not the way that IBM or Exxon or General Foods establishes its chain of succession. This is not the way they do things at Apple or Mobil or Wells Fargo. Why, even Manny's Lube and Muffler has a more carefully thought-out contingency plan in the event that Manny unexpectedly gets hit by a truck.

Thus we come to the interesting question of what this society thinks that it's doing by having Dan Quayle as vice president. Does *anyone* out there approve of this character? Are his hard-line, conservative beliefs that far out of line with the values of bedrock Americans? Is he really that dumb? Given that Dan Quayle *is* the vice president of the United States, *is* a heartbeat away from the office held by a man with an irregular heartbeat, and *is* the occupant of an office once held by the despised Richard Nixon, who went on to become president of the United States; the past-his-prime Dixiecrat Lyndon Baines Johnson, who went on to become president of the United States; the buffoonish Gerald Ford, who went on to become president of the United States; and the goofy, very nearly invisible George Bush, who went on to become president of the United States; this seems like a good time to take a closer look at the universally ridiculed Dan Quayle, and to pose the question: What is the meaning of this unfathomably strange public office he holds, and what does Quayle's occupation of it say about the society that put him there, yet keeps acting as if it didn't?

This may be a good time to pose such questions, but personally I would prefer if somebody else did it. By and large I would like to leave the serious questions about the significance of Quayle's career to more gifted observers and concentrate on such questions as these:

1. If I do pick bonds instead of stocks, should I be looking at long-term treasuries, intermediate corporates, or short-term municipals?
2. Why is Dan Quayle so interested in tort reform?
3. Isn't "tort" spelled with an "e"?

I do not mean to suggest by this that the following pages will be entirely devoid of historical detail and philosophical rumination. Far from it. At many points the reader's attention will be drawn to the fact that in the early 1940s Harry Truman was widely viewed as an intellectually deficient rube; that in 1962 Richard Nixon was thought of as a political zombie; and that in early 1988 George Bush was dismissed by many observers as a gawky fuddy-duddy ready to have his clock cleaned by Bob Dole.

The reader will further be reminded that Abraham Lincoln was despised and ridiculed by *members of his own cabinet*, and that Warren Harding once confessed that he had no idea whatsoever what he was doing in the White House. Clearly—to use Capitol Hill's favorite adverb—being labeled a clown by one's colleagues, as well as by the national press corps, has never been an insurmountable impediment to holding the highest office in the land, and raises many interesting questions about the nature of democracy.

But I will not be answering those questions, either. The questions I will be answering are:

1. Dan Quayle once told a reporter that he had never heard of Jim Morrison of the Doors. Through the intercession of professional psychics, is it possible to find out if Jim Morrison has ever heard of Dan Quayle?
2. What kind of medication is Marilyn Quayle on?
3. If the market goes down 300 points the day Dan Quayle becomes president, should I be buying at the end of the day, or should I stay on the sidelines until the whole thing blows over?

History is a truly wondrous thing that tells us about who we are, where we've been, and where we're headed. History abounds with tales of men like Dan Quayle who wait patiently in the wings for their big chance to prove themselves. Sometimes, as in the case of Harry Truman, Fortune favored them. Sometimes she didn't. Some of them would have been better off staying right there concealed behind the arras, where they couldn't get into any mischief. England's Edward II was such a bad king that although he ended his life impaled on a red-hot poker, many of his subjects thought he got off easy. No one can remember who Alexander the Great's second-in-command was, but he obviously didn't get the job done.

In more recent times, in our own country, the Republic has been governed by Andrew Johnson, an ineffective drunk; Warren Harding, an ineffective drunk; and Gerald Ford, who didn't even need to be a drunk to be ineffective. And it came close to being governed by Aaron

Burr, vice president under Jefferson, who was an out-and-out traitor. Yes, all the way back at the dawn of the Republic, the American people already knew that they were playing with fire in adhering to such an absurd line of succession. Yet we have done virtually nothing to correct it. This suggests either that the American government is such a perfectly oiled machine that it runs itself no matter who is in the White House, or that God, who already protects drunks and babies, also keeps watch over the fifty states. And it definitely raises a veritable host of interesting, thought-provoking questions about the nature of the electoral system.

But somebody else will have to answer these questions. No, this is not a book for the pundit, the savant, the serious student of the political process, or the policy wonk. Nowhere in these pages are there prescient comments by men named Kevin, Ed, or Fritz, or barbed asides by bespectacled women named Ann. If the reader is looking for exhaustive scrutiny of the role of Dan Quayle's Competitiveness Council in relaxing federal strictures mandating use of wetlands, he or she had better look elsewhere. The same is true for those seeking a tough, probing, sensitive analysis of Dan Quayle's vaunted bipartisan Job Training Partnership Act of 1982. I do not now give, nor have I ever given, a damn about the Job Training Partnership Act of 1982, nor for that matter the Job Training Partnership Act of any other year. And nobody else I know does, either.

The vice presidency, more than any other American political office, lends itself to an infinite number of inappropriate analogies. Critics of the institution scornfully haul out the NFL, noting that when a star quarterback such as Joe Montana or Randall Cunningham goes down with an injury, a capable veteran backup such as Steve Young or Jim McMahon steps into the fallen QB's shoes. In the political sphere, by comparison, when an Abe Lincoln or a George Bush goes down, he is replaced by a dud like Andrew Johnson or a (putative) dummy like Dan Quayle.

But this is an inappropriate analogy, because the vice president of the United States was never really intended to be a star-in-waiting. In previous eras, the appropriate analogy was to an elephants' graveyard. Today, the appropriate comparison is to the National Basketball Association's player development squad.

In the second round of the 1991 NBA draft, with all the top players from the college ranks already long gone, the Philadelphia 76ers drafted a little-known center from the University of Houston named Alvaro Teheran. Teheran had decent size and a nice touch around the basket, but he had no muscle on him, had come late to the sport, had not developed until his senior year in college, had played in a second-rate system, and was manifestly not ready for the pros. He was a moderately talented youngster who needed seasoning, a player who with time and patience might have developed into an adequate backup center. So the 76ers sent him to the Spanish Basketball League for a couple of years. Not long afterward, the Spanish Basketball League sent him back.

The U.S. vice presidency is the political equivalent of the Spanish Basketball League. It is, as Lyndon Baines Johnson once noted, a place where you send a youngster who needs seasoning. It is a place where you send a second-rater who might someday develop into an adequate backup. It is a training program for a mildly talented mop-up guy whom you hope and pray by all that you hold holy you will never have to put into a big game. The vice presidency is a reminder that life is not perfect, and that we all have to die. It's just that with some vice presidents, we might die a whole lot sooner.

THE HUMBLEST HOOSIER

I don't see the point to Quayle.

—Conservative writer who would
rather not be identified

Ninety-five percent of the stories that have ever been written about Dan Quayle read something like this:

ANYWHERE, U.S.A.—Dan Quayle, the dimwit playboy with the all-purpose face, who looks like the fourth lead in a spring-break movie, was in town yesterday to campaign for George Bush, his silver-spooned fellow scion who looks positively regal next to this bumptious Pat Sajak look-alike. The embattled, overprogrammed, gaffe-prone son Bush never had quickly got tangled in the thickets of his own rhetoric, and had to be rescued by his PTA-proper wife, the attractive but hardly stunning Marilyn Quayle, who abandoned her own burgeoning career as an aggressive Hoosier night-school lawyer in order to hit the trail for Quayle in her démodé hairdo, knee-length tartan skirt, and practical pumps.

The high-spirited, boyishly Hoosier bubblehead, who has continually taken a drubbing in the polls, was hoping to avoid another media feeding frenzy as Quayle-bashing reached seismic levels, but despite the peach-fuzzed laughingstock's threadbare attempt to give the impression of presidential stature, he self-incinerated in a cauldron of piffle, twaddle, and hokum as his prepackaged answers failed to dispel lingering apprehensions that he is a Tinkertoy politician, a Ferris Bueller manqué, a male bimbo, a pinhead dolt, and an empty vessel who entirely lacks *gravitas*.

Gamely mustering his puppylike, preadolescent energy, the incurably cheery Eddie Haskell look-alike, within the context of low expectations, attempted to show his mettle by standing in the fire and demonstrating that he had grown in office. But the incurably hostile press, furious at this Ken Doll's frathouse mien, his ebullient clichés, and his face untouched by life, teed off on Bush's vapid, sequestered, cocooned impeachment insurance, lambasting the gun-shy chowderhead with the microscopic attention span for his inept, banal mumblings. The chary, wary, edgy, telegenic pip-squeak in the lime green golf pants soon found himself out of his depth, and retreated to the safety of the *Hoosier Pride*, in the company of his prim, proper, prissy, pert Stepford wife.*

If it sometimes seems that these Dan Quayle stories have a generic quality, that reporters keep writing the same story over and over again, this impression is correct. There is, in fact, an all-purpose Dan Quayle story floating around the nation's newsrooms. It is called *TurboQuayle;* it runs on both the IBM PC (286 models and up) and Apple formats; and it requires at least two MB of memory. It costs $99.95 on the open market, but anyone who wants a copy can call me and I'll be happy to download it onto your unit for just $34.95.

TurboQuayle is actually two programs: an all-purpose Quayle-bashing story, which takes up 98 percent of the program's memory, and an all-purpose Quayle puff piece, which uses the remaining 2 percent. (For more information, call David Broder and Bob Woodward at *The Washington Post*). As a bonus, some versions come up with a supplemental program called "How to Write a Positive Dan Quayle Article." This requires a 386 chip, a minimum of four MB of memory, and a lot of nerve. It will also run you an additional $24.95. The all-purpose Quayle-bashing story looks something like this:

———

James Danforth Quayle, who was born on February 4, 1947, is the grandson of the **maverick/eccentric/ultra-right-wing** Eugene C. Pulliam, who started out as a police reporter and built an empire of conservative, small-town newspapers, including the **ultra-conservative/loopy/award-winning** *Arizona Republic* and the **ultra-conser-**

---

*All Quayle descriptions in this chapter taken verbatim from articles appearing in major newspapers and magazines between 1988 and 1992.

vative/inconsequential/non-award-winning *Indianapolis Star.* A **friend of presidents/champion of right-wing causes/maverick golfer,** Pulliam was once described by Bruce Babbitt as "the founding father of the Republican party in Arizona." With a fortune valued at **$600 million/$1.3 billion/a whole lot,** Pulliam liked to hang out with politicians, and politicians certainly didn't mind hanging out with the **eccentric Hoosier/maverick golfer/quirky right-winger.** But unlike Jim Quayle, Dan's **ultra-right-wing/tattooed/John Bircher** father, Pulliam had **eccentric/unpredictable/maverick** political beliefs that **are well documented elsewhere/are a matter of public record/we do not need to get into here.**

Pulliam liked golf so much that he moved to Florida, then Phoenix, each time buying **maverick newspapers/houses overlooking fairways/influence.** In Scottsdale, Arizona, where Dan's **Bircher/maverick/tattooed ex-Marine dad** Jim worked for his father-in-law's second-rate papers, the Quayles lived in a house on the eleventh hole of the **posh/elegant/whites-only** Paradise Valley Country Club golf course.

The **well-heeled/bleached-blond/sun-baked** Dan Quayle lived in this **Donna Reed/hopelessly bland/semitropical** environment from the time he was eight until he was sixteen, **frequently/incessantly/only** playing golf with his **kindly/attentive/maverick/ultra-right-wing** grandfather, getting his handicap down to seven by the time he entered high school. In 1963, the **eccentric/strange/unpredictable** Pulliam sold his **Bircher/wacko/tattooed ex-Marine** son-in-law the **tiny/drab/unnecessary** *Huntington Herald-Press,* and the family moved back to Indiana. When Pulliam died, he left Dan and his wife Marilyn **a portion of a huge family trust/more money than you can shake a stick at/a fortune valued at somewhere between $800,000 and $1.3 billion—hey, I'm not good with numbers.**

In this **sleepy/charming/prototypically Hoosier** hamlet of 16,000 people, the **peppy scion/overprivileged airhead/spoiled little rich kid** led a *Leave It to Beaver/Ozzie and Harriet/Rin Tin Tin* –type life, dwelling in a two-story frame house with a pool, a barn, and two **ultra-right-wing/Bircher/wacko fundamentalist** parents, including one with tattoos.

An **intellectual lightweight/classic late bloomer/complete**

moron, Quayle wasted his youth playing basketball and poker, and did not have the grades to get into college. But as **his family knew people/calls were made/luck would have it,** he was accepted into DePauw University, a **small, Methodist/charming/old-fashioned/ fifth-rate** school in rural Indiana where his dad and grandfather had also been students, and were trustees and donors. Quayle **captained the golf team/learned how to do the Deke handshake/messed up big time** and was only allowed to graduate after retaking his final exam in his major, political science, which he failed the first time around.

While his **maverick/Bircher/tattooed ex-Marine** dad was busy writing editorials supporting the war in Vietnam, his **lightweight/ vapid/featherweight** son was busy trying to get out of his military service. Although a lot of other young Hoosiers were having all kinds of trouble getting into the National Guard, **his family knew people/ calls were made/as luck would have it, there was a retired National Guard commander working right down the hall at one of his grandfather's papers,** and he got a job as a weekend warrior one week later.

Quayle's college grades **left a bit to be desired/really sucked/ weren't good enough to get him into law school,** but as **his family knew people/calls were made/luck would have it,** he was admitted part-time under a special, affirmative-action program to the University of Indiana night law school where he **knew the night school admissions dean/didn't set the world on fire/never actually saw the check his grandfather wrote to the law school shortly thereafter.** While commuting from his **quirky/maverick/elderly** grandmother's house, he met his **rigid/attractive but not stunning/horrid** wife, Marilyn, whose uncle had been the Indiana secretary of state. They were married ten weeks later.

Quayle wasn't much of a student, but as **his family knew people/ calls were made/luck would have it,** he got a job in the consumer affairs office of the state attorney general and then in the governor's office anyway. After receiving his law degree in 1974, he went back home and worked at a couple of **very demanding/incredibly interesting/no-show** jobs for his **Bircher/maverick/tattooed ex-Marine** dad. Two years later, **a group of extremely powerful Indiana political kingpins/the Fort Wayne Medicis/some guy named Orvas** asked the

shortpants mediocrity/opportunistic wimp/cheerful glamor boy if he would like to run for Congress against sixteen-year veteran Ed Roush. Quayle's **Bircher/maverick/tattooed** father said he had no chance of winning, but he won anyway.

The **chipper/contagiously upbeat/irrepressible** Quayle was a no-show congressman, nicknamed "Wethead" because he spent so much time in the House gym. But in 1980, the **surprisingly feisty/intensely competitive/consistently underrated** Robert Redford look-alike gave up his safe seat to take on eighteen-year veteran and one-time presidential candidate Birch Bayh whom he beat because of **high unemployment/abortion/out-of-state NCPAC money/Ronald Reagan.** He was reelected in 1986 by the widest margin in Indiana history.

In the Senate, the **junior Ronald Reagan/Kiddy Car Candidate/ Hoosier version of Mister Lucky** linked up with Teddy Kennedy to pass the $2.4 billion Job Training Partnership Act, and also helped Reagan get Senate approval of the controversial AWACs sale to Saudi Arabia. With his **pink hue/choirboy skin/Deke handshake,** he also involved himself in legislation involving tax reform, closing loopholes in nuclear arms treaties, reforming defense procurement procedures, etc. The positions of this **favored son/fortunate child/affable dunce** have been predictably right-wing: anti-kid, anti-black, anti-urban, anti-veteran, anti–gun control, anti-poor, pro-SDI.

The **inoffensive cheerleader/accident waiting to happen/miniature creature in a Republican petting zoo** was never thought to be a member of the New Right, generally melting away from such issues as abortion. Instead, he is a traditional midwestern conservative who believes in low taxes, weak regulation, strong defense, even lower taxes, support for freedom fighters in the Third World, less regulation, lower taxes, better *Murphy Brown* scripts. He does not care about acid rain.

Throughout his **charmed life/brilliant career/lifelong daydream,** the **likable ditz/Fourth Generation Deke/Huck Finn–like rube** has tried to militarize space, fighting long and hard for Star Wars. In 1987, when the **gritty pinhead/well-heeled mushmouth/cherry-cheeked poltroon** helped get a Senate proposal banning the testing of anti-satellite weapons killed, he told his **amazed/befuddled/confused/not terribly surprised** Senate colleagues: "I think eventually we will probably see agreements to establish self-defense zones in space that will actually divide up space between the Soviet Union, the United States, and other nations. If others come within our zone, then in fact they would be infringing on our territory."

George Bush selected the **untested/highly malleable/to the manor born** Quayle as his running mate on August 16, 1988, because he wanted to **placate the Republican right/reach across generational lines/show that he was his own man/piss off an entire country/get as many Dekes on the ticket as possible.** During the grueling campaign, this **male bimbo/boyish male lead/big man on campus** underwent a **baptism of fire/day of reckoning/*momento del verdad.*** At one point, the **goofy postadolescent/cuddly lapdog/supercilious pinhead** was asked to identify the chairman of the National Narcotics Border Interdiction System. **In over his head/unaccustomed to the rarefied air of the corridors of power/up the creek without a paddle,** Quayle confessed that he did not know. It was George Bush. Such gaffes seemed to strengthen the **lingering impression/unshakable conviction/nagging suspicion** that this **mechanical dolt/intellectual dwarf/hyperactive child** was **out of the loop/out of his depth/sealed shut in the body bag of his dreams.**

Quayle, who **occasionally calls to mind Tom Hanks in *Big*/possesses Robert Redford good looks/doesn't have much body fat on his intellect** had to be sent to candidate school to learn how to **emerge from George Bush's shadow/evince a patina of credibility/speak English.** The **butt of a thousand jokes/overrehearsed nebbish/cloistered numbskull** was lazy and inattentive. He confused the names of former astronaut Buzz Aldrin and Donald "Buz" Lukens, an Ohio congressman convicted of sexual misconduct, **using language like a Lego set/speaking in sentences that circled the runway/acting like he was memorizing answers for the big test.** Asked several times during his debate with the **craggy/well-respected/battle-scarred** Lloyd Bentsen what he would do if he suddenly had to take over for George Bush, he said that he would pray. Eventually, the **mesmerized/overprogrammed/totally wooden** ball of lint made the disastrous decision to compare his own term of office with Jack Kennedy's. We all know what happened then.

Since being elected vice president, the **handsome dilettante/politi-**

cal Galatea/overgrown Little Leaguer has fought for Star Wars, tried to persuade the president to resist quota bills, helped save Corey Aquino's ass, and campaigned for tort reform, congressional term limits, the space program, the Kurds, and Israel. Now **on the cusp of middle age/graying at the temples/incorrigibly pleasant,** Quayle has been most visible as head of the Council on Competitiveness, a **shadowy/anti-democratic/consistently underrated** seven-member organization whose job it is to **ease competitive barriers to American business/cut through nagging, bureaucratic red tape/water down federal regulations.** His ratings were low when he took office, and they are low now.

Mr. Quayle cannot spell.

I I I

THE BIG EASY

In the mid-1980s, the floundering New York Yankees were desperately
looking for pitching help from the right side. After scrutinizing various
free agents, then-president George Steinbrenner's eyes turned longingly toward San Diego, to a sturdy young righthander named Ed
Whitson. Whitson had been a moderately successful starter for the
Padres, with a lifetime record of 53 wins and 56 losses, and an earned
run average hovering around four runs per game. At no time in his
career was Whitson ever expected to mature into a Sandy Koufax or
a Juan Marichal. In fact, at no time in his career was he ever really
expected to mature into a Jerry Koosman or a Luis Tiant. Basically, he
was expected to be the next Rick Wise, or maybe the second coming
of Bob Knepper.

But if it is true that at no point in his career were truly great things
predicted for Ed Whitson, it is equally true that *good* things were.
These good things did not happen to Whitson in New York. Accus-

tomed to playing in front of smallish, unsophisticated, undemanding, and relatively civilized crowds in San Diego, where the Padres have a rich tradition of mediocrity, Whitson was never able to adjust to big-city pressure. He was wild, he was easy to hit, he was a sitting duck for lefties; the public made fun of him, and his *outspoken wife, who kept complaining about the awful way he was being treated by the media, only made things worse.* Eventually, the Yankees were reduced to playing Whitson only on the road, where he would be insulated from the venomous taunts of rabid, vulgar New York fans, and journalists *who don't know the first thing about baseball, but come on with this high-and-mighty attitude as if they were God's gifts to the world.* Eventually, Whitson was traded back to the Padres, where after a couple of so-so years, he picked up the jangled threads of his career and went back to being a relatively decent, if unspectacular, pitcher.

The eerie similarities between the careers of Ed Whitson and Dan Quayle—similarities that, admittedly, may not immediately spring to the reader's mind—are well worth exploring. They are worth exploring because, in a very real sense, Ed Whitson is the Dan Quayle of the diamond, just as Dan Quayle is an Old Executive Office Building version of Ed Whitson. Consider the facts. Both men flourished in cultural backwaters dominated by Republicans before making a fateful decision to expose themselves to the remorseless glare of the media spotlight in the East. Both men were viewed as rising stars of a tiny magnitude back home, but were treated as dim-witted incompetents in their new surroundings in the big city. Both men were torn to pieces by journalists who had attended eastern schools. Both men knew in their heart of hearts that when the train left for Cooperstown, they were not going to be on it. Both men had trouble with lefties, and would have been more than happy to end their careers playing .500 ball. Both men were hated by New Yorkers. Both men had leadership problems. Both men had wives who blamed their husbands' problems on the media and were foolish enough to say it in public for attribution.

This is the bald truth about Dan Quayle. He was a rotten congressman, a layabout who regularly missed floor votes and spent far too much time in the House gym playing hoops. But he was a *slightly* better-than-average senator who might one day have matured into a *somewhat* better-than-average senator. "Twenty years later, he would have been Gerald Ford," says Jacob Weisberg of *The New Republic.* Maybe a little smarter than Ford. But we should not lose sight of the fact that being a congressman is a lot harder than being a senator, that being a Republican congressman is a lot harder than being a Republican senator, and that being the junior senator from Indiana is kind of a joke job. As a minority whip raising hell in the House of Representatives, Newt Gingrich has a job that is infinitely more demanding than being a junior senator from Indiana. In any ranking of job difficulty, all congressmen, most governors, many mayors, the chairman of the Federal Reserve, and at least a handful of cabinet officials come long before senators. So do public health officials, a good number of police chiefs, and not a few fire chiefs.

"Any governor has a harder job than a senator," says Michael Kinsley of *Crossfire.* "Congressmen have a hard job because they have to do constituent service and raise money all the time and stand for reelection every two years. But being a senator is one step away from the dream job."

What's the dream job?

"Being vice president," says Kinsley. "Then you don't have to do anything."

"The Senate is the easiest important job in government," avers Richard Brookhiser of *National Review.*

Nevertheless, in the past two years, there have been periodic attempts to upgrade the Dan Quayle Story, to make it appear that Quayle was one hell of a senator; that GOP insiders knew all along that he was bound for glory; and that the national (i.e., liberal) press simply missed the big picture. Proponents of this theory have noted that Quayle's first two victories were smashing upsets: in 1976, he beat a sixteen-year incumbent in a House race that few experts thought he had a chance to win; in 1980, he gave up his safe congressional seat and beat eighteen-year veteran and one-time presidential aspirant Birch Bayh in a race no one thought he had a chance to win; and in 1986, he was reelected to the Senate by the largest margin in the history of the state.

Evidence to support the Quayle-as-diamond-in-the-rough theory has been trotted out by a number of conservative publications: *Commentary, The American Spectator,* and *The Wall Street Journal.* Through judicious use of the Library of Congress, adroit researchers have excavated such material as the 1985 edition of *Politics in America,* in which Quayle was described as "one of the 12 most effective but underrated members of Congress," and a 1985 issue of *National Journal* that dubbed Quayle one of the Senate's future leaders. In 1985, *Congressional Quarterly* described Quayle as a "pragmatic, thoughtful senator," while three years later, *The Almanac of American Politics* described him as a surprisingly hardworking chap who was willing to "dig into issues, do his homework, and come up with workmanlike legislative solutions to problems of government."

Moderately expensive NEXIS searches of library databases were also successful in exhuming mid-1980s articles from *major newspapers* written by *big-time reporters* that did not brand Quayle a moron. Quayle, it seemed, had received kudos as an emerging leader from no less a figure than Hedrick Smith of *The New York Times,* and had been deemed one of six "rising stars" by the *Chicago Tribune.*

These revisionist articles have been written with the intention of showing that Dan Quayle was an extraordinarily well-kept Republican secret and that the 13,000 journalists who were in New Orleans for the 1988 GOP convention—people whose delivery of *Congressional Quarterly* and *Politics in America* had been spotty at best—simply blew the story. Had they been reading *The Almanac of American Politics* or *National Journal** as they should have been, they would not have reacted with shock when Bush picked Quayle as his running mate that balmy afternoon. They would not have turned to one another and said, "Dan Quayle? Who the hell is Dan Quayle?" Instead, they would have turned to each other knowingly and said, "He's one of the 12 most underrated members of Congress, a hardworking guy who's willing to dig into the issues, do his homework, and come up with workmanlike legislative solutions to problems of government. Hats off to George Bush for a very savvy choice."

But this version of events is not true. The Quayle revisionist articles did not start appearing until the Humblest Hoosier had already been vice president for more than two years. Before Quayle was picked as

---

*By and large, Quayle revisionist articles tend to avoid less adulatory comments from publications like *The Almanac of American Politics,* comments such as "He doesn't seem particularly cerebral."

George Bush's running mate, he was just another blow-dried junior senator from Indiana, and that was it. (If you don't believe this, look in *The Readers' Guide to Periodical Literature* and see how many articles you find under "Quayle, Dan" between 1976 and 1988.) If Quayle was a well-kept secret, he was a secret that was being well kept from Republicans as well as from Democrats, from politicians as well as from journalists. "You had a lot of these Bob Forehead senators running around here," says Kinsley, recalling the Washington of the middle 1980s, "and he was one of them."

Quayle later said that his meteoric rise was one of the main things the press held against him. In their view, if Quayle hadn't been important enough or interesting enough to come around and interview during his first eight years in the Senate, then he had no business being vice president.

Quayle also said that one of the most personally shocking things about his treatment by the media during the 1988 campaign was that he had never gotten bad press back in Indiana. (Clearly, it helps to have a grandfather who owns all the important newspapers in your state.) In any event, Quayle mentioned his ingenious media theories to *The Washington Post*'s Paul Taylor, author of *See How They Run: Electing the President in an Age of Mediaocracy.* Taylor sort of goes along with the idea that reporters' shock and mortification at being surprised by the nomination accounts for a certain measure of their ferocity toward Quayle.

Nevertheless, he points out that some of the hardest body blows Quayle received after the nomination came from Republicans. Taylor stresses that immediately after the nomination, GOP figures as diverse as Bob Dole, William Cohen, Henry Hyde, and Jim Thompson all took potshots at Quayle, while defenses of the bland, dazed neophyte ranged from the inane (John McCain) to the stupid (Gordon Humphrey). Moreover, Quayle was treated like a runt during the campaign by Jim Baker and the rest of Bush's people, particularly campaign manager Stuart Spencer, who said, "I want him to step on his dick and then we'll own him again." The myth that the liberal media did Quayle in all by themselves is just that—a myth. George Bush took a poor, frightened, totally unprepared kid and hung him out to dry.

In 1978, Richard F. Fenno, Jr., a political scientist from the Univer-

sity of Rochester, received a grant to study the careers of several
generic young legislators. As luck would have it, one of them was Dan
Quayle. Between 1980 and 1986, Fenno got to spend quite a bit of time
with the senator and probably knows him as well as anyone alive
outside of Quayle's family and immediate circle of friends. In 1989,
after the election, he published his earlier, already compiled findings
verbatim in *The Making of a Senator: Dan Quayle.* Admiring of his
subject, Fenno feels that Quayle had the charm, grit, and coalition-
building skills to perhaps become the party whip a few years down the
road. "In the Senate, Dan Quayle was a comer." But Fenno also says
that the vice presidency wastes Quayle's abilities—coalition-building
—because it requires a skill he does not have, and is never going to
acquire. "Quayle has no rhetorical skills," says Fenno, "and he is never
going to be a great public speaker." Worse still, at the time Bush picked
him, the junior senator from Indiana had almost no experience in
dealing with the major media.

"I regard it as criminal that Bush sent him out there without
adequate preparation," says Fenno. "In a state like Indiana—in any
state except New York or California—you don't need to be a big media
star to be an effective senator. You don't have to develop any great
skills in confrontation; you fly into Indianapolis every couple of weeks,
handle a few easy questions from reporters, and then fly out. But you
put a guy like Quayle in a room filled with 700 hungry reporters who
have no story and it's a slaughter." He adds: "I think that sour grapes
from the Republicans really hurt him, too."

Richard Brookhiser, who covered the Republican National Convention for William F. Buckley's *National Review,* can recall precisely
what his reaction was when he and several other conservative writers
learned of Bush's choice that fateful afternoon in New Orleans. Like
just about everyone else in the Big Easy that week, Brookhiser had
fallen seriously behind in his reading of *Politics in America, The
National Journal,* and *Congressional Quarterly.*

"It was a shock; it was just incredulity," he recalls. "We didn't
believe it; we all just sort of scratched our heads and looked at one
another. His name had vaguely floated up in the margins of the Paula
Parkinson scandal, but that was really all I knew about him at the
time."

In the September 16, 1988, issue of *National Review*, Brookhiser informed readers that he had to phone a friend in Indiana to get a take on the Hoosier Who Would Be King. The friend said that Quayle had initially struck him as a typical big man on campus back when he was trying to unseat Birch Bayh in 1980, that he was "personable, popular, no burner of midnight oil." The man said that he now felt "Quayle knew what he was talking about, which I didn't expect." This is faintly complimentary stuff, but it does not sound like Socrates responding to a letter from Plato requesting more information about some guy named Pericles.

The American Spectator was similarly unimpressed by Quayle's selection. Though aware of Quayle's modest legislative accomplishments in the Senate, the *Spectator* felt that "in speeches, in interviews, Dan Quayle comes off as (how to say it?) something of a jerk . . . In interviews, the rudiments of understandable speech—things like subject-verb agreement and pronoun placement—fly off at once in a swift and brilliant flight, leaving him unarmed but for that patented pol's grin and a wide-eyed stare that could snuff out a candle."

The *Spectator* said that Quayle's acceptance speech was so slow that it reminded one of Bob and Ray's interview with "the President of . . . the . . . Slow . . . Talkers . . . of . . . America." Quayle, the magazine concluded, fit the mold of many up-and-coming Republicans: "probably hard-working and ambitious, but a bit too pretty; not stupid, but not exactly rocket scientists, either." As for the political drawbacks of being a blond, good-looking chap easily mistaken for a bimbo, the writer quipped: "I've met people in Hollywood who swear to this day that Jayne Mansfield enjoyed reading Kant. Maybe it's true. But who believes it?"

Brookhiser said that Quayle's acceptance speech was "quite bad," and when Gordon Humphrey, the crusty old conservative from New Hampshire, expressed jubilation at his nomination, beaming, "We're in the club," Brookhiser said, "It strikes *this* conservative that the club has rather comfortable standards of admission. Maybe Quayle would not drift off in a high wind, but I have yet to be shown."

Obviously, once the *fait* was *accompli*, a good number of conservatives closed ranks around Quayle. But they did not do so by using those NEXIS materials from *Politics in America*, which really don't play all that well in the heartland. Instead, they started drawing dubious parallels with other historical figures who eventually confounded low initial expectations. On September 16, 1988, former Jesuit John McLaughlin enthusiastically went to bat for the ostensibly callow youth in the *National Review*. Drawing powerful similarities to the life of John Fitzgerald Kennedy, McLaughlin noted that both Quayle and JFK were young men when they assumed office, had been helped tremendously by their powerful families, and had grown up without a care in the world. Both were elected in machine-controlled states, and both men had served a few terms in the House without much distinction. Although JFK had the heroic war record, Quayle was a much more effective senator, taking an active, bipartisan role in a number of areas. JFK, by contrast, had been a lazy, opportunistic, ineffectual legislator with a hazy, nebulous ideology.

"So what we see in the 41-year-old junior senator from Indiana . . ." wrote McLaughlin, "is a natural politician—not fully seasoned, to be sure, but well on the way. With these strengths, odds are that over the next two months he will develop his own following, becoming a real asset to George Bush. Time is on Quayle's side."

As usual, McLaughlin was wrong; Quayle cost Bush somewhere between two and three points at the polls in November. Still, with the election over, most conservative journalists were ready to give the Danny Quayle stories a rest for a while. That's when *The New Republic* stepped in. Realizing that sooner or later things would turn around for Quayle, but determined to delay it as long as possible, the nation's most influential political magazine announced the establishment of the Quayle Revisionism Award.

"Can journalists keep writing indefinitely that Dan Quayle is a moron, just because he is one?" the magazine asked rhetorically in November 1988, inviting readers to keep their eyes peeled for "revisionist Quayle stories, reporting newfound depths of wisdom, unexpected insights, and—extra points—growth in the job."

The first nomination went to B. Drummond Ayres of *The New York Times*, who wrote on Election Day itself: "The Dan Quayle who was elected vice president today appears to be a different man from the one who left New Orleans in August . . . He is a more seasoned and secure man now by his own analysis and in the judgment of those who know him best."

"Kinsley was trying to delay the inevitable, and I think he did delay it for around six months," says Rick Hertzberg, who succeeded Kinsley as editor of *The New Republic* in 1989. "For a while, people were too embarrassed to write the revision pieces."

So it would appear; in May 1989, *The New Republic* reported: "Word in Washington has it that some journalists would actually *like* to write flattering things about Quayle, but are afraid to, lest they be humiliated by winning our Quayle Revisionism Award."

What is most astonishing about all this is that at the very same moment that *The New Republic* was going out of its way to dismiss Quayle as a moron, *TNR* editor Fred Barnes was launching the Quayle revisionism process all by himself. Without completely and utterly toadying up to the vice president, Barnes quietly but persistently began feeding the magazine's readers the ostensibly reassuring news that Quayle was neither a loon nor a lunatic, and, anyway, he'd surrounded himself with good people. Quayle was so pleased by Barnes's pieces that he paid the mildly liberal publication a compliment in a March 31, 1989, interview with *The Wall Street Journal.*

"I used to, I've read, I read *National Review*—some," he said, in trademark fashion. "I used to read *Human Events.* Don't read it as much as I used to. *The American Spectator*—it's hard to get through *The American Spectator.* And *The New Republic.* I enjoy reading *The New Republic.*"

After reading these remarks, *The American Spectator* put Quayle on its cover, with a pair of huge, vacant blue eyes, dressed as a schoolboy with a flying beanie on his head, reading the magazine upside down. "Why Danny Can't Read" was the cover story, accompanied by an open letter to "The Interview Ace," in which the magazine was deliberately dumbed down for the veep. "Mexico City is the capital (C-A-P-I-T-A-L) of what country? No, Danny, not New Mexico."

The spoof did not go down well with the vice president, nor with many *American Spectator* readers. "Never in the 23 years of this magazine has it received a larger or more inhospitable response to a piece," wrote editor R. Emmett Tyrrell, who had known Quayle and counted him as a friend since the early 1970s, when they were among the youngest members of a supper club in Indiana. But Tyrell also pointed out that it was pretty hard for a conservative magazine to sell space to advertisers when the most conservative member of the administration went around telling the nation's most important conservative newspaper that he preferred reading the liberal *New Republic* to the conservative, ostensibly unreadable *American Spectator.* (Tyrell also noted that *The New Republic* immediately began using the quotes to woo advertisers who might otherwise have bought space in *The American Spectator.* One year later, *The New Republic* would refer to Quayle as "a dim-bulb Midwestern senator with subzero charisma." This time, no endorsement from Quayle.)

Obviously, Quayle and the media are not a great fit. Obviously, much of what he says about the press is naive. Yet, horrible as it is to admit, Quayle was dead right when he said that the 13,000 journalists should have seen his nomination coming from a mile away. They should have seen that the selection of Dan Quayle as George Bush's running mate was a lock from the word go. Bush didn't pick Quayle because he *wanted* to. Bush picked Quayle because he *had* to pick him. There was no one else to turn to.

On the surface this argument may sound a tad iconoclastic, a mite quirky. But the facts are irrefutable. We know today—because Bob Woodward and David Broder have told us so—that Quayle actively campaigned for the vice presidential nomination in the weeks and even months leading up to the Republican National Convention. He even considered running for the White House in 1988, but decided not to because of family obligations. We know that he had chatted with Bush in the Senate building, that both men had worked with media consultant Roger Ailes, and that the Bush and Quayle families had common friends. Never mind that three dozen other senators and congressmen and governors and mayors knew George Bush, had used Roger Ailes as a consultant, had common friends with the Bush Family, had been quietly campaigning for the vice presidential nomination, and had once entertained ditzy daydreams about running for the White House; all that matters is that Quayle let it be known to Bush that he wanted the vice presidential nomination, and that he wanted it pretty badly.

That wouldn't have been enough to get it under normal circumstances. George Bush is no dummy; he must have known about the National Guard fiasco; the drug rumors; the crummy grades in high school, college, and law school; the Paula Parkinson scandal; and all the rest of the baggage Quayle brought with him. Bush had also spent some time actually conversing in person with Quayle; it is impossible to believe that this fine, upstanding, well-read Yale graduate would not have noticed that Quayle's membership in the Great Books Club seemed to have lapsed after that initial ten-day introductory offer. He picked him anyway. *He picked him because he had no choice.*

Let's go to the videotape. It was part of the conventional wisdom in 1988 that the Republican party was stocked to the gills with presidential timber—Jack Kemp, Bob Dole, Alexander Haig, James Baker, Phil Gramm—as well as with presidential balsa, such as Bill Bennett, Pierre DuPont IV, and Pete Wilson. But for one reason or another, none of these men was acceptable to George Bush as a running mate. Bush and Dole hate each other. Bush and Kemp don't like each other, and, besides, Jack Kemp is the only Republican since Abraham Lincoln who gives a damn about black people, meaning no dice on the Willie Horton ads. Baker, like at least a handful of men before him going all the way back to John Quincy Adams, figured that it would be easier to springboard into the White House from the State Department than from the vice presidency. Phil Gramm is a prick. Pierre DuPont has a Roman numeral in his name. Alexander Haig worked for Nixon and used words like "vicar." Richard Thornburgh is hated by conservatives, despite his frequent attempts to impersonate them. Bill Bennett is an intellectual, a ballbuster, and once dated Janis Joplin. Pete Wilson (too moderate anyway) once had to be wheeled onto the Senate floor on a gurney so that he could cast a crucial vote on the catastrophic insurance bill. None of this stuff looks good on the eleven o'clock news.

The simple fact is George Bush got down to the GOP convention in August 1988 and found himself stuck between a rock and a hard place. He couldn't tap then-congressman Dick Cheney because Cheney had already had three heart attacks and comes from a small, politically insignificant state (Wyoming, which only has three electoral votes and is lucky to have that many). He couldn't pick Colin Powell because Colin Powell is black, and what kind of a country do you think we're running here? He couldn't pick Trent Lott, because Trent Lott wanted to run for the senate. He would have liked to pick Alan Simpson, but Simpson is a loose cannon, pro-choice, and comes from the same electorally useless state as Dick Cheney. He couldn't pick California governor George Deukmejian, because the last thing the GOP needed in a tight race was a ticket with two millionaires named George on it. He couldn't pick Phil Crane, because his name sounds too much like Daniel Crane, a congressional page–molester. Thomas Kean, the lame duck governor of New Jersey, was a possibility, but Kean talks like those Jessica Savitch–clone newsreaders—like he has pebbles in his mouth or something—and is just too twee, too preppy, too F. Scott Fitzgeraldy, too *too*.

As he looked down the list of unknown governors, uncharismatic congressmen, and unimportant mayors, Bush realized, to his chagrin and mounting horror, that he was up against the wall. And as he surveyed the list of prospective senatorial candidates, he realized that every single one canceled himself out for some reason. Some, like New Mexico's Pete Domenici and Oregon's Mark Hatfield and Bob Packwood, had real jobs running the United States of America and didn't want to spend the next eight years attending funerals in Costa Rica and preparing *The Vice-President's Task Force on Iron Supplements.*

And then there were people like John Chafee of Rhode Island, who not only came from a run-down, Mafia-controlled state but who had once lost a Senate race to Claiborne Pell, the Democratic ding-dong who believes in ESP, spends a lot of time visiting royalty in Liechtenstein, is a member in good standing of the International Association of Near-Death Studies, and who pals around with the psychic spoon-bender Uri Geller. He certainly wouldn't bring much to the ticket.

Neither would most of the other members of that august body, the United States Senate. Consider the possibilities:

Armstrong, William. (Colo.) Who dat?

Bond, Christopher. (Mo.) Who dat?

Boschwitz, Rudy. (Minn.) Yeah, great name.

Cochran, Thad. (Miss.) Who dat?

Cohen, William S. (Maine) Too liberal; voted to impeach Nixon; joke state.

D'Amato, Alfonse. (N.Y.) Don't ask.

Durenberger, David. (Mich.) Rumors about hitting the sauce and having affair with staffer; problems with Senate Ethics Committee; too liberal anyway.

Evans, Daniel. (Wash.) Who dat?

Garn, Jake. (Utah) Destroyed life as we know it on this planet by creating Garn–St. Germain Bill deregulating S&Ls. Has weird eyes. Evokes Mormon values. Short one kidney.

Grassley, Chuck. (Iowa) "Looks like an archetypal hayseed," says *Almanac of American Politics.* No thanks.

Hatch, Orrin. (Utah) Jake Garn, without the pizzazz.

Hecht, Chic. (Nev.) Moron.

Helms, Jesse. (N.C.) Racist scum.

Humphrey, Gordon. (N.H.) Married to woman who once raised money for organization that believes orgasms are vitally important to mental health. Comes from joke state. Rarely mistaken for Cambridge don.

Karnes, David. (Nebr.) Who dat?

Kassebaum, Nancy. (Kan.) Female. Daughter of Alf Landon, who got creamed by FDR in 1936. Bad memories. Female.

Kasten, Robert. (Wis.) Once arrested for drunk driving; business partner went to jail.

Lugar, Richard. (Ind.) Only serious rival to Alan Cranston in annual Senate Nosferatu Look-alike Contest.

McCain, John. (Ariz.) Took $112,000 campaign contribution from Charles Keating; went on Keating-paid vacations to Bahamas four different times.

McConnell, Mitch. (Ky.) Who dat?

Murkowski, Frank. (Alaska) Who dat?

McLure, James. (Idaho) Who dat?

Nickles, Don. (Okla.) Blow-dried airhead, once tried to appoint two bankrupt guys to be federal marshals.

Pressler, Larry. (S.D.) Dumbest Rhodes Scholar ever; dyes hair.

Roth, William. (Del.) Horrible wig, no Einstein.

Rudman, Warren. (N.H.) True believer, genuinely principled conservative, simply not a Bush kind of guy.

Specter, Arlen. (Pa.) Dreamed up JFK Magic Bullet Theory.

Stafford, Robert. (Vt.) Who dat?

Stevens, Ted. (Alaska) Joke state.

Symms, Steven. (Idaho) Dumb guy. Reportedly turned up on floor of Senate juiced up after taking secretary to lunch.

Thurmond, Strom. (S.C.) Racist octogenarian; has baseball bat in office to beat down erections after his death. Used to be a Democrat.

Trible, Paul. (Va.) Faked campaign ad to suggest he had been in the military. No rocket scientist.

Wallop, Malcolm. (Wyo.) Weird name, bald, joke state.

Warner, John. (Va.) Unbelievably dumb, got rich off divorce settlement in 1973, friend of Pat Robertson, once married Liz Taylor, just not acceptable.

Weicker, Lowell. (Conn.) Liberal, became famous by helping to end Richard Nixon's career.

That left only three men, and, unfortunately, all three were scions. *America hates scions.** It was bad enough that Bush was a scion, but if you were going to have two scions on the ticket, you had to be careful that at least he was a somewhat downscale scion. John Danforth, scion of the Ralston Purina fortune, was the wealthiest man in the Senate. Everybody had heard of Ralston Purina, so having a Purina scion on the ticket could give people the wrong idea about who was running the country. Now deceased John Heinz (Pa.) was the scion of the Heinz canned-goods fortune, and was thought to be worth $460 million. His last name alone gave away the whole shooting match. *The scions are coming.*

That left Dan Quayle. True, he was a scion of the Pulliam Family, but as scions go, that was a pretty obscure family to be a scion of. As

---

*One thing Republicans are very good at is avoiding potentially dangerous photo ops. An exception was on November 5, 1991, when newspapers all over the United States ran a photo of Barbara Bush, Nancy Reagan, Rosalynn Carter, Betty Ford, Pat Nixon, and Lady Bird Johnson walking side by side at the dedication ceremony for the Ronald Reagan Presidential Library in Simi Valley, California. It was quite a jolt. The average American goes through life thinking that he's living in a country dominated by glitzy, colorful ethnics such as Madonna, Michael Jackson, Magic Johnson, Bruce Springsteen, Oliver Stone, Barbra Streisand, and Michael Jordan. Then one day he wakes up and sees a photo like this and it hits him: "Oh, now I get it. *They* run this country."

scions go, he was the one who was closest to having the common touch, because he didn't sound like a scion. He hadn't been to private school, hadn't gone to an Ivy League university, didn't dress that well, and hadn't married a designer wife: Marilyn was definitely right off the rack. Moreover, although the Pulliam Family fortune was thought to exceed $1 billion, Quayle himself could only lay his hands on around $1 million of it at any one time. What's more, Indiana had always been a critical, toss-up state, and had a long history of supplying vice presidents (4) and vice presidential candidates (8), none of whom ever did the country much harm; none of whom ever did the country much good. Quayle was also more conservative than Danforth and Heinz, less preppy than Danforth and Heinz, better-looking than Danforth and Heinz, and looked less like a person who had been to Woodstock than any other member of his generation in the Senate. Everything about him sent a reassuring message to middle Americans. Thus, for Bush, it was a no-brainer. Quayle was the one.

How could the media have missed it?

I V

SYMPATHY FOR THE DEVIL

I don't presume to talk for everyone of my generation.

—DAN QUAYLE, in his August 18, 1988,
acceptance speech at GOP convention

We ended the previous chapter by asserting that George Bush tapped Dan Quayle as his running mate in 1988 because he literally had no choice. Obviously, many people are going to have a hard time swallowing this. They will continue to subscribe to one of the shopworn theories explaining Bush's odd, completely unexpected decision. One is that he did it to placate the right wing of the Republican party. But we know that this is not true, because choosing Quayle over Jack Kemp or Bill Bennett actually incensed the right. Another theory is that he did it to attract younger voters. But we know that this is not true, because Quayle's being on the ticket cost Bush the votes of many young people. Another is that he did it because of Quayle's good looks. We know that this is not true because Americans like hideous politicians. A fourth surmises that Bush did it because he wanted to surprise his own advisers, to mess with their heads. This theory makes the least sense, because Bush doesn't have a funny bone in his entire body, hates surprises, and only messes with black people's heads. The final theory is that he selected the Humblest Hoosier without giving any thought to what kind of candidate Quayle would make; that his advisers failed to vet Quayle properly to make sure that he wouldn't be a drag on the ticket; that it was all a big mistake.

The implications of this theory are too horrifying to contemplate. If

George Bush, on the very threshold of becoming the most powerful man on the planet, decided to pick a brain-dead running mate without any regard to his leadership abilities, and his advisers then okayed that choice, it would mean that we live in a capricious universe where events occur randomly, and where there is probably no God. This gets us into Ingmar Bergman, *Bridge of San Luis Rey*, Albert Camus, Woody Allen, what-is-the-meaning-of-life? territory, and I don't even want to think about *that.*

Fortunately, it *cannot* be the case that George Bush made his choice in an arbitrary and capricious fashion. Historians, economists, and political scientists assure us that events occur on this planet because they are a manifestation of sometimes imperceptible, but nonetheless overpowering, economic forces. The Visigoth invasions did not just happen; they were precipitated by deteriorating farming conditions back home in the lands Beyond the Pale, or something. The rise of Stalin, however unpleasant he may have turned out to be, was a reflection of the Russian peasantry's contempt for intellectuals like Lenin and Trotsky, an expression of their deeply racinated, centuries-old desire to be ruled by a ruthless autocrat. The rise of Hitler was a manifestation of the German people's desire to tame inflation, reorganize their economy, rebuild their decaying infrastructure, and kill all the Jews, gypsies, and homosexuals as a bonus. All of this is depraved and nasty, but at least it isn't aleatory. This leads to a raw, naked, yet somehow intellectually comforting, conclusion: *Life is mean, but it is not meaningless.*

Cynics may not be impressed by this, but when you sit down and think things through, it's really quite an inspiring thought. What it means is that no matter how stupid the universe (which includes Indiana) seems, there is actually a logic to it somewhere. "God is subtle, but he is not evil," said Albert Einstein, no Hoosier. This doesn't mean that awful things won't continue to happen—a return of the Black Plague, the destruction of the Rain Forest, another Neil Sedaka comeback—but at least we can go to bed at night knowing that there is some reason why these terrible things occur. We are not, in fact, as flies to wanton boys who kill us for their sport. We are more like birds to wanton girls who kill us for their brunch.

Axiomatically, this leads us to the conclusion that there is a formidable, well-camouflaged, but nonetheless logical, explanation for Dan Quayle's selection as George Bush's running mate. In fact, there are two. The first, already discussed, is that he had no choice. The second is infinitely more subtle, for in this instance the explanation is not political, economic, racial, or even religious. No, it is cultural. Of all the baby-boomer politicians who have been elected to high national office in the past decade, Dan Quayle is the one who least reflects the values of the Haight-Ashbury generation. A man who was obviously not born to be wild, Dan Quayle was tapped for the second slot on the GOP ticket because George Bush wanted to capture the votes of all those Americans who loath the 1960s and wish that they had never happened. Dan Quayle's ascendancy to the second highest office in the land is a subliminal expression of Middle America's intense desire not only to repudiate the 1960s but to purge any evidence that they ever happened.

Let us backtrack a bit and recapitulate the events leading up to Quayle's selection. Was it only yesterday that Bush got up in front of his supporters in New Orleans and said, "Do you want to know a secret?" Beaming with satisfaction, he said, "I've just seen a face, and he's blonde on blonde." But the face was Dan Quayle's. This was not a well-respected man. This was a little child, forever young, suffering from stage fright. "Mercy, mercy, mercy," cried many a Republican at the sight of this nowhere man. Worse still, Quayle's wife was no foxy lady; something in the way she moved suggested a space oddity. "Don't do it!" pleaded young Americans here, there, and everywhere, as their faces just sort of ghostly turned a whiter shade of pale. The country was at a crossroads, but Bush thought it would bring Georgie fame. Instead, the polls showed that Quayle could be the end. "Oh no, don't bring me down," moaned Bush.

Quayle, providing satisfaction for no one, just kept on trucking. Day after day alone on a hill, the man with the foolish grin was perfectly still. "He never listens to them; he knows that they're the fools," cackled his advisers. Moreover, he insisted, time is on my side.

Liberals at first were gleeful, warning Bush, "You're going to cry ninety-six tears." Then they had their 19th nervous breakdown. "Strange days have found us; strange days have tracked us down," they muttered. Shattered, yet seeking emotional rescue from the weight that had put them up on Cripple Creek, many said, "It won't be long." Surely, further on down the road Quayle would end the misery by saying, "I don't want to spoil the party, so I'll go." But no, the scary monsters just would not fade away. Leaving everyone else, well, helpless, helpless, helpless.

Now it is four years later, and Quayle is up for reelection. "Oh no, not a second time!" shriek Democrats in a state of manic depression, wondering how much you have to pay to avoid going through all these things twice.

Dan and Marilyn Quayle's estrangement from the 1960s—a generation they were in, but not of—is quite staggering in its awesome thoroughness. A man who is clearly no acquaintance of Ziggy Stardust, much less the spiders from Mars, Quayle has never taken a walk on the wild side, would not know how to bogart a joint if he tried, and has never felt the urge to get down and boogie all night long.

To a certain extent, that's perfectly all right; he is, after all, a hick from the sticks. But sometimes he tends to push it. In a 1989 interview with Maureen Dowd of *The New York Times,* Quayle recalled a question during the campaign about rock music.

"Some reporter asked me who I liked better: Jim Morrison or Jimi Hendrix," recollected Quayle. "I hadn't heard of Jim Morrison, so I took Jimi Hendrix."

This is weird. It's perfectly all right not to like Jimi Hendrix and/or the Doors; all sorts of perfectly normal, well-balanced, fortyish types in this country grew up preferring the Four Seasons and Dionne Warwick; they are the kinds of people who now play the soundtrack from *Les Misérables* at barbecues and ask, "What's the holdup on that new Abba album?" But when a person in his forties admits that he has never even *heard* of Jim Morrison, you have to start wondering about the quality of newspaper delivery in rural Indiana during the late sixties and early seventies.

Personally, I hold no brief for the Lizard King. He drank too much, wore tight leather pants, wrote truly awful poetry, sang weird songs about sleeping with his mother, and was known to occasionally whip out his cock in public. But one thing you had to give the guy: He was colorful. He made waves. He was the kind of guy who was hard to ignore, even if you were growing up in rural Indiana. So when Dan

Quayle said that he had never even heard of Jim Morrison, one question kept going over and over in my mind: Has Jim Morrison ever heard of Dan Quayle?

I know that the question seems a bit odd on first consideration. But it seemed to me that if Jim Morrison, dead for more than twenty-one years, nevertheless knew who Dan Quayle was, it would show not only how hip and *au courant* the lead singer from the Doors was but how thoroughly adrift from his own generation the vice president is. The only problem was: How was I going to find out?

To answer this question I knew that I was going to have to get into contact with people from the occult world and arrange a séance in which I could communicate with the rock star's dead spirit. This wasn't as easy as you think, even though I do live in New York. For one, anytime you're ditzing around with the occult you are running the risk of opening up the gates of Hell and causing the fires of perdition to rain down on yourself and on your children and on the children of your children yea down unto the very last generation. I was willing to take that risk. What had me more concerned was the possibility that I could be pissing away my money. Business transactions involving the necromantic universe never come cheap, and I didn't feel like shelling out hundreds and perhaps even thousands of dollars trying to track down the Lizard King unless I felt there was a pretty good chance of a payoff at the end.

That's where the White Plains Hotel comes in. One Sunday, as I was lying on the sofa wondering how I could find out if Morrison was even vaguely aware of the existence of Dan Quayle, my wife told me that a Psychics Fair was being held in the lobby of the White Plains Hotel that very afternoon. White Plains is the next town over from mine; I scooted over to the hotel to check out the zeitgeist.

The convention was your usual gathering of part-time clairvoyants, recession-hit astrologers, and pushy tarot card readers, but the price was right: $15 for a fifteen-minute session, $28 for a half-hour. I figured it was worth a shot, so I slapped down my $15, got my ticket stub entitling me to a fifteen-minute psychic consultation, and sat down at a table with a tarot card reader who went by the name of Dorothy. Dorothy was a plump, permed, chain-smoker in her middle thirties who didn't smile a lot. She was wearing stone-washed jeans and a nondescript tank top and, despite her impeccable necromantic credentials, looked a lot like every other working-class female from the suburbs. This is one of the things that I like about America, that even the Satanists and demon worshippers and tarot card readers drive Honda Civics and max out on their Diners Club card. It gives you a sense that we're all in this together.

I explained the nature of my visit—I wanted her to tell me if Jim Morrison, the lead singer from the Doors, knew who Vice President Dan Quayle was. I could tell from the look on her face that she didn't get many questions like this. Her expression seemed to say, "I'm used to dealing with screwballs, but they're *my* kind of screwballs. I'm used to dealing with people whose inquiries are coming from out of left field. But yours are coming from out of *deep* left field." I could see that. I could see that she was used to questions like: "What does it mean if the Fisher King turns up in the same row as the Maiden Crone?" and, "If the shadow of Merlin is in the sixth house of the Grim Reaper, should I play number 55678 in the New York State lottery next week?" I could see that my query had knocked her for a loop. But, being the consummate professional that she was, she hung right in there. She rode the tiger. I was impressed.

"Put your question in the cards," she instructed me.

"You mean, with a pencil and paper?" I asked.

"No, put your question in the cards."

"You mean, with my mind? Like, *psychically?*"

She nodded. I thought hard and long about Quayle and Morrison as she shuffled the cards. Then she began dealing them out. She was slow and methodical, and her face betrayed little emotion. Suddenly, while arraying the third row of cards, she stopped short.

"I'm getting the feeling that this person definitely knows about Quayle," she said. Jesus! I was on to something after all! But I still needed a bit more solid information before I could proceed to the expense of a séance or any other full-service occult extravaganza.

"How can you tell?" I asked.

"You see this card?" she said, indicating what I took to be the Fisher King. I did. "And you see this," she said, pointing to what seemed to be a woodsman clutching a bunch of faggots or swords or something. She looked up. "I definitely get the feeling that he knows him."

It made sense to me. Tickled pink, I got up to leave, but she stopped me. "You've still got ten minutes," she said, pointing to the egg timer beside the tarot cards. "You want the rest of the reading?"

I didn't.

On my way out of the hotel, I grabbed a few business cards advertising various services provided by other psychics working in the greater metropolitan area. I did so because my work was not yet over. Sure, I was pleased to learn that Morrison apparently knew who Dan Quayle was. But I'd been in this business long enough to know that a top-shelf, crackerjack, professional journalist doesn't go out and write that something is true after confirming it with just one source. That's not the way Bob Woodward and David Broder would do it. They would report it was true after confirming it with *two* sources. So I had to find myself a second source—pronto. In other words, I still had plenty of shoe leather and spade work ahead of me.

The next day, I started making some preliminary calls to see about arranging a séance. Here, I have to come clean and admit that this was the one part of the job that I wasn't looking forward to. The truth is, I'm a Catholic, and Catholics and the occult spell trouble. Even though I knew that pinning down the Morrison angle was pivotal to the success of my research, I was hoping that I could contact the spirit of the deceased rocker without having to attend a séance. Conjuring up the dark forces of Hell always creates the possibility, however slight, that Moloch or Baal or Mammon will get access to your ATM number and start wreaking havoc on your budget, perhaps by transferring your IRAs out of the conservative, blue-chip, well-managed Fidelity Magellan Fund and into Merv & Shecky's Emerging Paraguayan Small-Cap Convertible Debentures Fund.

What concerned me even more was getting the smell of fire and brimstone out of my clothes before I got home from the séance; my wife is already suspicious enough of some of the bars I frequent. So if it was at all possible, I was hoping to contact Morrison's itinerant spirit over the phone lines without having to subject myself to all the muss and fuss of a full-blown necromantic blowout.

The Rev. Maria D'Andrea (Ms. D., D.D.) seemed like a good person to start with. This congenial Long Island–based professional not only did psychic readings and hypnosis but could also perform rune castings.

Never having had my runes cast—though I did once have a girlfriend from northern California—I was pretty excited about our impending, transtelephonic psychic consultation. But when I phoned, Maria told me that she didn't do séances per se, and that in fact séances had become increasingly rare.

"Very few people do them now, because it's an extreme level," D'Andrea explained. "You can get the same information no matter what medium you use."

This was encouraging news, because it suggested that I might be able to contact the spirit of Jim Morrison without having to visit a witch or a sorceress or a warlock or a mystic seer or having to go to Los Angeles, all of which I find a bit on the scary side. D'Andrea told me my best bet was to call the Psychic Hotline, which costs sixty-five cents for the first minute and $2.25 for each additional minute.

I did—and I came away very pleased with the results. As anyone who's had experiences with 900-numbers will tell you, the operators on the other end can often pry loose a pretty fair piece of change by keeping you on the line with tantalizing bits of information, and you never realize what a sucker you've been till you get your phone bill at the end of the month. But nothing like that happened when I dialed Linda Sonnett at her 900-number in Elgin, Illinois. (I chose Sonnett because although there were fifteen psychics listed on the Psychic Network "900" Directory, none were based in Indiana. So I picked the next closest state, which begins with the same letter. Elgin is actually only 50 miles from Indiana, so it's certainly within easy psychic commuting distance of the Hoosier state.)

Sonnett immediately impressed me with her consummate professionalism. There was no song and dance, no carrot and stick, no bait and switch, no drum and fife when I got her on the line.

"I need to get into contact with Jim Morrison, the lead singer from the Doors," I explained. "A couple of years ago, Vice President Quayle told a reporter that he had never heard of Jim Morrison. I wanted to find out if Jim Morrison has ever heard of him."

"I heard 'yes,'" was the psychic's immediate response, which went through me like a stiletto. My heart beat like a hammer and my eyes welled full of tears. *"I don't know where I heard it, but I heard 'yes.'"*

"You mean you heard it from someone else?" I inquired, disbelievingly.

"I was interviewed locally and someone asked that question," Sonnett replied. "I happen to believe in angels and saints, even though I grew up in the Lutheran church, and people will ask, 'Well, how can a professional person like you do this sort of thing, and I have to explain it."

She lost me there for a minute. I couldn't figure out what angels and saints and Lutherans had to do with Jim Morrison and Dan Quayle. But one thing she said really kicked me like a mule bucking in its stall: the thing about queries from local reporters. Was it possible that someone—Broder? Woodward?—else had beaten me to the story, that someone else was hot on the trail of the Lizard King, trying to pinpoint his relationship with the vice president?

I came back to her with my Morrison inquiries, but the psychic kept drifting in and out of lucidity. Every time I asked her a question, she would recite a singsong necromantic rhyme that sounded like an occult limerick: "If you search for the power in ye / You will find the truth that is Thee." Or something to that effect.

Still, I had no reason to doubt her remarks about Morrison. *"I'm hearing mentally, right now, that I heard 'yes,' he had heard of him. He does know him."* Gosh, I said. Then I shifted gears. I pointed out that Morrison had died in France, which is a long way from Indiana, and wondered how he could stay in contact with current events so far from home. After all, if you died in Paris, wouldn't your soul stay there forever? And wouldn't your soul want to stay there, rather than going to someplace like Indiana?

"No," was her response. "As far as I can understand, it's like being in a different dimension. He's just moved to another level of reality. But he's aware of what's happening here."

That was fine. But I still had to feed her my fail-safe question. If she was just some hot babe working the psychic hotline circuit out in the middle of nowhere, it would make perfect sense for her to string me along and tell me whatever she thought I wanted to hear just to keep the meter running. It couldn't have been too hard for her to figure out that I *wanted* to be told that Jim Morrison knew who Dan Quayle was. So now I decided to go with a change of pace. I'd fed her my fastball. Now I was going to try the curve.

"Just one more question," I interjected. "Has Jim Morrison ever heard of Garret Hobart?"

"No," she replied without hesitation in response to my inquiry about the god-awful twenty-fourth vice president of the United States, who had served less than three years under William McKinley, and whose name was synonymous with vice presidential impotence. "No, not really. I'm getting no."

I guess that kind of sealed it for me. If Sonnett had told me that Jim Morrison knows who Garret Hobart was, I would have known she was lying. Nobody knows who Garret Hobart was: not journalists, not politicians, not raconteurs, not incredibly intelligent, plugged-in people like Norman Ohrnstein and Nina Totenberg, and certainly not some dead, dipsomaniacal rock star from L.A. Unless Jim Morrison was spending all eternity wandering around the Historical Society of Paterson, New Jersey, boning up on the life of its most famous political figure, there was just no way he could have ever heard of Garret Hobart. She was telling the truth.

Think about it then. Here's Jim Morrison, dead lo these twenty-one years, drifting around in the void, waiting for Armageddon, when his soul may be released from its ethereal chains and go to its final resting place forever. You wouldn't think a guy in that position would be all that interested in the American vice presidency. Yet, amazingly, Morrison knew who Dan Quayle is. On the other side of the coin, you have this pasty-faced ding-a-ling who grew up in the 1960s, when Morrison was doing all that neat stuff with his throbbing, tumescent manhood, and *Quayle has never even heard of the guy*. It doesn't add up. Unless Quayle is an extraterrestrial, he has to have heard of Jim Morrison. He must be lying. But why?

I spent a lot of time thinking about this question, and would never have cracked the mystery without the help of Garry Trudeau, the Pulitzer Prize–winning creator of the *Doonesbury* comic strip. When I visited with Trudeau, he was still heavily involved in the Brett Kimberlin controversy: the charge that during Quayle's first term in the Senate, the DEA had investigated him for buying drugs. I found it hard to imagine Dan Quayle using any drug more powerful than Robitussin, and, besides, if it did turn out that Quayle used to smoke pot or do Quaaludes, it would blow my elaborate theory about Quayle and the 1960s right out of the water. So I skipped the drug stuff and concentrated instead on some groundbreaking research Trudeau had done in the area of U.S. legislative hipness.

Basically, Trudeau cautioned me against assuming that just because Dan Quayle wasn't a happening sixties dude that his Democratic contemporaries were. During a savory Chinese dinner at his well-appointed studio, Trudeau interrupted my exposition of the Quayle-as-Cultural-Memory-Suppressant Theory to recount a truly alarming story about an experience he had had during the 1988 presidential primaries.

Back then, seeking to determine whether any of the candidates—Democrats or Republicans—had ever been happening cats, love machines, or party animals, or were merely the plastic people they seemed to be today, Trudeau asked each of the men seeking the highest office in the land: "Which was your favorite Beatle?"

Their responses were the stuff of gothic terror. Bob Dole said, "Ringo; he's the only one I can remember."

Alexander Haig, vicar of foreign policy, said, "I guess I liked the old drummer boy. I don't even know his name."

Joe Biden's response was, "I don't have a favorite. I never liked them."

I never liked them.

Jack Kemp said, "Paul. He was the leader, wasn't he?"

Michael Dukakis also voted for the smarmy mop-topped composer of such unsolved crimes as "Michelle" and "Yesterday." "Paul," said Dukakis. "I liked his wife."

He liked Linda Eastman. This was terrifying. But it wasn't the most terrifying thing. *None of them liked John.*

As anyone with a smidgen of intelligence knows, the correct response to the question, "Who was your favorite Beatle?" is "John." (George, said Trudeau, "would get you partial credit.") But no one purporting to be hip, with it, bodacious, funky, or having one's shit all together would ever have picked Ringo, much less Paul. These politicos were culturally marooned. That was perfectly acceptable in fiftyish, graying types such as Haig, Kemp, and Dole, who, after all, were old farts, and Republicans to boot. But how could a liberal Democrat such as Joe Biden or Michael Dukakis, who had grown up during the Age of Aquarius, not know that their generation's favorite Beatle was John?

Now we get to the eerie part. One of the presidential candidates *did* have a place in his heart for John Lennon. One of the presidential candidates *was* familiar with the work of Yoko Ono's husband. One *was* aware that the way to woo Yuppies was not to say that you liked Linda Eastman or that little drummer boy. One of the candidates *knew* that it was political suicide to say out loud that you didn't have a favorite Beatle, that in fact you had never even liked the most popular musical group in history who had lifted the hearts of an entire planet with their zany antics and lovable fab-fourishness. This man *knew* that the way you bridged the yawning chasm between the generations was to quote from a John Lennon song such as "Give Peace a Chance."

That man's name is George Bush.

It gets weirder. When George Bush actually included a line from Lennon's internationally celebrated anthem in a speech on the hustings in 1988, Jack Kemp went ballistic. Kemp thought it was inconceivable that a leader of the Grand Old Party would ever quote from a song by that mop-topped pacifist alien and drug addict.

"This is embarrassing, to have a Republican talking about 'Give Peace a Chance,'" said the former Buffalo Bills quarterback.

Obviously, no one seriously believes that John Lennon was ever George Bush's favorite Beatle. Trudeau says that Bush's use of the lyric was a clear case of "cultural pandering," not unlike all that stuff about Loretta Lynn and pork rinds and the Oak Ridge Boys. But Trudeau also recalls that it was when he heard Bush utter the line from the laconic Liverpudlian's song that he first realized that the Kennebunkport klutz had "a lock on the White House." Now then, where did the inspiration to use that line come from?

From Lee Atwater.

Even as I write these lines, I am sending duplicate copies of all my notes and files and research and videotapes to Mark Lane and Oliver Stone and Kevin Costner *just in case an accident befalls me.* Why? Listen up.

When people think of the legacy of Lee Atwater, they think instinctively of the vicious, negative campaigning, of the vile Willie Horton commercials, of the churlish attacks on Michael Dukakis and his wife. (Remember the stuff about Mike and the psychiatrist? Kitty and the flag-burning?) But that was only part of Atwater's contribution to his party, and by no means the most important part. What Atwater really brought to Republicans was an iconoclastic element of GOP pizazz, a conviction that it was possible to be a Republican without dressing, or even having a name, like Julie Nixon Eisenhower. It was Atwater who taught Republicans both young and old that it was possible to co-opt the cultural icons of the sixties generation and manufacture an aura of ersatz coolness. Remember the photos of Atwater and Bush playing guitar at that Blues Monsters postelection party in 1988? Remember Atwater duckwalking to "High Heel Sneakers"? Remember Atwater posing for a photograph with his pants down? This was not your average Republican. This was a dude who knew not only how to get down, but how to get with it.

By doing all this wild and crazy stuff, Atwater showed his fellow Republicans that it was possible to beat liberals at their own game. He demonstrated that a passion for rock 'n' roll was not philosophically incompatible with a burning desire to see the capital gains tax reduced from 28 percent to 15 percent. He showed his fellow Republicans that it was possible to be a Republican and still do the jerk and the pony maroni. In this sense, Atwater was a philosophical kinsman of such party-animal Republicans as P. J. O'Rourke, conservatives who were not afraid to admit that they'd smoked a little grass and popped a few pills back in the sixties.

Atwater was also a spiritual kinsman of such emerging hip Republican leaders as Governor William Weld of Massachusetts, a supply-siding, bureaucracy-purging, tax-slashing, free-market-venerating Republican who nevertheless can tell you not only who Semolina Pilchard was but what she was doing climbing up the Eiffel Tower. In 1991, Weld gave an interview to *The Boston Globe* in which he openly and enthusiastically discussed his affection for such groovy punk-rockers as Talking Heads and Elvis Costello—as well as Warren Zevon, Traffic, the Rolling Stones—and did it in such a way, with such detail and volubility and passion, that you could tell he wasn't faking it, that it wasn't just some PR gambit cooked up by his spin doctors. A spin doctor might have dreamed up Weld's enthusiasm for the Stones' brilliant 1971 double-LP *Exile on Main Street,* but no blow-dried nerd from Dartmouth could ever have cooked up Weld's remark that the recherché 1970s group Seatrain had recorded his favorite single of all time. And when the *Globe* asked who his favorite Beatle was, Weld knocked that big, fat, hanging curve right out of the park:

Let's do it by a process of elimination. It's not going to be Ringo. George was the best guitarist, but his solo albums are a little soupy for me. A lot of McCartney's music—although I think he's a great talent—is too saccharine for me. That leaves Lennon. He was the most revolutionary. He put more zip into it than anyone else.

Surely, anyone reading Weld's cogent remarks would feel compelled to say: There's something happening here; what it is ain't exactly clear. A Republican who got four out of four in the Favorite Beatle Quiz? A Republican who knew that the Rolling Stones were never the same after *Exile on Main Street*? A Republican who used to go home from working for Ed Meese at the Justice Department singing Talking Heads' "Once in a Lifetime," containing the words "This is not my beautiful house . . . this is not my beautiful wife"? The verdict was clear. *This was a man who had sold his soul to rock 'n' roll.*

But it was Atwater who made it acceptable for people like William Weld to breathe such opinions in public. The man was a legend. One night early in 1990, a couple of wiseass young reporters from *Spy* magazine decided to tail Atwater around the nation's capital to see if they could dig up any dirt on the GOP Godfather of Soul. As was only to be expected of such amateurs, the tail was a disaster—shortly after it began, Atwater actually jumped out of his limo and climbed into their car, declaring, "You boys seem to know where I'm going; why don't you give me a ride home?"

There then ensued a night of major league bipartisan weirdness for *Spy* reporters John Brodie and Bob Mack. Atwater led the young men into his den and proceeded to play them a demo tape he had just made with his idol B. B. King and other legends from this or that delta. "I'm bad, I'm bad, I'm the worst you ever had," Atwater sang, flailing away on air guitar. Later, he would expostulate on the artistic failings of Eric Clapton, pointing out similarities between Clapton and Supreme Court Justice Potter Stewart that had previously escaped the notice of *Rolling Stone, The American Lawyer,* and, for that matter, *Guitar Player.*

"You know, I love him and all that . . . but it's like Potter Stewart . . . you know it when you see it. He just doesn't quite get there."

Atwater then rattled on about his attempts to spring James Brown from the slammer, about his relationship with one of the Three Stooges, and about the relative virtues of various Muddy Waters LPs. The GOP chairman was obviously quite serious; when the lads interrupted him to ask about the future of the Republican party, he told them to shut up and listen to the guitar solo he was faking on a Stratocaster given him by bargain-basement Rolling Stone rhythm guitarist Ron Wood.

In feeding George Bush the line from John Lennon, Atwater was trying to bring the Republican party into the second half of the twentieth century, culturally speaking. But not every Republican was comfortable with the direction Atwater was taking the party. Not every Republican was comfortable with voting for a governor who admitted that he liked David Byrne numbers such as "Psycho Killer." Not every Republican was pleased at attending an election celebration where the entertainment was provided by Percy Sledge, Bo Diddley, Joe Cocker, Willie Dixon, Ron Wood, Dr. John, Etta James, and Stevie Ray Vaughan. Not every Republican was pleased at the sight of the president of the United States being dragged up on stage by Sam (No Dave) Moore, strapping on a guitar and pretending to trade sizzling, too-late-to-stop-now, incandescent blues licks with the chairman of the Republican National Committee.

You'd expect the Bob Dole and Robert Michel wing of the party to resent this stuff. They were old-timers, Glenn Miller buffs. Dole had gotten his arm shot up by the Nazis and didn't need this psycho killer nonsense. You'd also expect the Jake Garn and McCain types to resent this stuff; they were Vietnam vets with a real hard animus against the culture of the 1960s, with its horrid, recrudescent New Left undertones. What's more, the Doles and the Michels and the Garns and the McCains came from the heartland of America, from isolated rural states where none of those Sonic Youth or Dead Kennedys albums ever seriously threatened to go double-platinum.

What was harder to understand was the attitude of eastern urban Republicans, the ones who truly resented the Lee Atwatering down of the party. These were the guys who'd grown up in sophisticated places like Georgetown and Cambridge and New York City, and had gone to schools like Yale and Harvard and Dartmouth. Yet they hated this sixties stuff with a passion. They felt that it was ruining the country. They felt that it was a threat to civilization as we know it. And where was the greatest concentration of these people?

In the office of J. Danforth Quayle.

The facts are alarming. When Dan Quayle took office in 1989, he surrounded himself with an entourage of neoconservative wizards whose mission was to make him seem far more intelligent than he really was. This clique, numbering seven Ph.D.s (none from DePauw), included William Kristol, son of neocon founding father Irving Kristol, and a protégé of fire-breathing education secretary and drug czar Bill Bennett, as well as Carnes Lord, possessor of two Ph.D.s and proud translator of Aristotle's *Politics.*

These men were not party animals. As Charlotte Hays and Charlotte Allen point out in the December 1991 issue of *Spy,* several of Dan Quayle's closest advisers "subscribe to an arcane school of conservative philosophy known as Straussianism, after Leo Strauss, the late University of Chicago professor; other members include Allan Bloom and Francis *(The End of History?)* Fukayama. Straussianism is a kind of religion for high-octane conservative intellectuals, complete with a holy writ (Strauss's books and speeches) and even a schism between eastern and western Straussians. The school is especially appealing to philosophers, because its main tenet is that being a philosopher is life's loftiest calling; it tends to save its highest regard not for rulers but for those, like Aristotle and Machiavelli, who teach rulers."

Lee Atwater, who used to play guitar between five and eight hours a day from the time he was eight until he turned twenty-one, and who kept a guitar in his office at Republican National Committee headquarters, was not a member of either the eastern or western Straussian school.

"This was a guy who genuinely agonized over the implications of being a Republican and listening to Eric Clapton," says *Spy's* John Brodie.

Carnes Lord wasn't. Bill Kristol wasn't, either.

The implications of all this are too terrifying to be swept under the rug. When Dan Quayle took office in January 1989, Kristol and the boys forced him to start reading books by Plato and Machiavelli, and to quote ostentatiously from these works in embarrassing interviews with people from *U.S. News & World Report* and *The New Republic.* But they didn't give him any B. B. King records, nor any spanking-new compact discs featuring multicultural tribal chants fused with the quirky harmonies of David Byrne and the

Talking Heads. For the central characteristic of all Straussians—and this includes both the western and the eastern schools—is that they do not have the common touch. They do not get down and boogie all night long. They do not go to à go-go. They do not party till they puke. In their view, it's only rock 'n' roll, but they dislike it.

The record is clear on their extraordinary disdain for the masses. When Dan Quayle agreed to do a ninety-second appearance on the enormously popular CBS TV show *Major Dad*, Bill Kristol admitted that he had never seen the show. Allan Bloom's *Closing of the American Mind* is replete with furious tirades against the pernicious influence of rock 'n' roll. Francis Fukayama organizes his thoughts around Hegel and the obscure French intellectual Alexandre Kojeve, and uses words like *thymos*. His groundbreaking book, *The End of History and the Last Man* contends that all of human history is a slow but inexorable march toward the perfect society, which just happens to be this one. It is impossible to reconcile the contention that this is a perfect society and the last stage in the cultural evolutionary scale with the existence of Iron Maiden and Mötley Crüe. And do people with names like Carnes Lord, with two Ph.D.s from Yale and Cornell, really sound as if they ever owned a record featuring the searing, intricate guitar work of the immortal Carlos Santana?

I think it's pretty obvious what I'm driving at here. A drab, corny, old hack politician gets elected to the highest office in the land in large measure because of a successful masquerade as a man of the people who feels just as at home with the Beatles as with the Oak Ridge Boys. Shortly after he takes office, a rube from Indiana, who admits that he has never heard of Jim "Backdoor Man" Morrison and the Doors, takes over the post a heartbeat away from the presidency. He is surrounded by guys with names like Carnes Lord, all of whom have been heavily influenced by academics who loath rock 'n' roll and popular culture in general. And his staff is headed by a man who openly admits that he has never seen *Major Dad.* In 1990 Lee Atwater is incapacitated by an inoperable brain tumor. Not long after that, he dies.

I don't think his death was an accident.

I think somebody wanted him out of the way.

I'm not naming any names.

But I think you get the idea.
Something smells in Foggy Bottom.
I want that body exhumed.
I think the dude was iced.

V

HOW TO PROFIT FROM THE COMING AGE OF QUAYLE

It's all commerce.—RALPH GINZBURG

Back in 1987 I concocted what I viewed as a can't-miss get-rich scheme. The Iran-Contra scandal had just broken, taking center stage as one of the most ignominious interludes in recent American history. Naturally, I figured I could make a killing off the deal by buying up Ollie North autographs and selling them at vastly inflated prices once the full impact of the scandal had reverberated throughout the nation.

This would have been a disastrous investment decision, as I learned to my chagrin when I called my trusty autograph expert, Paul Hartunian, who operates out of Cedar Grove, New Jersey. Hartunian told me that in the eyes of history, Ollie North was a complete and utter nobody who would neither be admired, villified, nor remembered by posterity. "It's all ephemera; it's already disappeared," he said when I interviewed him for *Spy*, remarking that the only type of person crazy enough to think he could clean up by speculating in Ollie Northabilia was "the guy who's a taxicab driver by day and an autograph dealer by night." Plus me. Hartunian said the same was true for Elliott Abrams, Richard Secord, Fawn Hall, and all the rest of those scumbunnies who allegedly sold their country down the river for a few pieces of silver, plus some inexpensive home security equipment. Their autographs were worth nothing, maybe less. "To use your term 'shelf life,' " said the collector, "you could measure it in weeks, even days."

From that conversation and several others conducted over the next three or four years, I learned a whole lot about the vagaries of the autograph market. For example, I learned that Son of Sam autographs were a bad investment because the monstrous psychopath, having first ruined the lives of his six victims and their families, had then made life miserable for autograph collectors (hoping to put their kids through college by selling their David Berkowitziana) by flooding the market with tiny snippets of paper reading:

I AM THE SON OF SAM AND I KILLED SIX PEOPLE.

I learned that Charles Manson autographs, once worth as much as $250, had tumbled to barely $50 or $60 because the verdict of history— that he was nothing more than a mass murderer—had caught up with him. And I learned the most important lesson of all: that the autographs worth the most money are the ones scrawled by people who exerted a profound influence over the course of history, usually to the benefit of humanity. For this reason, Hartunian explained, the signatures of the Mike Milkens, the Ivan Boeskys, and the Dennis Levines had no more than ephemeral value. These folks were garden-variety sleazeballs whose influence over the course of history was evanescent. The only bad people whose autographs were worth anything were the *really* bad people, monsters whose actions profoundly altered the course of history: Adolf Hitler, Josef Stalin, Attila the Hun, and, to a lesser extent, Lee Harvey Oswald and Sirhan Sirhan. (Attila the Hun's John Hancock is kind of hard to come by these days, but so is Sirhan Sirhan's.)

Here, Hartunian set forth a basic rule of thumb: When buying an autograph, never consider what your neighbors Chuck and Shirley think about the person who wrote it. Consider what people named Jean-Paul, Didier, Gabrielle, Simone, and Fifi are likely to think about that person.

"People in France have never heard of Mike Milken," Hartunian told me in 1989 when I interviewed him for *Forbes*. "It's the question you have to keep asking yourself: What do they think of this guy in France? Elvis Presley changed history. They know him. The Beatles changed history. They know them. But who ever heard of the Beach Boys? Who ever heard of the Turtles?"

One other thing that I learned from Hartunian was that the autograph-collecting community is an amazingly prescient handicapper of political elections. George Bush autographs were already going for $65 late in 1987; Mike Dukakises and Rich Gephardts were going for $10, proving that the market already knew that Bush had the inside track on the White House, while Dukakis and Gephardt were dead on arrival. After the Broder-Woodward hagiography of Vice President Dan Quayle appeared in *The Washington Post* in January 1992, it seemed like a good time to check in with my collector friend and find out how the vice president's fortunes were faring.

"Talk about the rise of the phoenix," said Hartunian. "When Quayle first became vice president four years ago, you couldn't give his autograph away. But early this year, autograph collectors started to see some legitimacy there. I recently sold a signed letter, containing some mildly interesting comments Quayle had written, for eighty-five dollars. Since then, I've gotten over forty orders for Quayle. That told me two things: that collectors see him as a legitimate vice president and a legitimate candidate for the White House in 1996, and that I had priced the letter too low."

Interestingly, Hartunian says that the revival in Quayle's fortunes actually preceded the laudatory Woodward-Broder series.

"It started in the fall of '91, but it really took off when he went after Mario Cuomo and said, 'Take that.' All of a sudden that somehow legitimized him in the eyes of collectors, and I started getting calls. If I get two or three calls for something I put in my catalog, that's about average. If I get four or five, I know something's going on there. But if I get thirty or forty calls, it tells me that I missed the mark and underpriced the item. And that's what happened with Quayle."

(Technical note: When buying items autographed by Dan Quayle, make sure that you either get a letter bearing his signature or a photograph. Scraps of paper with his name scrawled on it are virtually worthless, as is anything lacking in some kind of historical context. According to the Fall 1991 issue of *The Manuscript Society News*, Quayle has a habit of turning up at public functions and scrawling an imaginary signature with his fingertip, while an aide traveling in his wake distributes "preautographed" business cards. These cards are nearly worthless. A final note: Many pols use a device called an "autopen" to crank out thousands of seemingly genuine signatures. Autopen signatures are worthless.)

Hartunian stresses that vice presidential autographs *always* retain a certain value, because the entire universe of specimens is so tiny. There have only been forty-four veeps in our history, so *any* vice president's autograph—even Garret Hobart's—is going to be worth something, if only to collectors who want a complete set. But in Quayle's case it is not simply a matter of collectors buying up Quayle to round out their vice presidential collections. Beginning in late 1991, the dealer began to sense that "a number of people have begun heavily speculating in Quayle. They do view him as a contender for the presidency."

Are these individuals or institutions?

"Always individuals," says Hartunian. "Institutions have an institutional mentality, which means that they always buy materials at the worst possible moment. They buy Zachary Taylor letters right *after* Zachary Taylor's body has been exhumed and the theory that he was poisoned gets laid to rest. Institutions are a poor predictor of the market."

Speculators, on the other hand, are not.

"They are really super at handicapping elections," says Hartunian. "They know that George Bush is a virtual lock to be reelected in 1992, and they know that the chances of Quayle being dumped are very low because it would be too politically risky for the president. They're not stocking up on Bush now because the price is too high. But they are buying Quayle; I have a waiting list of forty people who will buy anything I can get."

It is widely believed that political figures as diverse as James Baker, Phil Gramm, and, of course, Pat Buchanan are gradually positioning themselves for a run at the White House in 1996. The realization that Dan Quayle may very well have the inside track on that office is only slowly beginning to dawn on the public. Collectors, on the other hand, have known this for at least a year, and are already placing their money on Quayle. This is reflected by the amount of speculative interest Hartunian has detected in materials signed by Secretary of State James Baker.

"Zero," says Hartunian. "Nobody believes he has a chance of becoming president."

What about Phil Gramm?

"Zero. Just nothing. Absolutely nothing. Nobody believes it."

What about Buchanan?

"He's in the same category as Jesse Jackson. No one seriously thinks he has a chance of ever being president of the United States. But there might be some interest in him as a spoiler. A signed autograph would bring about ten dollars."

Hartunian says that the earliest tipoff to the outcome of the 1992 election was the distinct lack of interest in Democratic materials among collectors in the spring. "It's so cheap, you can buy scads of this stuff," he notes.

What is most fascinating about the boom in Quayleiana is that the value of the materials is not necessarily predicated upon the vice president's continuing in office.

"If Bush were to dump Quayle, he would probably go underground for a while and come up for air in 1996. He would be like Jimmy Carter in 1976. What was Jimmy Carter before he ran for the White House? He was governor of Georgia, a nothing, a nobody. Politically, he was not on the scoreboard; remember 'Jimmy Who?' Then he became an American folk hero. Quayle could do the same thing."

What's more, Hartunian feels that Quayle's being dumped from the ticket could create a wonderful buying opportunity for investors willing to hunker down for the long haul.

"If Quayle got dumped, a lot of people would start unloading their materials. At that point, speculators would move in, figuring that if Quayle were elected in 1996, the price would go through the roof. The downside is: They could be dead wrong. I speculated on Humphrey in 1968."

Taking the long view, does Hartunian think Quayle will ever be president?

"Personally, I have my doubts," he admits. "That's primarily because of his image. When Richard Nixon was vice president, there were plenty of jokes about him, but they had a kind of intellectual edge to them. The jokes about Quayle are mean jokes, like 'Did you hear that the vice president has a new plane? Airhead One.' The jokes are *ridiculous* jokes. Still, he's made a big comeback. When he first took office, I thought he was dead in the water."

———

Death is the next subject that must be considered, specifically the death of President Bush. As far as I can determine, it is impossible to find anyone who believes that a Dan Quayle ascendancy to the White House would be a good thing for the stock market. The only question is: How far will the market go down, and how long will it stay down?

John Neff, the wise old sage who manages the mammoth Vanguard Windsor Fund, says that a sudden Quayle ascendancy would cause the market to lose 10 percent of its value, and perhaps more. "Markets are the captive of momentum," explains Neff. "The momentum would be downward."

Mario Gabelli, who manages a family of mutual funds with $2 billion in assets, agrees that the market would tank if Quayle should suddenly step into Bush's shoes, sharing Neff's view that the collapse would bottom out at about 10 percent. Marc Perkins, chairman of the Tampa, Florida, brokerage house Perkins, Smith also expresses that view, but insists that by the end of the day he would be wading into the market as a buyer. Victor Sperandeo, a veteran trader at Rand Management and author of *Trader Vic: Methods of a Wall Street Master*, also agrees that the initial reaction of the markets would be "a horror show: 10 percent minimal." But unlike Perkins and Neff, he feels that the sell-off might occur over a period of days, rather than in a single, twenty-four-hour stampede for the exits. And, like Perkins, he would take advantage of the sell-off to cover his short positions and go back and buy "some things that I really like. But would I be a buyer in the first hour after the drop? No."

Sperandeo's comments underscore a very important point: that a sudden Quayle presidency would be very good news for short-sellers. Shorts-sellers are people who borrow the stock of companies that they think are overvalued, then sell the stock, and wait for the price to collapse so that they can buy back the stock at a lower price and replace the borrowed securities. Usually, short-sellers wait for hyped, dud stocks to collapse of their own accord, but a Dan Quayle presidency would be a bonus because it would spark a huge, immediate sell-off in cruddy, overvalued stocks.

All this notwithstanding, not every short-seller views a Quayle meltdown as the answer to all of his prayers. "Would the market drop 300 points if Quayle became president?" laughs Joe Feshbach, the most famous short-seller in America. "Yeah, maybe, but that would probably mean the market would drop from 6000 to 5700."

Mike Murphy, a bear who built his reputation in the 1980s with two irreverent, savvy newsletters, *The Overpriced Stock Service* and *The California Technology Stock Letter*, suspects that any sell-off would be short-lived.

"I think it would be transient, the Kennedy reaction," says Murphy. "The market would immediately go down 250 points, at which point they would shut it down, and when it reopened it would be down 400 points because of margin squeezes. But it's a one-day event; the market goes down, but the next day it rallies. Look, how many companies' cash flow is going to be affected by Dan Quayle's becoming president or not?"

Steve Kibbey, a money manager for Centurion Capital in Dallas, feels that the possibility of a serious dip in the market is a clear and present danger any time the averages achieve the historically anomalous levels they reached early in 1992. Interviewed in February 1992, when the market was "an incredibly risky environment" (trading at about twenty times earnings), Kibbey noted, "Americans don't like uncertainty. I don't know anyone who's talked about this possibility [Quayle stepping in for Bush], except in the most cursory fashion, but my feeling is that you'd have a short-term dip in the market. Some people would immediately come back in as buyers, because they've been trained to buy on the dip. But whether prices would stabilize remains to be seen."

Sperandeo also feels that the rout would be temporary.

"The market would sell off for two main reasons," he says. "One, Quayle is not looked at as a man of substance. The vice president is, of course, a parrot; you don't really know what he stands for. But the more important consideration is that it would increase the possibility that the Democrats would take over the White House. And Clinton and the rest of those guys are anti-business."

Sperandeo's comments are valuable for two reasons: because they underscore the widely held perception on Wall Street that Democrats are bad for business, and because they show that even though people inside the Beltway know that Dan Quayle is basically a younger, slightly more intelligent version of Ronald Reagan, with solid, right-wing political credentials, people outside the Beltway don't know anything about his political beliefs at all. They just know him as Dan Quayle.

"People would be terrified," says Shad Rowe, a Dallas hedge fund manager who writes a regular investing column for *Forbes.* "But in the long run, it might not matter that much. Remember what we read in our history books about Chet Arthur in the White House? People couldn't believe it. But maybe it doesn't matter."

How long would the market stay in the doldrums after a post-Bush meltdown? Murphy says that it might take a while for the market to regain its momentum, but doesn't feel that Quayle need forever remain a captive of his horrible image. "There's a sense that any Republican is better for business than any Democrat," he explains. "Before Reagan, that wasn't true: The market actually did better under Democrats than under Republicans. But if you ran those numbers today, you'd probably find that they're pretty close. So even though Quayle has this image problem, the first time he does something right, all will be forgiven."

Sperandeo agrees that the market would come back in its own good time, but not with enough of a vengeance for the longs to break out the champagne.

"Ever since Lincoln, every time a president has died or had a heart attack, the market has always recovered," says the trader. "Would it come back full? No, I don't think so."

Both Murphy and Perkins feel that the government is too enormous and amorphous to be dramatically affected by any single politician, no matter how competent, no matter how inept. "The president is the prisoner of his advisers," says Murphy. Perkins, who is contemptuous of Washington in general, doesn't think that the president, the vice president, the speaker of the house, or anyone else on Capitol Hill has much power to affect the American economy.

"The federal government is a metastatic blob, run by twenty-eight-year-old blond-haired graduates of Princeton and Dartmouth, that consumes everything in its path," reasons Perkins. "People like Quayle come to Washington and find out that they are incidental. The twenty-eight-year-old blond-haired graduates from Princeton and Dartmouth give them position papers telling them how to vote. And they vote that way. The twenty-eight-year-old blond-haired graduates of Princeton and Dartmouth are the ones who run the country."

Kibbey feels that the key point in all this would be whether a Quayle presidency immediately stampeded foreign investors and caused a collapse of the dollar. "If the dollar fell apart and interest rates exploded, that would absolutely slaughter the market," Kibbey says. "A lot of people are looking for us to lead the world out of the recession, and if that confidence in the United States were ever destroyed, you could have a problem."

Noting, like Neff, that markets are creatures of momentum, Kibbey adds, "If you're familiar with Chaos Theory, you know that any particular grain of sand could be the one to set things off. Well, we don't know if Dan Quayle is that grain of sand."

That pretty much sums up the attitude of folks in the highly volatile stock market. But what about the more sedate bond markets? How would they react to the news that Dan Quayle had replaced George Bush as the forty-second president of the United States? Joe Mysak, editor of *The Bond Buyer*, the New York authority on municipal bonds since 1891 (no one can remember who was the authority *until* 1891), has this to say, "The first hour after the news is announced, the market—and here we're talking about the Treasury bond market, because everything else follows suit—is off two points, maybe two-and-a-half. By the end of the day, the market is off maybe a point; the next morning everything goes back up. The bond market is a lot more relaxed than the stock market."

What does that mean?

"The bond market knows that it almost doesn't matter who's president. This isn't the kind of country where the Republicans get into power and go out and shoot the Democrats, or vice versa. So at the end of the second day the bond market is off maybe an eighth of a point."

Mysak also feels that the president is largely incapable of dramatically altering the powerful economic tides that engulf us every day of our lives.

"Consider such a disaster as Jimmy Carter," says Mysak. "Carter exacerbated a few things and made things worse than they were, but a lot of things that happened were really beyond his control. So, in a certain sense, it doesn't really matter who's in the White House." He pauses, then remarks, "I think it's kind of reassuring."

Reassurance is precisely what the markets need in times of national emergency, says Paul Montgomery. Montgomery is an extraordinarily prescient interest-rate forecaster who works as an analyst for Legg Mason Wood Walker in Newport News, Virginia. The publisher of a highly idiosyncratic newsletter called *Universal Economics*, Montgomery enjoys a cultish celebrity among market cognoscenti because of the esoteric barometers of market sentiment he has developed over the years. One of these is the *Time* Magazine Cover Story Indicator, derived from the premise that by the time the world's most popular and influential general-interest magazine does a cover story about a trend, the trend is just about over. Thus, if *Time* magazine, written by smart generalists, but generalists all the same, decides to do a bullish story about the stock market, it's probably time for investors to head for the exits. Conversely, if *Time* does a story lamenting what tough economic times we all face, it's probably time to wade into the stock market with cash in both fists.

The Indicator, research shows, is accurate more than 80 percent of the time, going all the way back to October 28, 1929, when the magazine put Ivar Kreuger ("The Match King") on the cover. At the time, Kreuger was the second wealthiest man in Europe, a financial titan who had just lent the French government $75 million to stabilize the franc. October 29, 1929, was Black Tuesday, the day the world fell apart, and also the day that Kreuger's stock began its horrifying plummet from $38 a share to a paltry $5 two years later when Kreuger committed suicide.

Montgomery, who has also found that *Business Week* cover stories provide a virtually infallible contrarian indicator (always buy when the brain-dead *Business Week* says to sell, and vice-versa), believes that the market would take a grievous, short-term beating were Quayle to step into Bush's shoes in the next four years. But he stresses that the effect would probably be just that: short-term.

"It would be a terrible blow to market psychology," says Montgomery, "but it wouldn't destroy it unless the market was ready to go anyway, unless the underlying technical factors were so weak that it was ready to go. When John F. Kennedy died he was a beloved figure, whereas Lyndon Baines Johnson was pretty much thought of as a lowlife. But I remember that when Kennedy died the market went down and then it came right back up. The market does what it's going to do."

Montgomery does point out one major difference between 1963 and 1992: The economy LBJ inherited when Kennedy died was a robust one, while the Bush-Quayle economy is in fairly bad shape, with a vastly overvalued stock market poised at the very precipice of disaster. (It should be noted that when Dwight Eisenhower had his heart attack in 1955, the market also had a massive sell-off, despite the relatively good health of the economy. When Truman succeeded FDR in 1945, just as the Nazis were being ground into the dust, the market actually went up, as it did when the lightweight Calvin Coolidge succeeded the poltroonish Harding in 1923. But in both of those cases, the economy was in good shape.)

For a left-wing market perspective on all this, we turn to *The Left Business Observer,* the offbeat newsletter put out by New York economist Doug Henwood. Though Henwood despises the vice president, describing his rise to power, or near-power, as "a sign of the absolute debasement of the American ruling class," he doesn't think a Quayle takeover would necessarily be disastrous for the market.

"The president himself is not terribly important," he says, echoing the comments of Perkins, Gabelli, Murphy, and Rowe. "There's a permanent government that does everything."

It would be absolutely irresponsible to conclude this section without considering the opinions of our good friends to the north. In Canada, as in the Lower Forty-eight, it is almost universally agreed that the sudden appearance of Dan Quayle in George Bush's boots would trigger a merciless stampede.

"October of '87 would seem like just a practice run for this," says Pierre Panet-Raymond, a Montreal money manager. "I think that the reaction might be overblown, but we could easily see the market give up 700 or 800 points."

That's the *eastern* Canadian viewpoint on the matter. But what about the *western* Canadian viewpoint? For this we turn to Dave Pescod, a broker in Edmonton, Alberta, famous for the largest shopping mall in the entire solar system, and for little else. Pescod does not think that the market rout would be quite as complete as his colleague from the despised eastern provinces suggests.

"You guys would all bail out and we'd get creamed too, because we're just the tail that wags the dog," says Pescod. "But I don't know how long the effect would last, or how bad it would be. After all, some of the guys that you people elect down there aren't so, how shall I say it, *gifted.* Like, say, Jerry Ford, or your little friend from Georgia. Nice guys, with their hearts in the right places, but not too sure how all the levers work."

———

What can we learn from all this? The most obvious, long-term investing strategy is to make a list of the types of industries that would probably fare well under a Quayle administration and start buying them as soon as it looks like he's going to step into Bush's shoes. Conversely, one should make a list of industries that would fare poorly during a Quayle administration and prepare to short them as soon as the new president gathers up the fallen Kennebunkportian scepter.

Obvious buys would include manufacturers of golf equipment, blue-chips based in Indiana (Eli Lilly, for example) that are likely to benefit from a Hoosier presidency, purveyors of wholesome entertainment (Disney, for example), and brewers, since it is virtually certain that a Quayle presidency would spark an immediate, protracted increase in the amount of drinking that takes place in this country. Stocks that would make obvious candidates for short sales would be book publishing companies.

But a savvy investor can also do well with a more eclectic approach to investing, particularly on the short side. Look at it this way: If you think that President Bush is looking a bit peaked, make a list of incredibly putzy companies with no earnings, no dividends, no sales, or no products, and short them. Biotechnology companies purporting to be working on a cure for AIDS, mutual funds specializing in unlisted securities in Outer Mongolia, and just about any company whose name ends in -osis, -isis, or -unex, or begins in aqua- are *always* good shorts. Once your short positions are in place, it's simply a matter of waiting for Dan Quayle to take office, watching the stock market collapse, and then covering your short positions and taking your profits. You may never have to work another day in your life.

But what if you're a long? What if you're one of those people who's bullish on America, who views short-selling as a cynical, un-American practice, as the investment equivalent of child molesting? Is there a realistic way to hedge your portfolio against the kind of short-term cataclysm a Dan Quayle presidency would bring on? The answer, sadly, is no. Traders regularly use a device called stop-loss orders to hedge against declining stock prices, mechanisms that theoretically ensure that a stock trading at, say, 32 will automatically be sold off once it declines by 10 percent. But stop-loss orders, notes Alan Abelson, editor of *Barron's*, only work in "orderly markets." Abelson explains that if the stock is trading at 10 and the stop-loss order is 8, "that doesn't help you if the next buy order is at 7." In short, once the market begins its descent into the abyss, you will have to rely on your own wits to get out quickly.

If it's any consolation, an analyst for a major money management firm says that big investors would be hurt just as badly as small ones in the event of Bush's death.

"Most money managers don't use stop-loss orders because they're glued to the screen waiting for stocks to move an eighth of a point," he explains. "But when you have a major cataclysm, it's all a big pension fund manager can do to get his broker to return his phone calls. You just have to grin and bear it."

Of course, there are many people in this country who refuse to believe that a Quayle presidency would result in a mere market correction of a few hundred points. Some people honestly believe that a Quayle presidency would cause the market to collapse, wiping out trillions of dollars in stockholder value, and dragging down the entire global economy with it. One well-traveled harbinger of doom told CNN that the moment Quayle takes over from Bush the market will give up 600 points. Naysayers such as this are not swayed by arguments such as those we have heard above, arguments in which professional money managers, who handle hundreds of millions of dollars of trades every day, explain that the person occupying the White House has very little effect on the real forces that drive the stock market: earnings, sales, profit margins, price/earnings ratios, cash flow. These people need to have things spelled out for them. They need to be shown precisely why a Dan Quayle presidency is not going to wipe out their portfolios.

Here is that explanation. When Dan Quayle was nominated as George Bush's running mate in August 1988, he took a severe pounding from the press. That pounding lasted from August of 1988 until the day of the election, and only started to abate in the spring of 1989. Although the vice president has continued to be treated with contempt and derision in many newspaper and magazine articles in the four years that have passed since then, his image as a simpleton has not been perpetuated primarily by the press. It has been perpetuated primarily by stand-up comics and talk-show hosts such as Jay Leno, David Letterman, and Arsenio Hall.

Let's get a little analytical here. When George Bush and Dan Quayle were elected on November 8, 1988, the Dow Jones Industrial Average stood at 2127.49. In the next three years it rose more than 1300 points to surpass the 3400 mark, in one of the most astonishing bull markets in history. Throughout that period the comic broadsides of Jay Leno and David Letterman directed at Dan Quayle have had no direct financial impact on the markets, because the stock market does not care about the vice president of the United States, and cares even less what stand-up comics think about him. However, if Dan Quayle were to become president, for whatever reason, those barbs and taunts would play a crucial, and perhaps decisive, role in shaping the attitude of the American people toward their new leader. Moreover, those barbs and taunts would play a crucial role in forming the attitudes of the tens of millions of individual investors who have money invested in the stock, bond, and mutual fund markets.

Here's where the genius of the capitalist system comes into play. In a worthless, oppressive, stupid society like, say, Romania or El Salvador, stand-up comics are marginal characters who don't have a whole lot of cash to spread around in investments. Because they don't have a whole lot of cash, a lot of real estate, a lot of stocks, they have no personal stake in the economic well-being of their nations. They are free to mercilessly pillory their national leaders, thus causing the amused populace to lose confidence in them, thus causing the financial infrastructure to collapse.

In America things are different. Jay Leno, David Letterman, and Arsenio Hall are millionaires many times over. They have tax shelters. They own real estate. They probably own stocks; they almost certainly own long-term government bonds exempt from both state and local taxes. As a result, they have a direct financial stake in the economic well-being of this society and a direct personal stake in the smooth, uninterrupted functioning of the capital markets. And because of this, if and when Dan Quayle does become president, they will have a vested interest in making sure that the stock market does not collapse. To put a fine point on it, it will be in their best interests to lay off the new president of the United States.

What we are talking about here is a little-known portfolio management principle called the Carson-Agnew Comedic Circuit Breaker Theorem. This is a theory that states that upon the ascendancy of a clownish vice president to the highest office in the land, all of the influential stand-up comics in the nation will immediately receive urgent calls from their stockbrokers, portfolio managers, accountants, or wives warning them to *knock off the jokes*. These calls will make clear, in no uncertain fashion, that continued ridicule of the new president will set off a market meltdown that will wipe out overnight more than 50 percent of the wealth that the stand-up comic or talk-show host has amassed over the long, hard years of struggle when nobody wanted to give him a break, when jobs were hard to come by, and you were happy just to get a meal and a place to lay your head at night. The calls will make clear that it would be in the best interests of the stand-up comic not only to stop making fun of the president but to start making fun of his adversaries. And to make *a lot of fun* of his adversaries.

What is most fascinating about this theory is its relevance to the current situation. On January 8, 1992, while dining at a state function in Japan, George Bush leaned forward, vomited, and fell to the ground. For a moment, it seemed that the Age of Quayle had begun. A few days later David Letterman announced that he was laying off Dan Quayle jokes for a while.* Coincidence, you say? A vote of confidence in a

---

*The main reason that elected officials are required to put their stock holdings in blind trusts is to avoid conflicts of interest caused by unusual buying opportunities. For example, if the president were to become so ill that the vice president had to assume his duties, the vice president would know about the impending bloodbath in the markets long before anyone on Wall Street would. Having been told that he would be assuming office within a matter of hours, at which point a petrified nation would send the Dow Jones Industrial Average plummeting 300 points, Quayle could instruct

fellow Hoosier? Then consider this. On Super Bowl Sunday, January 26, 1992, I spoke with Jay Leno on the subject of Quayle jokes. I asked what gave. And Leno informed me that he too was getting tired of doing Quayle jokes.

"You can only do so many of them before the audience gets tired," said Leno. "After two, they become redundant." Then he added, "Teddy Kennedy is more susceptible to humor than Quayle is." There could be only one reason for Jay Leno to say this: Leno had seen those haunting video clips of the chief executive seemingly barfing his way into the hereafter. Leno had briefly come face-to-face with the realization that Dan Quayle might suddenly become president. Seconds later he had gotten a call from his broker explaining the dire reverberations on his own financial well-being if the jokes about Quayle continued. He immediately turned up the heat on the Democrats. He knocked off the Quayle jokes.

The conclusion is inescapable. *Jay Leno sees the handwriting on the wall.* And the handwriting reads: *"Dan Quayle, forty-second president of the United States of America."*

Jay Leno knows which side his bread is buttered on.

Hail to the Chief.

---

his broker to "sell everything" and avoid a massacre, or could even tell his friends and relatives to make a killing by shorting everything in sight in expectation of a huge market meltdown. This is the sort of stuff people used to do all the time during the Reagan administration.

V I

THE VERDICT OF HISTORY

Obviously, while Quayle was at school, he was something of a playboy; as much can be said of the young Churchill, the young Waugh, and the young Augustine.

—*National Review*, September 30, 1988

Immediately after monstrous tragedies occur on this planet, there is a very brief period during which everyone tells the truth when discussing them. For the first twenty-four hours after Pearl Harbor is bombed or Rome is sacked, nobody comes out and says, "It's about time" or "So what?" It takes at least twenty-four hours before even the most jaded revisionist can bring himself to proclaim that the sinking of the *Titanic* is a blessing in disguise because it will make navigators more attentive to icebergs, or that a massive earthquake in San Francisco sends a reassuring message to Americans because only a handful of people died, whereas if it had happened in Armenia, the casualties would have run into the millions—proving that the emergency warning system works! In the wake of a total catastrophe, even the most astute spin doctors find themselves suddenly rendered speechless.

This is precisely what happened when George Bush announced that Dan Quayle would be sharing the ticket with him in the 1988 presidential election. Predictably, Democrats reacted with a mixture of glee (how could he be so stupid?) and horror (what if these guys win?) that Bush would select such a bland, obscure, apparent pinhead as his running mate. But this is precisely the way that Republicans—even right-wing Republicans—reacted as well. The immediate reaction of most people on the right was the same as that of most people on the left: Who is this guy Quayle, and why is Bush doing this to us? (You can look it up.)

This evanescent moment of naked candor lasted about a week. Then, once the media feeding frenzy regarding Quayle's National Guard service, his weekend spent with *Playboy* model and resourceful lobbyist Paula Parkinson, and his mysterious academic record got underway, Republicans closed ranks, viewing an attack upon *him* as an attack upon *them*. Ingenious arguments defending the vice-president-to-be were manufactured at a fever pace. The most plausible ones were those advanced by amateur historians who ransacked the pages of history looking for famous historical figures who started out with as many public relations problems as Dan Quayle, yet lived to overcome them. This seemed like a wonderful idea, until Quayle was foolish enough to compare himself favorably to the martyred John F. Kennedy during his otherwise satisfactory vice presidential debate with Lloyd Bentsen.

Quayle's gaffe notwithstanding, the idea of pillaging history books for image-enhancing analogies is an inspired one, so much so that it is now time to return to the annals of history for another round of ransacking to see if there are any good ones that the spin doctors missed.

In defending Dan Quayle's dismal, academic record (he had a 2.16 GPA at DePauw), assorted pundits and Quayleophiles have pointed out that Franklin Delano Roosevelt, John F. Kennedy, and Ronald Reagan were all pretty rotten students back in their college days, as were the aforementioned Lion of Britain, the young Waugh, and Saint Augustine, who dissipated his youth seducing an astonishing number of Nubian harlots in the fleshpots of Sodom before getting on with his life's work: dreaming up the Just War Theory at precisely the same moment that the Vandals were clambering over the walls of Hippo, where he happened to be living. It was really the Just (in time) War Theory.

If it is fair to invoke the names of FDR, JFK, Winston Churchill, Saint Augustine, and the young Waugh (whoever that was), in an attempt to characterize the vice president as a "classic late bloomer," then it is equally fair to delve even deeper into the history books to ferret out relevant historical analogies between the life of Dan Quayle and the lives of the great men of history. And if we are looking for examples of important historical figures who did not show early promise, the examples are eye-opening and plentiful. Mohammed was an undistinguished camel thief with virtually no upward mobility before he founded the world's most popular, if unpredictable, religion at the age of fifty-two and became a hero to billions, though not to Salman Rushdie. Joan of Arc was a daft teenage peasant who used to complain to her parents that she was being lobbied by a trio of chatty angels before she strapped on a suit of armor and helped to drive the hated English out of France forever.

In recent years, revisionist psychologists have advanced theories that the divine Ms. Arc's angelic voices may have been caused by a rare, medieval hearing disorder, or that she was the victim of an elaborate prank carried out by furloughed commedia dell'arte performers trying to keep up their chops until the feudal market for performance artists picked up. For this and other reasons, feminists have hesitated to adopt Joan as a full-fledged role model, deeming it unwise to overlook the fact that the peasant girl grew up in rural France, where people start drinking cognac at five o'clock in the morning. All this notwithstanding, it is impossible to underestimate Joan's intellectual influence on Camille Paglia, her theatrical influence on Jane Fonda, and her sartorial influence on Madonna.

There are many other examples of complete nobodies who rose from the out-basket of history to become political colossi. Before delivering King Charles I's head to the executioner's block, Oliver Cromwell was a diffident, fortyish, unambitious farmer most famous for saying "No man goes so high as he who knows not where he is going." Before he stepped into his father's shoes, Henry V—immortalized as Prince Hal in Shakespeare's *Henry IV* (as opposed to Henry Tudor, who was immortalized as Henry VII in Shakespeare's *Richard III*)—was thought to be a ne'er-do-well jock and party animal who would amount to absolutely nothing. (Bear in mind that at the beginning of *Henry V*, it is the French dauphin's sneering coronation gift of a crate of tennis balls that really gets young Henry's dander up.)

But when the time finally came to get serious, Henry ditched his whoring wino friends, stopped sleeping with comely wenches, and went on to become one of the greatest kings in English history. Indeed, at the very end of Act I, Scene II, in *Henry IV, Part I,* the young prince, who is still very much in his *Animal House* mode, tells the audience that his adolescent dissipation is a calculated effort to make him seem more serious once the transformation occurs:

> So, when this loose behavior I throw off
> And pay the debt I never promised
> By how much better than my word I am,
> By so much shall I falsify men's hopes;
> And like bright metal on a sullen ground
> My reformation, glittering o'er my fault,
> Shall show more goodly and attract more eyes,
> Than that which hath no foil to set it off.
> I'll so offend, to make offense a skill;
> Redeeming time when men think least I will.

The parallels with the life of Dan Quayle literally leap off the page. Like Henry, who wasted his youth playing tennis, Quayle wasted his youth playing golf. Like Henry, who was accused of hanging out with drunkards, Quayle was accused of hanging out with drug dealers. Whereas Henry cavorted with sexually active opportunists like Falstaff, Quayle cavorted with sexually active opportunists like Paula Parkinson. Henry had a powerful, conservative family from whom he inherited England. Dan Quayle had a powerful, conservative family from whom he inherited Indiana. Before entering politics Henry had never held a job his dad hadn't arranged for him; ditto Dan Quayle. The last job either Henry V or Dan Quayle held before entering the public arena was working for their dads.

What's more, like Henry V before him, Quayle now finds himself rising from the ashes of his own reputation and "imitating the sun." As was the case with the black sheep Henry V, it is precisely because Quayle made such a horrible first impression back in 1988 that he is now garnering kudos from all sides; it is the contrast with those early disasters that makes him shine today.

It is true that Dan Quayle made a perfect fool of himself that fateful afternoon on the paddlewheeler the *Natchez Queen* in New Orleans when he ripped off his jacket, dashed to the front of the anachronistic vehicle, and began flailing his arms madly and babbling nonsense as George Bush looked on in disbelief. Quayle's idiotic gesticulating and numbskull banter has been captured for posterity on film, and nothing can ever be done to expunge the record.

Yet here, once again, history is kind to the vice president, providing us with innumerable examples of famous men who made perfect fools of themselves the first time they were thrust into the national spotlight, yet who lived long enough to erase that bitter memory and ascend into the pantheon of the immortals. In 1754, the immature, dermatologically ravished George Washington, just twenty-two at the time, helped set off the French and Indian War by firing on a French fort not far from Pittsburgh, precipitating a humiliating military engagement that concluded with Washington in the hands of his enemies. The following summer, Washington was serving as Major General Edward Braddock's aide-de-camp when the British officer's command of 1,459 men was torn to pieces by a smaller army of 150 French militiamen and perhaps 1,000 Indian allies. Until recently, most historians familiar with the incident were convinced that the carnage would have been even worse had the Indians not taken time out to flay and castrate their captives, engaging in the kinds of depraved, primordial, widely reported activities that used to give Native Americans a really bad reputation. But that was before Kevin Costner came along and showed that this was all hearsay.

These early debacles did not prevent Washington from becoming commander-in-chief of the American rebel forces twenty years later when the War of Independence broke out, during which time he lost battles right, left, and center in the greater New York metropolitan area before heading south to lose the Battle of Germantown in the greater Philadelphia metropolitan area plus many other undistinguished engagements before the French finally bailed him out at Yorktown and allowed him to become the most famous and important man in American history.

Winston Churchill is an even finer example of a future legend whose debut in the spotlight was preposterously inglorious. We know (for *National Review* tells us so) that Churchill was not a particularly adept student. But nothing in his deplorable academic record could have prepared the nation for his dismal initial efforts as first lord of the British Admiralty in 1915. That was the year that the forty-year-old Churchill decided it would be a really neat idea to sneak up on the Germans through a narrow strip of land in the Dardanelles called Gallipoli. The ensuing carnage (250,000 of His Majesty's troops died) left a permanent blot on Churchill's record and had the unintended, but nonetheless catastrophic, effect of inspiring a movie that helped launch Mel Gibson's career. The unspeakable horrors at Gallipoli also contributed directly to the penning of a truly ghastly Australian folk song called "And the Band Played Waltzing Matilda" that was later immortalized by a lethal Irish rock group called The Pogues, all of which is at least as horrifying as anything that took place that horrible summer in Sulva Bay. All in all, young Churchill has a lot to answer for.

If we are seeking a truly spectacular example of a legendary historical figure who at first seemed to be a bit of a chowderhead, we need look no further than Otto von Bismarck. According to *Bismarck: The Man and the Statesman* by A. J. P. Taylor, Otto von Bismarck was an indifferent scholar who did not show any real get-up-and-go until he was already in his thirties, and who tried to get out of his military service by *telling his superiors that he had a pain in his arm.* When he did report for service, he proved to be a perfectly awful soldier, even though he was given special treatment by *friends of the family,* and was regularly invited to the royal palace nearby for *boozy rave-ups.* Despite his remarkably pacific experiences in the military, he would later become a hawk on defense, sparking the Franco-Prussian War of 1870, and creating the Prussian war machine whose unbridled ambitions would lead directly to the First World War.

Well, now.

Bismarck *got into politics by accident* after being selected as a member of his local diet as an alternate in case one of the regular members got sick. A poorly read rustic from the dreary spud kingdoms of Prussia, he was *heavily influenced by religion and his wife* and utterly despised the *liberal, intellectual circles of Berlin.* He was also smart enough to recognize that being in his company was no raucous chuckle-fest. "I have the unfortunate nature that everywhere I could be seems desirable to me, and dreary and boring as soon as I am there," he once said. In short, like Dan Quayle, he knew his limitations.

Before we vacate Mount Olympus, let us dwell for a moment on the easy-to-overlook parallels between the lives of Alexander the Great and the Humble Hoosier. When Alexander was a callow, impressionable youth ignorant of the ways of the world, his father, King Philip of Macedon, hired as Alexander's personal tutor a pretentious foreign intellectual from a once-mighty nation that had fallen on hard times about seventy years earlier. When Dan Quayle was a callow, impressionable, newly elected vice president of the United States who was ignorant of the ways of the world, George Bush hired as Quayle's personal tutor a pretentious intellectual from a once-mighty nation that had fallen on hard times about seventy years earlier. Philip hired Aristotle, who hailed from Athens; Bush hired Henry Kissinger, who hailed from Germany. Both men had thick accents and thought they knew everything. Both men got up a lot of people's noses.

What was their influence on their youthful mentees? Bertrand Russell contends that Alexander viewed Aristotle as a boring old fart, and rarely listened to anything he said. As for Quayle, after listening to Kissinger's spiel about détente and linkage and balance of power and the end of the Cold War and the importance of being civil to the Russkies, the new vice president went out and called the Soviets a pack of imperalistic scumbunnies until Jim Baker told him to shut up.

This, however, is the only obvious comparison between Alexander the Great and Dan Quayle.

Clearly, not *every* callow, impressionable youth who has suddenly come to power down through the ages has panned out as well as the celestial Alexander. History also supplies us with many examples of kingdoms that disintegrated as soon as a strong, popular leader died or ceded power to a younger, weaker man. Marcus Aurelius is universally revered by historians as one of the most sagacious, cultivated, and humane of the Roman emperors. But his son Commodus was a monster, murdered in his sleep by his own servants who'd decided that if they didn't murder him in his sleep, he would murder them in their sleep. Good help, even back in the days of the Roman Empire, was hard to get.

Another edifying example of a nation that fell into disarray when a callow youth took power is England in the Middle Ages. After a lengthy period of wise, imaginative rule by tribal chieftains with colorful names such as Egbert, Ethelwulf, Ethelbald, Ethelbert, Edward, Edmund, Edred, Edwig, and Edgar, England's House of Wessex fell into the hands of Ethelred the Unready. He was unready—and the Danes cleaned his Wessex clock.

The same can be said of the sons of Charlemagne. When the mighty Frankish potentate slipped this mortal coil in 814, he was succeeded by his well-meaning but incompetent son, Louis the Pious. Louis immediately wrecked everything his father had spent his entire life accomplishing by carving up the Carolingian Empire into three states, soon to be ruled by his sons Charles the Bald, Louis the German, and Lothair, one of the few rulers from the Dark Ages who had no nickname. Their intense rivalry led to years of Frank unpleasantness, culminating in the very brief reign of Louis the German's son Charles the Fat (nephew of Charles the Bald), who was finally succeeded in power (if not in official office) by Count Odo of Paris, King of the West Franks. (None of this has anything to do with Alcuin of York or Charles the Stupid.)

As we move along through the annals of history, we can find many other supremely unpleasant examples of mighty empires that fell on hard times when they came into the hands of second-in-commands who were entirely out of their depth. And here, it must be said, the analogies with the life of Dan Quayle are sometimes disturbingly ominous.

Edward II of England was a *self-centered playboy* with a *rotten public image* who whiled away his time in *public displays of athletic prowess* until civil war erupted. Though Edward died a horrible death, getting a red-hot poker shoved up his rectum, none of his subjects seemed to object. This is one of the many ways in which the Middle Ages differ from our own era. Ten years after Jimmy Carter was driven from office by a populace that clearly loathed him, public opinion polls confirmed that the attitude of the American people had softened, that the American public had come to respect and even admire the banished thirty-ninth president. Ten years after Edward II was driven from public life on the tip of a red-hot poker, the public still seemed to think he'd gotten what he deserved.

Another intellectual lightweight who sealed his fate through ostentatious public displays of his membership in the leisure classes was Louis XVI of France. When Louis ascended to the French throne in 1774, he was an untested youth of twenty married to a *strange, mean, ambitious woman with a weird hairstyle whom everybody hated.* Uh-oh. Louis XVI had inherited his throne from the bland caretaker king, Louis XV, who had himself succeeded the enormously powerful and well-liked Louis XIV, the legendary Sun King who had hopelessly bankrupted the nation through a *debt binge* that fueled a monstrous *real-estate boom.*

Gee.

———

That pretty much covers the area of callow youthfulness and lack of experience in big assignments. Now, how about intellect? It is a matter of public record that Quayle was a rotten student as an undergraduate at DePauw University. (During the 1988 campaign, there were even reports of a hushed-up plagiarism scandal back in his college days, but the allegations were subsequently proven to be without merit. This, of course, is mere nitpicking, anyway; Martin Luther King was a plagiarist, and *he* has a holiday named after him in most civilized states, so what's all the fuss about?)

Several of Quayle's professors have been unsparing in their criticism of his academic performance. "I looked into those blue eyes and I might as well have been looking out the window," Professor William Cavanaugh told *Time* during the 1988 campaign. "He was vapid, ordinary, and relied on his personality to cut corners," chimed in another. In Quayle's defense, as a youngster he was not getting much parental supervision; his mother told *The Saturday Evening Post* in 1989: "I always felt Danny's grades were good."

The vice president himself has been of two minds on the subject of his retrograde academic achievements and the seemingly inescapable conclusion that the Quayle pound note may be short a few shillings. On several occasions he has dismissed demands that his alma mater release his college grades, declaring the matter "irrelevant." But in a more conciliatory mood, he once said, "I was a less than serious student in college. If I had to do it over again, I would be far more serious."

He added, "I did play a lot of golf. But I don't believe that is any reflection on my ability to lead this nation."

Is that a valid position for the vice president to take? Is education really all that important? Are brains sometimes overrated? What, after all, is the verdict of history regarding intellectual lightweights who have suddenly been thrust into positions of immense importance? Well, in his unjustifiably neglected book, *Understanding Stupidity: An Analysis of the Premaladaptive Beliefs and Behavior of Institutions and Organizations* (Mount Pleasant Press, Orient, N.Y.), James F. Welles, Ph.D., brother of *Business Week* editor Chris Welles, points out that in the late sixteenth century the Duke of Medina-Sedonia was actually promoted to the rank of Supreme Commander in Politics and War *after* he had screwed up as Admiral of the Spanish Armada and ruined Spain forever. This would seem to indicate that intellectual deficiencies culminating in epic national disasters need not always be a drawback to success as a politician.

"The craftier politicians have found that while stupidity may lead to unpopularity, popularity may lead to stupidity," writes Welles in his crisp, concise fashion. "And that this is the most effective way to succeed in politics."

Lamentably, as Welles notes, the literature on the history of dim bulbs is scanty, so other examples of tremendous rewards for intellectual deficiency are not that easy to find. There may be some in Leopold Lowenfeld's 1909 classic *Über Die Dummheit*, or in Max Kemmerich's seminal 1912 study *Aus der Geschichte der menshlichen Dummheit*, but I have no way of knowing, as I don't speak German and can't find the books in my library. The only book in English that deals specifically with the subject is Walter Pitkin's *A Short Introduction to the History of Human Stupidity*, but that was published in 1932, long before Quayle took office, and I couldn't find that one either.

Welles, for his part, has many interesting insights: "American stupidity cannot be fully appreciated as a stagnant, torpid force, but must be perceived in the dynamic context of a linguistic current ever at odds with the realities of life." This is a valid point, yet the author's condescension toward intellectually impaired politicians betrays a shocking ignorance of the many occasions in Western history in which historical figures widely perceived to be muttonheads, bozos, jackasses, or addle-brained pinheads still managed to outsmart their adversaries and rise to incredible heights of power. When Angelo Giuseppe Roncalli was elected pope back in 1958, he was generally thought to be a fat, good-natured idiot, not unlike Saint Peter, the first pope, who was generally thought to be a thin, good-natured idiot. (Jesus Christ, the Son of God, handpicked Peter, an unsuccessful fisherman, to replace him as head of the Catholic church, in large part as a way of expressing his personal contempt for intellectuals. This is one of the more obvious ways in which George Bush resembles Jesus Christ.)

Roncalli, who has gone down in history as Pope John XXIII, was elected supreme pontiff because he was the only candidate who everyone else didn't despise. Moreover, the College of Cardinals was convinced that they could manipulate this congenial dunce into doing whatever they liked because he would owe them eternal gratitude for giving him such a great job.

"They say and believe that I am a fool," Roncalli once wrote in his journal. "Perhaps I am, but my pride will not allow me to think so. This is the funny side to it all."

Funny, indeed. By the time of his death five years later, Roncalli was universally revered by Catholics and non-Catholics alike, who viewed him as a sweet, gregarious man of peace, and one of the greatest popes in history—even though no one thought that he'd gotten very much smarter during his five years as supreme pontiff.

The lesson Quayle must learn from this is that if Pope John XXIII could do it, anyone can do it. Why, just look at the Roman emperor Claudius! Throughout most of his adult life, the shy, quirky grandson of the pederast Tiberius was written off as a stuttering buffoon who would never amount to anything. Yet, upon his succession to the throne vacated by the murdered madman Caligula, Claudius reigned for thirteen years, doing a more than adequate job in the judgment of most historians, before being knocked off by Nero and his wicked mother, Agrippina, who also happened to be Claudius's wife.

We will conclude this brief historical survey with a series of potentially illuminating references to three other historical figures whose careers bear startling resemblances to Dan Quayle's: Peter Abelard, Saint Bernard of Clairvaux, and Ivan the Terrible.

Ivan the Terrible rates a mention because he symbolizes the dangers of supposing that just because a person is smart and talented and shows promise as a young man that he will necessarily grow up to be a great leader. Ivan, crowned as tsar at the age of seventeen, was an entirely satisfactory ruler until his mid-thirties. Then he suddenly began murdering everyone in the immediate vicinity, including the inoffensive Prince Viskavati, whom he ordered hung from a gallows and sliced into tiny pieces.

While the prince was languishing in his death throes, Ivan was busy raping Mrs. Viskavati, and his son, Ivan junior (whom Ivan senior would later murder), was busy raping Viskavati's eldest daughter. It was a horrible display. In Ivan's defense, he was suffering from syphilis at the time, and, according to Russian legend, apologized on his deathbed for having condemned tens of thousands of his countrymen to be boiled in hot oil, and impaled on spikes, or gnawed on by famished rats. "It wasn't me; it was my disease," Ivan is reputed to have said. "I'm not a bad person getting sicker; I'm a sick person getting better."

The case of Saint Bernard is worth considering because of his curious relationship with his contemporary, the famous scholar Peter Abelard. Bernard, a celebrated French monk, was an ascetic of unchallenged piety. But he was also a bit of a dummy. Peter, on the other hand, was one of the greatest intellectuals of his age. But he liked the late-feudal babes. The result? Whiz-kid Peter Abelard ended up in an obscure monastery with his penis chopped off, while Bernard helped organize the Crusades and reform the Church, and ended up as a saint, getting to sit at the right hand of the Creator. (Well, somewhere in the immediate vicinity.)

What does this prove? It proves that brains aren't everything, a lesson that cannot be taught often enough. In our own age we have seen how John Sununu, arguably the smartest Lebanese-American the state of New Hampshire has ever produced, ended his career by getting banished to, well, New Hampshire. We have seen how Alexander Haig, an incredibly smart man, ended up working for both Gerald Ford *and* Ronald Reagan. We have seen how Bill Kristol, brilliant son of brilliant writer Irving Kristol and brilliant historian Gertrude Himmelfarb, had to work for Marilyn Quayle's husband. In the words of John Fitzgerald Kennedy, who wasn't much of a student: Nobody ever said that life was fair.

TO THE HOOSIER STATION

Crosby asked me what my name was and what my business was.
I told him, and his wife Hazel recognized my name as an Indiana
name. She was from Indiana, too.

"My God," she said, "are you a *Hoosier*?"

I admitted I was.

"I'm a Hoosier, too," she crowed. "Nobody has to be ashamed
of being a Hoosier."

"I'm not," I said. "I never knew anybody who was."

—KURT VONNEGUT, JR., *Cat's Cradle*

I t is, we are assured, a gentle land that surrenders its secrets demurely,
with the blushing grace of a comely maiden on her wedding night. It
is the gracious, placid heartland nurtured by the Shawmucky, where
the poky old *Wabash Cannonball* chug-chug-chugs its way down
through Raintree County, right past Pumpkin Vine Pike, before reach-
ing its destination in Kokomo. It is a tender bower of joy and serenity,
where even the battlefields drenched in the blood of the white man—
and the red—bear soft, evocative, peaceful names: Tippecanoe, Vin-
cennes. It is the land called Indiana, the glorious Hoosier state.

We know not whence comes the term Hoosier. According to Walter
Havighurst's *The Heartland*, the seminal work on the mighty civilization that flourishes in the states of Ohio, Indiana, and Illinois, the term
may have originated with the nineteenth-century Indiana prizefighter
Aaron Short, who had an annoying habit of pummeling his opponent
to the canvas and then towering above him bellowing "Hurrah for the
Hoosier." This was a troubling moment for the victims, who would not

have known what Short was talking about in the best of times; groggy from the pounding they had just been subjected to, they were now completely at sea. In fact, reports Havighurst, the phrase "Hurrah for the Hoosier" meant that Aaron was proclaiming himself the mighty "husher" who could "hush all comers."

Other etymologists disagree. Some say the word Hoosier comes from the Anglo-Saxon term *hoo*, meaning a hooty rustic. Others say it may derive from the last name of the legendary nineteenth-century canal foreman Sam Hoosier, who always hired shovelmen born on the Indiana side of the Wabash. There is also a faint possibility that the term comes down to us from the southern American expression *hoozer*, meaning a lean, mean frontiersman, or even from the Indian word *hoosa*, which means "corn."

"Whatever its origin," writes Havighurst, "the name has had a lasting appeal for Indiana people, and has acquired a quite enviable aura. For more than a hundred years, it has continued to mean friendliness, neighborliness, an idyllic contentment with Indiana landscape and life." According to this Hoosier hagiographer, there was once a Kentucky man named Pritchard who had relocated to Indiana in his youth and was completely bowled over by everything he found there. Later in life, a friend asked how old he was. Going on fifty, Pritchard replied. The man observed that Pritchard had to be older than that because he, personally, had known him for forty years. At which point Pritchard replied, "Well, I did live for twenty years in Kentucky, but I never counted that." Quoth Havighurst: "He was a genuine Hoosier."

Mighty are the Hoosiers and noble are their deeds! Here it was that William Henry Harrison broke the back of the Shawnee Nation forever when he defeated the valiant Tecumseh at the Battle of Tippecanoe in 1811. Here it was that Wilbur Wright, who would later give man wings, first crawled. Here lived, prospered, died, and is buried Booth Tarkington, poet laureate of the Hoosier bourgeoisie, whose chef d'ouevre, *The Magnificent Ambersons*, inspired one of the greatest motion pictures of all time. And was it not in Kokomo that Elwood Hayes took a horseless carriage out for the first spin around the block in American history? (Yes, it was.)

It was also right smack dab in the middle of the Hoosier state that James Whitcomb Riley penned the most popular poem in the history of the Republic: "An Old Sweetheart of Mine," as well as such classics as "The Ripest Peach," "When the Frost Is on the Pumpkin," "When the Green Gits Back in the Trees," "The Old Swimmin'-Hole," and "Thoughts for the Discuraged [*sic*] Farmer." Here it was that Knute Rockne, perhaps the greatest football coach of all time, first suckled a Hoosier bosom. Here it was that Hoagland "Hoagy" Carmichael was suffused with the breath of God, providing him with the inspiration to pen anthems such as "Stardust" and "Georgia on My Mind." As Havighurst writes: "Nowhere did the moon shine so bright as on the Wabash, nowhere was such contentment as lay over the Indiana fields when the frost was on the pumpkin and the fodder in the shock." Not to mention the hoarfrost on the giblet.

Truly, it is a land that has history in its soil, tradition in its marrow. It is the native land of astronaut Gus Grissom, basketball colossus Larry Bird, and novelists Lloyd C. Douglas and Lew Wallace, who, legend has it, wrote his towering epic *Ben-Hur* while nestled beneath the brooding maternity of a capacious beech tree in the sleepy town of Crawfordsville, Indiana. Yes, there was a time, less than a century ago, though few Americans are aware of it today, when the Hoosier literati dominated American arts and letters.

The brightest star in that pantheon of Hoosier cognoscenti was Edward Eggleston, who got the whole thing rolling in 1872 when he published his remarkable book *The Hoosier Schoolmaster.* This touching chronicle of rural life in southern Indiana in the years preceding the Civil War transformed the author into a national treasure, and led inexorably to the triumph of *The Hoosier Schoolboy,* which inspired Maurice Thompson's *Hoosier Mosaics,* which in turn inspired Meredith Nicholson's *The Hoosiers* and *A Hoosier Chronicle.* Many other books with similarly inventive titles followed, as Hoosier writers dominated American letters until well into the twentieth century. Their delicate charms, their zest, and the subtle allure of their homespun philosophy were best summed up by a genial old woman in *A Hoosier Chronicle* who declared: "It's all pretty comfortable and cheerful and busy in Indiana, with lots of old-fashioned human kindness flowing round."

La nouvelle vague hoosière did not end with that first generation of Indiana cultural titans. Right after them, at the turn of the century, came such towering figures as Charles Major, author of *When Knighthood Was in Flower;* Booth Tarkington, who penned *The Gentleman from Indiana* and *Love at Seventeen;* and Gene Stratton Porter, who bequeathed his countrymen the unforgettable *Freckles,* for which we are all grateful.

The Hoosier state is a land that has given much to the Republic: many poets, songwriters, fine athletes, and more vice presidents than you can shake a stick at. These include Schuyler Colfax (veep during Grant's first term), Thomas A. Hendricks (Grover Cleveland's veep in 1884), Charles W. Fairbanks (Teddy Roosevelt's veep), Thomas R. Marshall (two terms under Woodrow Wilson), and, of course, Dan Quayle. And that's not even mentioning the four Hoosier vice presidential candidates who were defeated in the general election: George W. Julian (who ran on the Abolitionist and Free-Soil ticket in 1852); Joseph W. Lane, who ran with John Breckinridge in 1860; William H. English, the second-stringer with Winfield Hancock in 1880; and John W. Kern, who ran with William Jennings Bryan against Taft and James Sherman in 1908.

And even those Olympians who were not born there grew up strong and straight in the land of Hoosier. William Henry Harrison lived there. So did Wendell Willkie, inexplicably the only presidential candidate that Indiana University has ever produced. Abe Lincoln spent a good portion of his early life there. So did Benjamin Harrison, the twenty-third president, and the closest the Hoosier state has ever come to sending a native to the White House. (He was a Buckeye by birth.) Yea, the tendrils of Hoosieriana run deep beneath the tree of American civilization. Thus, Vonnegut's charmingly voluble character Hazel is right on target when she tells the narrator of *Cat's Cradle:* "I don't know what it is about Hoosiers . . . but they sure got something. If somebody was to make a list, they'd be amazed."

———

They'd be amazed, all right, but maybe not for the reasons Hazel thinks. For all is not peaches and cream, milk and honey in the Land of the Hoosier. No, there is a dark side, a disturbing side, a sinister side, and if we scratch beneath the surface just a bit, we will be perplexed—and even horrified—by what we see.

We should be aware, for example, that it was in Indiana in 1924 that the Grand Dragon of the Ku Klux Klan, the monstrous D. C. Stephenson, took control of the entire state government and maintained it for the next two years. This was a dark, dark moment in the history of the Republic, when some 4.5 million Americans pledged fealty to the Knights of Darkness—and nowhere did the serpentine coil of the Klan clasp tighter than in Indiana. Stephenson, a ne'er-do-well traveling salesman, who was born in 1891 and died in 1966, took control of the Klan in 1922, and within two years had built an organization so powerful that it took control of the governor's mansion, many seats in the state legislature, and all but one of the state's seats in the U.S. House of Representatives.

According to Richard K. Tucker's *The Dragon and the Cross*, Stephenson himself amassed an immense fortune, thanks to his hefty cut from the initiation fees and sheet and hood sales to the hundreds of thousands of Hoosiers who joined the shadowy organization during these dark times, not to mention the 250,000 others who had joined the Military Machine, a sinister organization inside the sinister organization.

It's all pretty comfortable and cheerful and busy in Indiana, with lots of old-fashioned human kindness flowing round.

There is more, much more: During the 1924 Democratic convention, a pro–Ku Klux Klan candidate named William G. McAdoo actually managed to hang around until the hundredth ballot. And Stephenson himself entertained serious dreams of winning a trip to the White House until he found himself embroiled in a murder scandal that resulted in his being imprisoned for thirty years. Indeed, it was only the demise of the Grand Dragon that caused the Klan to be repudiated in the Hoosier state. Otherwise, these folks were going places.

How do Hoosiers explain this underside to their history? According to Jeannette C. Nolan, author of *Indiana*, it's all innocent stuff: Hoosiers are just plain, old-fashioned, dyed-in-the-wool "joiners."

"They will join anything," she writes. "The state abounds in clubs: social, fraternal, church, musical, literary, charitable; clubs of sportsmen, needlewomen, collectors, genealogists, travelers, amateur poets. Combined with this instinct for belonging is a special, childish enthusiasm for secret orders. Perhaps along with intolerance of Jews, Negroes and Catholics, it was the lure of robes and rituals, passwords and parades with flaming crosses that drew Hoosiers in such appalling hordes into this fanatical organization."

Right.

Another disturbing item on the Hoosier rap sheet is the number of certifiably strange and/or unpleasant people who were born there. Theodore Dreiser, far and away the most depressing novelist in American history, a man who never had anything good to say about anybody, was born there. So was Paul Dreiser, his brother, who, when he was not busy penning songs like "My Gal Sal"* and "On the Banks of the Wabash" (the official state song of Indiana), would parade around the Dreiser brothers' hotel room in Manhattan with a towel draped from his erect penis. This contributed to the deep sense of sexual dysfunction that brother Ted would feel for the rest of his life. It also made Theodore vomit.†

It is a point of interest that the hotel in which Paul Dresser (he changed his name when he became a songwriter because he thought it sounded catchier) used to induce fraternal nausea in the Hoosier Zola by parading his betoweled roger around the room was the Hotel Martinique, catty-corner from Macy's department store in Manhattan's Herald Square, an establishment that would become a famous hellhole in the late 1970s, a crime-ridden welfare hotel in which dreams, and not a few West Indian illegal immigrants, died. It is, to this very day, a ferociously depressing place to hang one's hat, so it is not terribly surprising to find that the morose Theodore Dreiser once called it home.

In defense of *les frères Dreiser*, it should be noted that the lads' parents, John and Sarah, were psychics whose home was regularly visited by supernatural creatures. Vera Dreiser says that the supernatural visitors weren't very nice: "They tumbled tables, they spilled food, they entered the children's beings, causing them to speak in unfamiliar tongues, words of the devil." Unexpected appearances of grim and

---

*Despite its seemingly innocuous title, "My Gal Sal" actually deals with the composer's deep and abiding passion for the mistress of a famous bordello.

†For more information on Dreiser's legendary sexual adventures, including his twenty-year affair with the notorious Thelma Cudlipp, consult the riveting memoir *My Uncle Theodore* by his niece, Vera Dreiser.

satanic creatures partially exculpates Theodore for his promiscuity and gloominess, and Paul for his obsession with his cock. Nothing, however, can mitigate Paul's responsibility for writing songs like "On the Banks of the Wabash."

Theodore and Paul Dreiser were by no means the most confused people to spring from Indiana. Eugene Debs, one of the founding fathers of American socialism, was born there. Ditto colorful bank robber and psychopath John Dillinger. Professional strange youth James Dean, who used to go into leather bars and invite men to put out their cigarettes on his chest, was a Hoosier. So was Jim Jones, the psychotic cult figure whose murder of a congressional delegation led by California congressman Leo Ryan in 1978 led to the suicide of 909 members of his Guyana-based People's Temple, including numerous children. According to Jeannie Mills (formerly Deanna Mertle), author of *Six Years with God*, Jones ruled his clan primarily through sexual blackmail. One of his techniques was to force a man who didn't like oral sex to go down on a menstruating stranger while one hundred or more people—including the man's wife—looked on.

In addition to taking all their money and dignity, Jones used to brainwash the children of his adherents by having them chant: "We cut off the penises of capitalists and people who believe in God." Actually, this doesn't sound all that different from the lyrics of the heavy metal band Guns 'N' Roses, whose sociopathic lead singer, W. Axl Rose, grew up in Lafayette, Indiana. Rose (né Bill Bailey), has become famous by precipitating a riot in which hundreds of thousands of dollars of damage was done to a brand-new arena; by being arrested for assaulting a female with a wine bottle; and by inviting publishers of famous rock 'n' roll magazines to provide him with instant sexual gratification by performing oral sex on his Hoosier protuberance. *It's all pretty comfortable and cheerful and busy in Indiana, with lots of old-fashioned human kindness flowing round.*

Consider, in addition, the illustrative case of Michael Jackson, the aspiring extraterrestrial and androgynous Diana Ross impersonator, who sleeps in a bedroom filled with E.T. dolls and owns the remains of the Elephant Man. He's a Hoosier. So is his sister, LaToya, who once posed for *Playboy* magazine with a python snaked between her legs, and then wondered why everybody in her family got so upset. So is

David Lee Roth, formerly lead singer with Van Halen, which once destroyed their dressing room in a rock amphitheater because the management had neglected to remove all the brown M&M's from the candy dish the band was eating from, and *Van Halen hates brown M&M's!*

Also a Hoosier is John Mellencamp, who started his life as "John Mellencamp," then changed it to "John Cougar" when he started his career as a rock star; then figured the "Mellencamp" would add a nice little spin to it, so he changed it to "John Cougar Mellencamp." He has recently decided to drop the "Cougar" altogether and become a movie star using the name his parents gave him. As image changes go, this may turn out to be the niftiest idea since Wendell Willkie blazed a trail across the pages of American history in 1940 by campaigning against the Promethean Franklin Delano Roosevelt under the sobriquet "The Barefoot Boy of Wall Street." That *really* helped.

The Mellencamping of John Cougar and the Wendelling of Willkie is certainly a topic that warrants our attention here, for there seems to be a deep, proud Hoosier tradition that stipulates: Nobody gets famous in this state unless he or she has a really strange name. George Barr McKutcheon. Booth Tarkington. W. Axl Rose. Edward Eggleston. David Lee Roth. Kurt Vonnegut. Deanna Mertle. LaToya Jackson. Cole Porter. Thelma Cudlipp. Bear in mind that the Senate seat won by James Danforth Quayle in 1980 had been occupied for the previous eighteen years by a man named Birch Bayh, who had won the seat from an eighteen-year veteran named Homer Capehart. J. Danforth Quayle got into politics at the behest of a Hoosier bigshot named Orvas Beers, and the principal influence in his life has been his grandfather Eugene C. Pulliam, a conservative who simply hated people like Birch Bayh and, were he alive, would probably hate the current occupant of the governor's mansion—Evan Bayh—even more. In Indiana, even the fictional characters—Carrie Meeber, Kilgore Trout—have weird names. Jesus, what kind of name is Ben-Hur?

There are other disturbing footnotes to Indiana cultural history. Prozac was discovered by Eli Lilly scientists in 1972—the year Dan discovered Marilyn. Booth Tarkington's novel *The Magnificent Ambersons* was turned into the movie that ruined Orson Welles's career in

Hollywood, depriving his countrymen of many great films. Kurt Vonnegut, despite his great success as a novelist, was ultimately subjected to one of the cruelest fates any American man of letters has ever known: having Geraldo Rivera as a son-in-law. Madonna spent three months in Evansville, Indiana, filming a movie about an all-girls baseball team, and couldn't get MTV. She likened the experience to visiting Prague, Czechoslovakia. During the McCarthy era, Mrs. Thomas J. White, a member of the Indiana State Textbook Commission, declared that "there is a communist directive in education now to stress the story of Robin Hood. They want to stress it because he robbed the rich and gave it to the poor. That's the communist line. It's just a smearing of law and order." And Edward Eggleston's *The Hoosier Schoolmaster* was not first published in Indiana, nor for that matter in the United States. It was published in France in 1871, the year after the Franco-Prussian War, under the title *Le Maître d'Ecole de Flat Creek*. This is never a good sign. Nothing good ever comes from France.

How do we account for this strange mixture of gullibility, mediocrity, and weirdness? Let us essay a pharmacological explanation. Indiana is a state where people believe that cancer can be cured by applying ear wax to the surface of the malignancy or, failing that, by applying the remains of a dried toad sautéed in a quart of unsalted butter to the oncologically menaced area. It is a state where people believe that epileptic fits can be cured by drinking cow parsnip in pennyroyal tea, that hemorrhoids can be shrunken with Ben-Gay, that athlete's foot can be cured by letting a dog lick your feet, and that arthritis can be cured by applying a mixture of essence of pokeberry juice and Karo pancake syrup. It is a state where people believe that rheumatism can be cured by killing, skinning, and drying a rattlesnake, mixing the skin with whiskey, and drinking the resulting elixir.

These are not the sneering insinuations of a mean-spirited Gothamite. They are the conclusions of no less a figure than Varro E. Tyler, author of the seminal work *Hoosier Home Remedies*, which contains 750 folk remedies still being used in the state of Indiana, only one of which is designed for alleviating the pain of gout. Why so few remedies for the affliction of bon vivants? Tyler, once president of the American Council on Pharmacal Education, feels that this shows that "there was probably little high living among the Hoosier pioneers."*

The sense of estrangement from reality that has become a hallmark of Hoosier life was never more in evidence than during Dan Quayle's August 18, 1988, acceptance speech at the Republican National Convention. That evening, Quayle said the usual things about winning one for the Gipper, the insidious threat posed to America by the likes of Teddy Kennedy and Michael Dukakis, and the rock-solid covenant that he and George Bush had established with the American people on the subject of taxes.

But then he said something puzzling about the great state of Indiana. He said, "In Indiana, they call us 'Hoosiers,' and if you saw the movie *Hoosiers*, you have a feeling for what life is like in the small towns of our state. My hometown of Huntington is a little bigger than the town in the movie, and the high school I graduated from was a little bigger than the one that fielded the basketball team in the film. Still, I identify with that movie *Hoosiers*, because it reflects the values that I grew up with in our small town. We believe very strongly in hard work, in getting an education, and in offering an opportunity to our families. We love basketball, we love underdogs, but most important we love our country."

Here we come to the crux of the connundrum, to the heart of the hoax of Hoosier hokiness. If Dan Quayle grew up in a town like the one in *Hoosiers*, and if the values of that small town are the ones that he values, it is bad news for the rest of us. In *Hoosiers*, Gene Hackman plays a down-at-the-heels high school basketball coach who comes to the poky little town of Hickory, Indiana, to coach the basketball team. He is treated with fear, hatred, and contempt by the narrow-minded, bigoted residents of the farming town, who loathe outsiders. So great is their antipathy toward Hackman, who has just spent twelve years in the navy, that they actually hold a town referendum and vote him out of office. His job is saved only when a talented but moody holdout from the team says that he will rejoin the squad only on the condition that the hated Hackman be retained as coach.

*For more information on this topic, consult *The Vascular Plants of Indiana: A Computer-Based Checklist* by Theodore J. Crovello, Clifton A. Keller, and John T. Kartesz. (The American Midland Naturalist and University of Notre Dame Press, 1983)

It's all pretty comfortable and cheerful and busy in Indiana, with lots of old-fashioned human kindness flowing round.

The movie has many other troubling elements. One of Hackman's assistant coaches is a shotgun-toting dipsomaniac played with consummate verve by all-purpose wacko Dennis Hopper. Hackman, we learn, was fired from his last job as a college coach because he punched one of his players. And the denouement of the film is the implausible triumph of this seven-man hick roundball squad over the big-city favorites (a team that features many players of the *black* persuasion). The film, therefore, with its subliminal racist message, can rightly be called *Rocky Pumps the Jumper*, in that it portrays on film in a fantasy world something that could never occur in real life: the victory of a bunch of redneck scrubs over talented black urbanites. Quayle's affection for the film *Hoosiers* underscores his antipathy toward booming metropolises such as New York City, which he has repeatedly described as a failure. The vice president seems to suffer from the delusion that if New York is a failure, Fort Wayne must be a success.

The movie also underscores Indiana's profoundly unhealthy attitude toward sports. Indiana, despite having several large cities, has no major league baseball team. In states like this, cornball sports such as college hoops flourish. Aficionados of college sports claim that it is superior to the pros because the players show such enthusiasm, diving for loose balls and wearing their hearts on their sleeves while wholesome, perky girls in short skirts kick their legs merrily nearby. But what they're really saying is: *College ball is the last time we'll ever get to see our third-rate plowboys play.* College basketball, and its evil stepchild high school basketball, is a slow, dull, low-scoring form of entertainment designed to neutralize the skills of talented basketball players, almost all of whom are black. It is a sport controlled by colorless, middle-aged white men in plaid blazers who design Byzantinely somniferous offenses that rely on holding the ball and keeping it out of the hands of the good kids so that every game ends up with a score like 65–57 or 78–72, as opposed to the 123–122 scores you get in the pros. In college basketball, black athletes who perform the sort of spectacular acts that are routine in pro basketball are often forced to sit on the bench by coaches named Dean, Duane, Drew, and Tubby, who are angered by their "schoolyard" play. College basketball, whose popularity has a lot more to do with gambling than with the inherent allure of the sport, is to pro basketball what municipal bonds are to stock index options. Yes, Terre Haute's most famous citizen, Larry Bird, is one of the greatest basketball players of all time; but he didn't become famous in Indiana, but in Boston, as a Celtic. Yes, Isaiah Thomas is one of the fifty greatest players of all time, but he didn't become famous in Indiana. He became a star in Detroit, as a Piston. He played basketball for two years with Indiana University's sociopathic coach Bobby Knight, won a national championship, then got the hell out of there.

Indiana sports are, well, strange. The abysmal Indianapolis Colts used to be the awesome Baltimore Colts, who put the National Football League on the map when they played the New York Giants in the greatest championship game of all time back in 1958. But the Colts literally snuck out of Crabcake Corners in the dead of night in 1984, as the owner backed up a truck and cleared out all the trophies won during the Johnny Unitas and Raymond Berry glory years. The coach of the Indiana University basketball team is a lunatic once arrested in Puerto Rico for assaulting a cop. The star forward of the old Indianapolis Pacers—George McGinnis—had the strangest shot in the history of professional basketball: He unleashed the ball on the way *down* from his jump. The most famous athletic squad in the state is the Notre Dame Fighting Irish, a football team from a Catholic university whose mascot is a leprechaun and whose players all have names like Raghib Ismail and Hiawatha Francisco, whose most famous coach was named Knute Rockne, and whose second most famous coach was named Ara Parseghian. *You figure it out.*

Anyway, *Hoosiers.* It is deeply troubling that Dan Quayle should refer so affectionately to a movie that lionizes coaches who hit their own players, bigoted townspeople who despise outsiders, and booze-crazed ex-jocks who like to hang out with teenage boys. What can we learn from all this? Well, for one, we can assume that Quayle probably never saw the picture, or, if he did, that he wasn't paying very close attention.

But we can learn something else as well: that the statewide confusion about the true nature of the Hoosier is not a fluke that some mean-spirited son of a bitch from New York or Los Angeles dreamed up. For while Hoosiers think of themselves as helpful, harmless, and a tad hooty, history tells us that they are also cruel, mistrusting, and bizarre. The state that gave us such solid citizens as Booth Tarkington and Larry Bird also gave us such grotesque, troubling figures as Jim Jones, Axl Rose, and Michael Jackson. And it gave us one other character whose profound strangeness is a dozen times more disturbing than theirs, a truly gothic American archetype whose sublime weirdness makes LaToya Jackson, James Dean, Theodore Dreiser, the Imperial Wizard of the Ku Klux Klan, and Jim Jones seem as normal as, well, David Letterman.

It gave us Marilyn.

V I I I

EMBRACE THE SERPENT

There is one thing worse than being a violated man. Being a
violated man's wife. — GARRY WILLS, *Nixon Agonistes*

———

Arrogance results in psychoses and neuroses, and how once a
person gets locked into a psychotic condition through arrogance
. . . from that point on, they need medication and often they
need to be sent to an institution to be totally retrained for
society. — ROBERT THIEME, JR., *Satanology*

hold no truck with opportunistic mudslingers whose japes and catcalls
draw attention to Marilyn Quayle's lack of conventional American
pulchritude. Not for these pages are vicious, *uncalled-for attacks* such
as P. J. O'Rourke's likening Marilyn Quayle to a "Cape buffalo," nor
cruel, heartless barbs about her anachronistic hairstyle, her serviceable
shoes, her titanic overbite, or her "1940s librarian look," which won her
an appearance on Blackwell's Worst Dressed List a couple of years ago.
I will only say, purely in the interests of journalistic accuracy, that
when *U.S. News & World Report* says of the Second Lady, her "long
chestnut hair and large blue eyes make her more attractive than her
pictures," *U.S. News & World Report* lies.

I do not refrain from attacks on Marilyn Quayle's personal appearance out of some cryptic, misguided, démodé sense of male chivalry,
nor out of any fear that Dan Quayle, once he has left public office, may
wander into my neighborhood and kick my butt. Nor do I refrain from
such personal attacks out of a gnawing fear that Quayle agents provoca-

teurs in the fashion industry might pen nasty appraisals of my own spouse's serviceable shoes and conservative, British coiffure. Instead, I find myself in the company of those, such as Jay Leno, who believe that the spouses, children, and close relatives of politicians are inappropriate targets for the satirist's tongue or pen.

"I don't do jokes about Barbara Bush and Marilyn Quayle, or about their kids," says Leno. "They're not elected officials, so I lay off them."

I agree wholeheartedly with this code of ethics, with a single exception: politicians' relatives who fervently court derision, prosecution, and even assassination because of their spectacularly unacceptable public behavior. In this group I would include sleazeballs (George Bush's son Neal); people who drink rubbing alcohol during national elections (Kitty Dukakis); bon vivants (Willie Kennedy Smith); lawyers who went to Wellesley (Hillary Clinton); and anyone whose last name is Carter. But that's *it.* Therefore, in this book there will be no *jokes* about Marilyn Quayle.

There will, however, be *remarks.* For if it is mete and just to refrain from personal attacks on the spouses of highly placed officials, it is perfectly fair to make comments about them once they assume policy-making roles—either by embracing high-profile causes, or by busting their spouses' balls. Spouses such as Joan Mondale, Barbara Bush, and whoever is married to Pat Schroeder generally stay out of the limelight, and do not invite our scrutiny or criticism. Strident, militant, meddlesome, or ethically suspect spouses such as Eleanor Roosevelt, Nancy Reagan, Marilyn Quayle, and John Zaccaro do. Since we know that Marilyn Quayle is intimately involved with the management of her husband's career, and since we know that taxpayers foot the bill for her six-office suite in the Old Executive Office Building, we are perfectly within our rights to make certain inquiries into her background and personality. This right has been greatly amplified ever since Marilyn Quayle decided to publish a novel charged with inflammatory political allegations: that journalists are tools of the Republic's enemies, that Democrats are buffoons, that only Star Wars can preserve America from the hellfires of Armageddon.

In discussing Marilyn Quayle, then, there are two questions that need to be addressed: (1) Is she really more intelligent than her apparently dim-witted husband; and (2) Is she as insane as she seems to be? The first question arises from the widely held belief that *any* spouse of Dan Quayle's would have to be the brains of the family; the second arises from Marilyn's admittedly exotic religious upbringing, most particularly her decades-long indoctrination in the work of the shadowy, dispensational premillenialist preacher Robert B. Thieme, Jr.

Marilyn (née Tucker) Quayle's curriculum vitae is generic upper-middle-class American. She was born on July 29, 1949, in Indianapolis to a pair of doctors, to whom she almost immediately proclaimed her decision to become a lawyer (she has since described this decision as an act of "rebellion"). Marilyn's grandfather was a Republican circuit judge and her uncle was Indiana secretary of state, so this was not a childhood filled with hardship, much less adventure. In grade school, she won such a breathtaking number of Girl Scout honor badges that one of her sisters nicknamed her "Merit," a moniker that has stuck to this very day. She got her B.A. in political science in 1971 from Purdue University, where she formed a pom-pom girl squad called the Pep Girls and served as student-body treasurer.

Poms pommed, she moved on to night school at the University of Indiana, where she met Dan in 1972. They fell in love under the most remarkable circumstances—while working at the state attorney general's office on a redraft of Indiana's death-penalty laws, an event that was certainly not a red-letter day in the history of African-Americans. They were married ten weeks later on November 18, 1972, by Kent Frandsen, the associate dean of students. (On November 18, 1988, scant days after Dan was elected vice president, Frandsen died of a heart attack, a tragedy his widow attributes to the deadly pressure of having to withhold information about Dan's grades from the press. Dan's grades were really bad.)

The Quayles received their law degrees in 1974; indeed, it has become a fixture of Marilyn's legend as a tough, determined woman that she had the delivery of her first child induced ten days early so that she wouldn't miss her bar exam. For the next three years, she practiced law in Dan's cubbyhole of a hometown, while her husband worked as associate publisher (associate publishers are people who go to lunch) of *The Huntington Herald-Press,* owned by Quayle's dad. In 1976, Dan was elected to Congress, and Marilyn settled into her role for the next fifteen years as supermom and all-round harpy, raising three children (Tucker, Benjamin, and Corrine) in whatever free time she had from making life miserable for anyone unfortunate enough to work in her husband's office.

Supposedly, 1988 was the year Marilyn was going to resume her career—such as it was—but the hand of fate changed all that when her husband was selected as George Bush's running mate. At this point, Marilyn decided that practicing law would cause too many conflict-of-interest problems, embarrassing her husband, whereas writing a crackpot, right-wing novel would not. She also gave some thought to taking the senatorial seat vacated by Dan in 1988, but decided that this would create huge problems if she were ever forced to vote against the president.

Throughout Dan's career, Marilyn has been at center stage, approving campaign photos and literature, encouraging him to talk to dumb local reporters rather than smart ones with national reputations, and grabbing her husband's arm when he's making a fool of himself as a signal that he should put a lid on it. Today, she has an office right across the hall from his in the Old Executive Office Building, making it hard for her to keep the low profile that some members of Quayle's staff would like her to keep. In her free time, she engages in such traditional Republican hobbies as jogging, swimming, tennis, horseback riding, and Bible study, but for some strange reason, she does not golf.

A mean-spirited, vindictive, temperamental person who hates the press, Marilyn covertly attended Republican charm school a couple of years back, and learned the all-purpose image-massaging technique: crying in public. She used the brink-of-tears routine to maximum effect during a 1991 interview with David Broder and Bob Woodward, when she realized that they were planning to repeat to their *Washington Post* readers the wonderful anecdote about her removing Dan's photo from a wall, mutilating it, and then kicking it all around her office one day.

Other tried-and-true PR gambits that Marilyn has mastered include: telling a few jokes about herself at the National Press Club, changing her hairstyle, finding a worthy cause, and making sure everyone knows that she has never had a pedicure. Her first cause was disaster relief, which eventually got put on the back burner due to its devastatingly ironical undertones; her latest cause is breast cancer, the disease to which her mother succumbed at the age of fifty-six after repeatedly failing to have a mammogram.

Marilyn Quayle is a woman who has made a career out of quietly resenting her husband's success, a woman who has lately benefited from a curious form of perverted feminism that chastises left-leaning women who stay home and raise their children, or left-leaning women who both raise children and have a professional career (Hillary Clinton), but commiserates with right-leaning women who oppose the Equal Rights Amendment and abortion, and who sit at home for decades at a time complaining about what marvelous careers they could have had if it weren't for their goddamn husbands. (For the record, I am not sure how much the American Bar Association has missed out on just because one less lawyer with a night-school degree from the University of Indiana is patrolling the corridors of justice.)

"She wound up subordinating herself to the public official whose chief responsibility is subordination," Gail Collins wrote in *New York Woman* not long after the 1988 election. "No wonder she looks angry." Deborah Werksman, cofounder of the irreverent, Quayle-bashing newsletter *The Quayle Quarterly*, is even more abusive.

"Marilyn gets up and pretends to be a—quote-unquote—professional woman," says Werksman. "She would never call herself a feminist, but she talks about her career in law and being a professional and being treated like a professional. And yet she's no Lynne Cheney. She put her own career on ice sixteen years ago and put everything into her husband's career. So she's a real right-wing woman. Yet she insists upon her professionalism. In a sense, one can see that Dan's career has frustrated her in some sense. Marilyn's trying to have her cake and eat it, too."

Marilyn's particular cake is one in which there is no shortage of fruit. She grew up in a state where Gideon International still gives high school students a copy of the Good Book upon graduation, which really comes in handy if your name happens to be Bernstein or Heifitz. As a matter of fact, Huntington, Indiana, is one of the towns where such Bibles are distributed; Dan Quayle got one in 1967.

But Marilyn did not grow up in rural Indiana; she grew up in Indianapolis, once known as "Naptown." Still, Indiana is a state where there's enough weirdness to go around for everyone—and there was certainly plenty in the Tucker household. Though Marilyn now attends a Presbyterian church in Virginia, she grew up under the influence of Colonel Robert B. Thieme, Jr., a somewhat mysterious minister from Houston, Texas, who occasionally turns up in the pulpit wearing his air force uniform.

Thieme, a dispensational premillenialist, is the pastor of the Berachah Church in Houston, Texas, and president of R. B. Thieme, Jr., Bible Ministries. Dispensational premillenialists are people who believe that mankind has already entered the final stage in human history, and that only Christians and converts to Christianity will be saved when Armageddon occurs. Dispensational premillenialists are kind of hazy about dates, but they are fairly certain that Armageddon will not occur until after we have suffered seven (consecutive) years of tribulation. It is not clear when these seven years of tribulation will arrive, but we were well on our way to year number five when Jimmy Carter was evicted from the White House in 1980. Had he continued in office, Armageddon would have occurred on approximately February 1, 1984—the day the prime rate would have hit 187 percent. This would have meant that the Baltimore Orioles would have won the last World Series in history, contradicting W. P. Kinsella's prediction in *The Iowa Baseball Confederacy* that the Chicago Cubs would win the last World Series before Armageddon.

Now well into his seventies, Thieme is probably the most influential dispensational premillenialist in America, having recorded more than 7,000 hours of lectures "covering most of the Bible verse by verse" in cassettes with titles such as "Scar Tissue of the Soul," "Satanic Plot No. 1," and "Slave Market of Sin." Much of his material is good, old-fashioned, reds-under-the-beds, fire-and-brimstone stuff; he calls the welfare system "satanic"; thinks black slaves should have counted themselves lucky to have been brought to this country; loathes the United Nations and the World Council of Churches; shows war movies at the church on film nights; and doesn't have much time for liberals, gays, union members, feminists, or people who are not dispensational premillenialists.

Thieme's influence on the Quayle family became an issue during the 1988 campaign when Marilyn—remember, *she's supposed to be the smart one in the marriage*—let slip to the press that she had grown up in a house where the tapes were played virtually nonstop. In September 1988, she told the *Louisville Courier-Journal:* "I read Dr. Thieme's literature, and I do find him very good, and enjoy listening to his tapes." She also said that she and her husband had occasionally listened to the tapes while visiting her father, and that she had used them in her own children's education. A month later, she told *Newsweek* that she knew nothing about Thieme's extremist political views, that her parents had only gotten interested in his preaching as an "intellectual exercise" because of his literal interpretation of the Bible. Dan chimed in that neither he nor Marilyn listened to the tapes anymore, and that, anyway, they had never played them for their kids. Thieme says that arrogance is the worst sin a Christian can commit. I still think it's lying.

The subject of Thieme became a further cause of concern, at least to liberals, when it was revealed that not only the Tucker parents were dispensational premillenialist buffs but so were two of Marilyn's sisters, including Nancy Tucker Northcott, the sibling who just helped Marilyn write her goofball thriller, *Embrace the Serpent.* Northcott told the press that their late mother, Mary Alice Tucker, used to play Thieme's tapes "all day, every day" when they were growing up. For years, Northcott has hosted a tape group at her house in Tullahoma, Tennessee, and she and her husband have taken their families to Thieme conferences many times.

This is where things stood shortly before the election in 1988 when, just to round out the whole dispensational premillenialist shebang, word got out that Dan's parents, Jim and Corrine, were also fans of Rev. Thieme. Yes, Corrine and Jim have attended many Thieme conferences and listen to Thieme tapes "every Sunday and sometimes more." And Corrine has admitted that back in the 1970s Marilyn used to bring over tapes that had belonged to her mother. So it's pretty clear that when the Quayles and the Tuckers get together for a Fourth of July picnic, the subject of the Four Horsemen of the Apocalypse is going to pop up sooner or later.

In his defense, Thieme is not a one-dimensional crank, as he sometimes has been depicted in the press. He is not a smarmy, blow-dried, publicity-hounding shill like Jerry Falwell or Pat Robertson, nor does he appear to have gotten into the dispensational premillenialist racket for the money. Whatever else he may be, Robert B. Thieme, Jr., is not Mr. Entertainment. His interminable sermons, captured for posterity on the thousands of tapes he sends, free of charge, to anyone who requests them, are merciless harangues in which he rants and raves about specific points of Christian doctrine. His sermons are loaded with foreign terms and his own curious neologisms: "the Arrogant System of Cosmic One," "the right lobe of the soul," "the *gnosis* stage," "the *epignosis* stage," and that perennial favorite, the "divine dynasphere."

Thieme is probably the only living native of Beverly Hills, California, who holds it as a fundamental article of faith that all true Christian doctrine "has to go into the eight compartments of your right lobe." And he definitely is the only native of Beverly Hills, California, who can tell you who the Volscians, the Sabines, and the Etruscans were.

Thieme has been taken to task in the past for padding his résumé and purporting to have a command of foreign languages that he does not in fact possess. Garry Wills, in a 1989 article that appeared in the fey, doomed periodical *Wigwag*, took a sober, balanced look at Thieme, portraying him as less of a dangerous wacko than as an eccentric. Wills made clear that Thieme was not a song-and-dance huckster like Falwell or Robertson, but an intense, devout, somewhat scholarly sort who thought of himself as a serious theologian and intellectual. Nevertheless, Wills concluded that he was an "intellectual phony" who had lied about his military writing career, lied about turning down a Rhodes scholarship, lied about his academic credentials, and pretended to know Greek a whole lot better than he actually did—which the hoi polloi in his congregation had apparently never noticed. *Riff-raff.*

Thieme has predictable hatreds: liberals, Muslims, Russians, feminists. But every so often he comes in with a curve, as when he declares that a substantial number of Holy Rollers are in fact psychotics. He adds: "There are millions of psychotic people in this country, and it's increasing every day . . . and part of those millions—and a good part of them, are born-again Christians." You'll get no argument from me there. And in an extreme departure from the precepts of Falwell, Robertson, et al., Thieme vehemently defends the individual's right to privacy, even extending that philosophy to the explosive issue of abortion.

"An abortion is a private matter between a patient and a doctor—

and that's all," he declares on one tape. "And no one has the right to attack one of these things in any way or to stand outside a clinic and harass people. This is terrorism in the making."

Although he has often been portrayed as a pedantic, humorless sort, Thieme actually says some pretty funny things. For example, in *Satanology: Arrogance and Antagonism,* he uses what amounts to a spiritual hydraulic system to compute the "units of pressure" that are imposed on a Christian by various events in his or her life:

> So you have the unit factor. You have 10 units of pressure as a single person. You have 500—immediate—500 units as a married person. As a person having that pressure, if you have children, well then it'll go out of sight. Everytime you have a child, add 5,000. A dog or a cat . . . a cat would be about three units; cats seem to grow up quickly and handle themselves. A dog, depending upon the dog, could be anywhere from 5 to 10 units. And I understand that some people are taking pigs as pets, so maybe some day we'll analyze that one.

Coming from a full-time, professional harbinger of doom, this is pretty zany material.

———

Even if Thieme were as authentically bizarre as some people have made him out to be, there would still be something unfair about the attempts to depict Marilyn as a wacko just because she grew up in a house where his venomous tirades against everything that the Democratic party stands for were played twenty-four hours a day, every single day of the week. So what if Marilyn and her friends on the right grew up listening to Robert B. Thieme, Jr., with his grim view of the universe? Kids on the left grew up listening to Black Sabbath, the Grateful Dead, Canned Heat, and the Velvet Underground. Marilyn grew up listening to tracks such as "Scar Tissue of the Soul," while liberal kids had "Cocaine," "Heroin," "Manic Depression," and "The Pusher." Marilyn listened to "Satanic Plot No. 1." Liberal kids opted for Frank Zappa albums with such heartwarming titles as *Hot Rats* and *Weasels Ripped My Flesh.*

Marilyn gets all this grief because of listening to apocalyptic jeremiads about death and destruction and demons and the fires of Hell, while healthy, well-balanced left-wing kids are considered to be perfectly normal despite spending their youths listening to fine, instructive, uplifting tapes such as *Their Satanic Majesties Request* and *Sticky Fingers.* This is totally unfair, as the following chart comparing representative works by the recording artists Robert Thieme, Jr., on the one hand, and the Rolling Stones, on the other hand, makes clear.

Satanology, No. 1	***Their Satanic Majesties Request***
Mentions Satan	Mentions Satan
Comes in cassette format	Comes in cassette format
Deals with sin	Deals with sin
Talks about drugs	Talks about drugs
Pretty good seller	Pretty good seller
Still in catalog	Still in catalog

Indeed, the stunning comparison can be expanded to include a side-by-side, try-and-buy comparison of the amazing similarities between the driving forces behind these two recordings. Consider:

Robert B. Thieme, Jr.	***Mick Jagger***
Wears weird clothes on stage	Wears weird clothes on stage
Likes to show off	Likes to show off
Has prominent nose	Has prominent nose
Does SRO shows in Texas	Does SRO shows in Texas
Demure wife; no Nicaraguan progeny to speak of	Married to leggy blonde; has a kid who's half-Nicaraguan

As far as I'm concerned, it is no sin to have grown up in a household where one's parents constantly played bizarre, ultra-right-wing tapes dripping with hatred of liberals, union members, and homosexuals. It's still better than having parents who made you listen to *The Best of Jerry Vale* or *Vic Damone Goes Mambo!,* like mine. Nor is it a crime to arrive at voting age without ever having sat in a dark room listening to a badly scratched copy of "In-A-Gadda-Da-Vida." For some Americans, adolescent rites of passage involve Carlos Castenada and the Electric Prunes, while for others, the sacred liturgy consists of dog-eared copies of *The Yearling* and vastly overplayed 45s of "Cherish" and "Big Girls Don't Cry."

The right expresses its insanity through religion; the left expresses its insanity through art. But neither poses a direct threat to this bouncy, jovial society. Unlike Muslims, who actually practice what they preach, or what they have preached to them, making vital day-to-day decisions based on the precepts of the Koran, Americans use religion and rock 'n' roll to let off steam.

Right-wingers don't really believe that Armageddon is nigh; if they did, what are they doing in thirty-year Treasuries? Left-wingers pay zillionaires like Bruce Springsteen enormous sums of money to sing songs about how they're not going to take any more of this shit from their corporate bosses. Then they report for work the next morning and take some more shit from their corporate bosses. Dispensational pre-millenialism and rock 'n' roll are each a crutch used by their fans in an effort to control things that no one can control. But no one in his right mind would ever take either of them seriously. God certainly doesn't.

Marilyn Quayle is also the victim of an East Coast bias against WASP, fundamentalist religions, whereas political figures—or their wives—who practice Catholicism, Judaism, or any of the assorted BMW religions like Episcopalianism get a free ride. I grew up as a Roman Catholic, listening to all sorts of mumbo-jumbo taught by men in capes in dark rooms filled with the smell of incense. I was taught that Saint Lawrence, after being roasted for hours on an open grill by his Roman captors, wisecracked, "I'm done well enough on this side; you can turn me over now." I grew up being taught that the Blessed Virgin Mary had dropped off a personal letter to the pope with some trainee shepherds in Fatima, Portugal; that both Jesus Christ and his mother Mary were born to virgins; that a priest can turn ordinary bread and wine into the body and blood of Christ; and that if you are wearing a brown cloth object called a scapular around your neck when you're hit by a car, you will eventually go to Heaven. How is this stuff any stranger than what Marilyn grew up believing?

The countervailing argument, of course, is that Catholic and Judaic theology is largely apolitical and nonideological, whereas the ministry of Robert B. Thieme, Jr., is a ministry of fear, charged with hateful, ultra-right-wing suspicion of foreigners, feminists, liberals, unions, and homosexuals. This is true, but these can hardly be called nonmainstream positions in the environment in which Marilyn Quayle grew up. For a set of beliefs to be deemed officially "weird," they have to involve things that only a tiny percentage of the general population practices, such as competitive dwarf-tossing or Morris dancing. But out where Marilyn Quayle comes from, *everybody* believes that Armageddon-is-nigh.

Richard Brookhiser, author of *The Way of the Wasp,* has thought long and hard about the issue of ostensible WASP weirdness, and believes it is a canard.

"Ronald Reagan was skilled at presenting himself as normal," says Brookhiser, "but he was actually a very peculiar person. Many, many Americans—far more than we are willing to acknowledge—are peculiar. There are lots of people like Marilyn Quayle out there. That kind of peculiarity is really quite normal among Americans; the country was founded by religious fanatics."

On the basis of these statements, I would argue that, by a very narrow margin, Marilyn Quayle should be acquitted of all pending charges of weirdness, estrangement from reality, and insanity. However, I *would* recommend that she be kept under surveillance.

———

This then brings us to the nettlesome subject of Marilyn's alleged intelligence. There has long been a theory that Marilyn Quayle is the smart person in the Quayle marriage; *Vanity Fair* even described her as "an underused national asset," as "a full-time Svengali" who "constantly looks as if she were itching to run Chrysler, on alternate Tuesdays." Of course, that's the sort of thing that *Vanity Fair* would say. *Spy* noted the irony in tributes such as this, pointing out that Marilyn, a genuinely unpleasant, haughty, unattractive person, has had a small measure of success in improving her public image, whereas her husband, a genuinely nice man, is still profoundly disliked and ridiculed by most Americans and almost all journalists.

Much of this willingness to back off the Second Lady derives from the conviction that Marilyn really is quite bright; a number of people who have worked with her have described her as brilliant. I don't think too many of these people have read her book, *Embrace the Serpent.* After reading this book, it's impossible to believe that Dan Quayle is the dumbest person of the family, because in writing her novel, Marilyn Quayle has committed the one unforgivable crime: *She has put it all down on paper.* As long as your public statements are transmitted through the media, you can always claim that you were misquoted, that your comments were taken out of context, that the videotape was deliberately edited to make you look bad. Once you write a full-length novel expressing your own thoughts in your own—or your sister's—words, there's no place to hide.

After reading *Embrace the Serpent,* my suspicion is, yes, Dan Quayle has access to far more intellectual firepower than his wife, and is a smidgen closer to Sir Isaac Newton and Pliny the Elder on the evolutionary scale than Marilyn. After reading *Embrace the Serpent,* my suspicion is that Justice, the Quayles' venerable old Labrador retriever, may be smarter than Marilyn Quayle. And Justice is buried out back, behind the vice president's mansion.

I make these allegations for a number of reasons. Oh, forget the loopy, McCarthy-era politics—journalists are traitors, Congress has made it impossible for the American intelligence forces to function, Democrats are morons—you sort of expect this from a Hoosier tennis lady who obviously doesn't get out of the house very often. No, what's really unnerving is the fact that the wife of the vice president of the United States isn't aware that the Soviet Union has—how shall I put this?—sort of collapsed. Which makes a *thriller* about a Soviet takeover of Cuba seem sort of—how shall I put this?—dumb.

Embrace the Serpent (originally entitled *Rage of the Lambs* or *Silence of the Emerging Republican Majority* or something) is a disarmingly moronic thriller that deals with the death of Fidel Castro. After Castro dies, everything would seem to be in place for his drug-dealing madman of a brother Raul to launch an attack on the Star War–less United States with chemical weapons. But Raul is bumped off by the Russians (remember them?), and a commie stooge named César Valles is installed in his place. Operation Romanov races toward its breathtaking conclusion with the help of a Pulitzer Prize–winning editor (a pinko cretin, in Marilyn's lexicon, who only won his Pulitzer because of material fed to him by a Soviet spy) from what is obviously *The Washington Post.* The editor assures the left-leaning, duncelike president of the United States that the dupe Valles is an all-right guy, whereas José Moya, a genuine insurgent and *friend of democracy* recently sprung from the slammer by the Forces of Good, is actually a Soviet puppet. (Marilyn and Sis never really explain why an American president would think that a man who had spent twenty years in Castro's prison would be a commie puppet; this isn't usually the way things work. But hey—they're Hoosiers.)

The Soviets, of course, are in league with Iran, which is secretly hoping to plant nuclear weapons in Cuba so that it can obliterate the United States. Meanwhile, the Cubans will be selling our kids so many drugs that we will forget to spend money on Star Wars and our enemies will overrun our fun-loving but basically misguided democracy. The only thing that stands between the Home of the Brave and the Apocalypse is a valiant, conservative senator from Georgia and a woman who went to Georgetown law school. In the biggest hoot of all, the senator happens to be black.

At the beginning of Chapter 2, Marilyn and Sis cite a remark once made by Thomas Jefferson: "The man who reads nothing at all is better educated than the man who reads nothing but newspapers." Coming from someone whose last name is Quayle, such references to education, newspapers, or Thomas Jefferson seem terrifyingly incongruous, if not out-and-out suicidal. One almost wishes that Congress would pass a Federal Anti-Chutzpah Statute, barring authors from citing the Founding Fathers unless they can demonstrate that their IQ is within seventy points of the person being quoted.

The most charitable thing one can say about their book is that the girls started writing it two years ago, before the Soviet Union had fallen apart, and already had too much stuff on the word processor to start from scratch. (It should also be noted that Sis lives in Tullahoma, Tennessee, where the news that the Soviet Union has imploded may only just have arrived.) Obviously, the book should have been rewritten or deep-sixed as soon as it became historically ludicrous. But publishing houses don't care about things like that, because they know that the target market for books like *Embrace the Serpent* is not the same as the target market for *The Iliad*. The market for *Embrace the Serpent* is made up of people who think that Thomas Jefferson was a member of a 1970s Norman Lear sitcom about an upwardly mobile black family. Moreover, the publisher probably figured that most readers buying a book co-written by a person named Quayle would have been disappointed if it wasn't stupid.

Marilyn and sister Nancy have a prim, dainty writing style, with no sex and almost no profanity: "We want to know what's going on before everything hits the fan." The closest they get to a real, live swear word is "bitch," a word with which Marilyn is, presumably, not entirely unfamiliar. As might be expected, the girls favor Sagamore-on-the-Wabash expressions such as "hornswoggle."

The love scenes involving the freedom fighters are absolutely hilarious: " 'And you, my sweet one,' Moya said, running his finger lightly over her lips, 'you're lovelier than even my dreams of you. If only we could spend these minutes enjoying each other. Oh, my darling,' he whispered, one hand caressing her face, his other arm holding her protectively, 'I want to hold you, to feel your nearness.' "

Embrace the Serpent is the kind of book so magically unintelligent, with such painstaking obliviousness to detail that no one at its publisher's seems to have noticed that the Cuban characters spend the first 269 pages speaking English like Sergeant Garcia or José Jimenez or Manuel the Waiter from *Fawlty Towers* before suddenly erupting into Spanish:

" *'Tengo que hablar con Señor Victor Rojas.'* "

" *'El señor no esta aqui.'* "

But even when the Freedom Fighters do speak English, it's the kind of English that suggests the direct linguistic influence of *The Three Amigos* or *The Mark of Zorro:*

" 'He was a patriot, and he died a patriot's death, bravely and with honor,' " Moya said. " 'I grieve not only for you, Alejandro, who has lost a beloved father, but for Cuba, which has lost a courageous son.' "

This intensely autobiographical book shows Marilyn and Sis to be deeply resentful of people who went to eastern schools, people who enjoy classical music and the arts, people who are sophisticated, and people who get regular newspaper delivery; in short, the cultural elite.

The publication of *Embrace the Serpent* signals the continuing decline in the power and prestige of the Executive office. This is a decline that began with Watergate, was interrupted for a brief time during Reagan's first term, and then picked up steam once the ineffectual George Bush took office. Were LBJ still in office, and had Muriel Humphrey gone out and written a book with her sister that would have embarrassed the entire administration, Johnson would have gone down the hall and wrung the Happy Warrior's fat little neck. Reagan would have been more discreet; he would have had Lyn Nofziger wring the vice president's grubby little neck. Under Reagan, Vice President George Bush was given specific instructions: "Stay the hell out of the way for eight years, and then we'll let you be president." Bush complied. But now that he is president, for some inexplicable reason, Bush allows his image to be smeared not only by his feisty but cerebrally impoverished vice president but by his daft wife as well.

Meanwhile, back in the Beltway, no one seems to know quite what to make of all this.

"There's some sort of free pass given to people in the administration because of all those books that came out under Reagan," says Rick Hertzberg of *The New Republic.* "Can you imagine what the reaction would have been if Rosalynn Carter or Joan Mondale had written a book like this?"

Perhaps Marilyn cannot help herself. For in a very real sense, Marilyn Quayle is a clueless person. She makes a point of letting journalists know that she buys soap and shampoo at the Price Club, then spends $590,000 redoing the vice president's mansion. She goes out of her way to let people know that her daughter Corrine often wears hand-me-down clothes inherited from a friend, then appears in *Vogue* attired in riding gear. She pouts publicly that Dan's grandfather did not believe in inherited wealth, making the Quayles virtual paupers, then demands that a reporter for *Women's Wear Daily* be chucked out of a function at the private school the Quayle children attend— even though the reporter is in attendance because her children also attend the same school. She makes a major show of cutting Dan's hair and hemming Tucker's pants and telling *The Saturday Evening Post* that she's never had a pedicure, then goes gallivanting—very nearly causing a riot—in Manassas National Battlefield Park the weekend the government was closed in October 1990 because of the budget standoff.

(Things got worse when the National Parks Service agreed to build a horse stable at Manassas to accommodate the Quayles.) It's obviously too late for Marilyn to learn anything about liberty, equality, and fraternity, but it would be nice if she took some of that taxpayers' money and got Nancy Reagan's charm coach to teach her thematic consistency.

In any case, the more you get to know her, the more you can understand why Dan spends so much time golfing. "You have to know Mr. Dewey very well in order to dislike him," a wit once said of Thomas Dewey. Ditto Marilyn Quayle.

I X

IN HOKE SIGNO VINCES

Ever since fancypants incumbent Martin Van Buren was accused of perfuming his whiskers, wearing a corset, and drinking expensive wines during the campaign of 1840, it has been incumbent upon American politicians aspiring to high national office to cultivate an image of ferocious ordinariness. Dozens of millionaire presidents have claimed to have been born in a log cabin, a shotgun shack, a lean-to, a barn, a humble abode, or a tumbledown Quonset hut located, it goes without saying, on the wrong side of the tracks. This tradition was initiated by William Henry Harrison, a war hero who was actually born on a huge Virginia plantation of some 2,000 acres, but who won a trip to the White House by purporting to drink hard cider and wear a coonskin cap while sitting in the shade of his log cabin. Harrison was at least as well-heeled as the patrician that he unseated, and has gone down in history as the first president whose image was created almost entirely by his handlers. Washington and those guys didn't need handlers.

After a knavish campaign in which a long-suffering nation was deluged with log-cabin teacups, log-cabin songbooks, log-cabin sing-alongs, log-cabin sunbonnets, and fancy dance-steps such as the Harrison hoe-down, Harrison caught a cold while delivering a dreary two-hour outdoor inaugural address during a March gale and perished thirty-one days later. The unedited version of the speech, before Daniel Webster took an axe to it, contained seventeen separate references to obscure Roman politicians, to this day an outdoor American record. But there was nothing in the fatal peroration that made people view Harrison's death as an irretrievable loss to the nation.

Taking their cue from the duplicitous Harrison, the Machiavellianally down-home Lyndon Baines Johnson, and the theatrically rustic Jimmy Carter, the Quayles have worked hard to project an image of spectacular ordinariness ever since Dan entered public life in 1976. As a freshman senator in the early 1980s, Dan regularly could be seen tooling around Capitol Hill in his beat-up old orange Plymouth Horizon. Supposedly, the garish vehicle had trouble getting up hills and was blighted by an air conditioner that was always going on the fritz; indeed, money that could have been spent repairing the air conditioner or replacing the transmission was probably spent on press releases keeping the media aware of the troubled status of the air conditioner and the desperate condition of the transmission.

This aura of rehearsed chintziness has not entirely disappeared since Quayle has assumed the second highest office in the land; as vice president, he has occasionally showed up for important government functions sporting a dress shirt with a badly frayed collar. When asked by hard-hitting journalists why he didn't simply stop off at National Brands Outlet and pick up some new threads, Quayle replied that he was just plain cheap.

Ostentatious cheapness has long been a motif in the history of this family. When the Quayles moved from Virginia to Washington after Dan became vice president, Marilyn told *The Saturday Evening Post* that it "sparked a household debate" over what was "worth paying to have moved." On the grooming front, it is a matter of public record that for the longest time Marilyn would cut both her own and her husband's hair, only ending this practice after friends cautioned that her barbering tended to make the Quayles look even younger and less serious than they actually are.

After being elected vice president, Dan and oldest son Tucker started getting their hair cut at the Senate barber shop at $4.50 a crack. The unimpeachable source *People* magazine has reported that Marilyn buys personal items such as shampoo and soap at the Price Club wholesale warehouse, while daughter Corrine "often wears hand-me-down clothes from a friend in McLean, Virginia." What's more, when *People* visited Marilyn at her McLean home in 1990, she was busy hemming a pair of Tucker's pants. (Prefrayed trousers badly in need of hemming in front of impressionable journalists can be purchased at Common Touchables, a Georgetown boutique specializing in cunning but wholesome Republican props.)

Obviously, the twin burdens of fame and power have forced the Quayle household into a lifestyle with which they—solidly middle-class folk that they are—feel a tad uncomfortable. These days, the Quayles live in a thirty-three-room Victorian mansion nestled on the grounds of the Naval Observatory in Washington. Dan earns $166,200 a year, and also gets an annual house allowance of $183,000, plus $75,000 to cover expenses. He has a huge staff, five offices, a chauffeured limo, a helicopter, and access to Air Force Two—a Boeing 707, with a crew of more than a dozen. For reasons of personal and national security, the three Quayle children attend private school, where they are probably the only children whose mother still hems their clothing in public.

The Quayles have been aided in projecting a just-plain-folks image by numerous champions in the media. Writing in *National Review* in September 1988, libertarian Neal B. Freeman said of the veep: "His current circumstance is more Dagwood Bumstead than Robin Leach. Mom carpools the Rockwellian kids around the suburbs in a Ford van, and Dad takes his turn at coaching the girls' softball team."

These charming touches—carpools, softball teams, shabby attire—may have been cribbed from the *faux bourgeois* zillionaires who flourished on Wall Street in the Age of Milken. Back in the 1980s, no *Manhattan, Inc.* or *Fortune* profile of Shearson Lehman Hutton chairman Peter Cohen—the guy who botched the $25 billion takeover of RJR Nabisco and ran his company right into the poorhouse—was ever complete without mentioning Cohen's devotion to his daughter's softball team. *See?* the stories seemed to be saying, *he has the common touch.* John Mulheren, the colorful risk arbitrageur arrested outside his Rumson, New Jersey, home while allegedly on his way to bump off his old pal Ivan Boesky, was rarely seen in public without his trademark leather pants and sockless feet. *You have to admit: He has the common touch,* the articles seemed to suggest. *After all, he doesn't wear socks.* Another notorious *sans-chaussettes* was Keith Gollust of Coniston Partners, the trio of corporate raiders who in 1988 came within an eyelash of taking over Gillette. *I am not wearing socks,* Gollust's big, beautiful smile seemed to say to mesmerized magazine readers. *Therefore, I must be just like you. Now, give me all of your money.*

The central question in the Quayle family's decades-long masquerade as ordinary, middle-class people is whether the entire clan truly believes that money's tight and they're all going to have to pull in their belts a few notches, or whether it is all an elaborate charade. Dan, after all, grew up in a house on the eleventh hole of the Paradise Valley Country Club in Scottsdale, Arizona, where he played golf as a child with his grandpa, the most powerful man in Indiana. Sometimes, Dwight D. Eisenhower, president of the United States, tagged along. When Quayle, who used to play forty-five holes a day as a kid (taking salt tablets to ward off the effects of the heat), played a round of golf in 1990 with *Sports Illustrated* writer Rick Reilly, he told a highly illuminating tale about his childhood. According to Reilly, young Quayle was caddying for Judy Kimball in the LPGA tourney at the course. Kimball was one shot off the pace when she staggered onto the eleventh hole, and wanted to use a five-wood for her second shot. Quayle didn't think that was such a good idea. She did. So Dan said, "Look, I live on this hole. There's no way you can get a five-wood to the green. You have to take a four-wood." Kimball still didn't think it was such a great idea, but she finally broke down and took his advice. She also took a nine on the hole.

There are several things that can be learned from this incident. Even at a very early age, Quayle was not shy about offering advice to his betters, advice that could turn out to be disastrous. But there is another, more important, point: Most people who drive to work in a beat-up old Plymouth Horizon with an air conditioner on the fritz, attired in a shirt with a badly frayed collar, never had a chance to patrol the links in Dwight D. Eisenhower's shadow or offer advice to any golfer on the

LPGA tour about how to play a hole that happened to be in his own backyard. Most people are driving those cars and wearing those shirts because they have to, and don't have the foggiest idea which club to use on any hole on any course on the planet.

Dan has always insisted that he is heir to but a tiny portion of his grandfather's estimated $600 million fortune, and is worth only perhaps $1 million. (Conservatives become apoplectic when journalists describe him as being worth $50 million—which would make him a fat cat—when he is only worth a paltry $1 million—which makes him a piker.) Whatever the case, it is clear that Quayle's descendants stand to inherit a fortune from trust funds that have been set up in their names by their great-grandfather. Thus, if Dan himself is not fabulously wealthy, he certainly knows a lot of people who are, and knows that his children will never be so hard-up that they have to debate what furniture to move from one house to the other. Wealth is when you have to explain angrily what percentage of the interest on your grandfather's $600 million fortune you are *not* entitled to.

All this notwithstanding, Quayle has generally handled the issue of wealth quite well—by avoiding the subject. Not so his wife. The daughter of two doctors, the granddaughter of two influential Indiana pols, and the wife of a man whose grandfather owned $600 million, plus all of Indiana and half of Arizona, Marilyn has repeatedly become quite testy when the subject of family wealth has come up. According to one report, Marilyn wrote her abysmal novel *Embrace the Serpent* only to raise money to put her kids through college. This may not be a calculating gesture on her part; there is reason to believe that Marilyn Quayle may be genuinely confused about the differences among the various economic classes in America. There are, after all, nuances, and those who have led sheltered lives in the Hoosier hinterland may not be aware of them. Therefore, as a public service, and with nothing but the Second Lady's own personal edification in mind, we present the following handy chart.

HOW YOU CAN TELL IF YOU'RE WEALTHY OR NOT

Wealthy People	*Not-So-Wealthy People*
Have shopped at Price Club	Shop at Price Club
Have hemmed kids' clothes	Have hemmed kids' clothes
Have driven a beat-up old car	Drive a beat-up old car
Have gramps worth $600 million	Have gramps on welfare
Grew up on eleventh hole of golf course in Scottsdale, Arizona	Grew up in Milwaukee
Know, or are, scions	No scions in family

There is another chart that may also be of some assistance in apprising the socioculturally marooned Marilyn of her true economic status. Every four years, presidents and vice presidents are required, by force of custom, to go out and meet the people. At some point in the campaign, contact with blacks is inevitable. Not even Republicans can avoid this kind of thing. In the course of these meetings, a host of unappetizing, cardiovascularly toxic foodstuffs will be ingested; homage to Jackie Robinson, Martin Luther King, and Michael Jordan will be elicited; remarks to the effect that deep down inside we are all brothers under the skin will be made. At some point, the urge to invoke the beat-up old orange Plymouth with no air conditioning will become overpowering, as will the overwhelming desire to complain about skyrocketing prices that have forced the family to begin shopping at Price Club. *At all costs, these urges must be resisted.* Many black people have a keen sense of socioeconomic distinctions and can immediately recognize when they are in the presence of wealthy people masquerading as just plain folks. The following chart explains why:

Well-to-Do White People	*Ordinary Black People*
Drive beat-up old Plymouths	Drive beat-up old Plymouths
Hem kids' clothes	Hem kids' clothes
Haven't read Kierkegaard	Haven't read Kierkegaard
Deeply concerned about tort reform	Not losing much sleep over tort reform
Recognize that you should really use a number 5 to get onto the green, and should resist the temptation to blast out of there with a number 4	Kind of hazy on this stuff

Fell in love while working on rewriting Indiana's death penalty	Never seriously considered as candidates to rewrite death penalty of Indiana, or death penalty of any other state, for that matter
Claim to like Garth Brooks	Not big, big Garth Brooks fans

When wealthy politicians do this sort of stuff in front of blacks and colorful ethnics, it kind of makes sense: They're grasping at straws and simply want to get out of the neighborhood without getting blamed for crack or AIDS or Newark or something. But why wealthy politicians feel that they must put themselves through these grueling sackcloth-and-ashes ordeals in front of other white people is not immediately apparent. Americans, by and large, are not uncomfortable with the idea of being ruled by rich white people; it is certainly preferable to being ruled by poor blacks, middle-class Puerto Ricans, or anyone from the Dominican Republic. Bush, a spoiled rich kid, and Quayle, a spoiled rich kid, are no different from most of our presidents and vice presidents.

Of our truly great presidents, only Lincoln and Jackson were not to the manor born; Washington, Jefferson, Madison, both Roosevelts, and Woodrow Wilson were all loaded, as were such second-rankers as Monroe, the two Adamses, both Harrisons, Taft, and JFK. Of our forty-one presidents, thirty-three were born into the upper or upper-middle class; only three were actually born poor. And many of the presidents who weren't loaded when they emerged from their mothers' wombs made sure that they were loaded by the time they got into politics. Viz: LBJ.

It should also be borne in mind that poverty has always been stigmatized in this country. Americans don't mind if you were *born* in a log cabin, but they hate it if you *stayed* there. Millard Fillmore, who really was born in a log cabin, was a hopeless bozo who served sixteen forgettable months as vice president, then wasted more than two and a half years of his own and everyone else's time as a spineless, conniving, ineffectual chief executive, then rounded out the performance by disgracing himself as the presidential candidate of the xenophobic, anti-Catholic third party, the Know-Nothings. Andrew Johnson, born in a log cabin and the poorest president we have ever had, showed up in an advanced state of inebriation for his own inauguration as Abe

Lincoln's second-in-command, and later came within one vote of being impeached by the Senate. Richard Nixon, born on the wrong side of the tracks, ended up becoming Richard Nixon.

As for vice presidents, Richard Johnson used to tell people that he was "born in a cane brake and cradled in a sap trough." The American people rewarded him by voting him out of office. *The cane brake material is fine,* the American people seemed to be telling Johnson, *but the sap trough stuff is really pushing it.* Clearly, there is no advantage to being poor when seeking high political office. In fact, there is no advantage to being poor, period.

And yet high-level American politicians *do* feel embarrassed about their wealth, and are constantly going out of their way to don raffish attire and sheepishly affect an utterly unconvincing solidarity with the masses. No one seriously believes that John Kennedy could have enjoyed visiting coal mines in West Virginia. No one seriously believes that George Bush enjoys eating pork rinds. Yet every four years, after forty months of behaving like the insensitive patricians that they are, the lads are back out there on the hustings making fools of themselves. Why?

To understand this phenomenon, we must backtrack a bit and examine the deeply ingrained tradition of American hokiness. This tradition dates from the early 1800s, when pioneers from the eastern shoreline, their hearts set on making a new life for themselves in the golden West, began plodding their way into Injun territory. While moseying through the amber waves of grain, beneath the spacious skies, poised scant feet above the purple mountains' majesty (where the grapes of wrath are stored), the pioneers would while away their time by singing songs such as this:

> Come all ye Yankee farmers who wish to change your lot,
> Who've spunk enough to travel beyond your native spot,
> And leave behind the village where Ma and Pa do stay,
> Come follow me and settle in Michigania—
> Yea, yea, in Michigania.

Why did the early pioneers chant such inane twaddle? In part, because they had been told by grizzled Acadian fur traders that Indians would flee in terror before white men armed with such lusty japes. But an even more overpowering reason was a sense of what cultural historians now refer to as "Conestoga campiness." The pioneers knew that their songs were hokey crap, but it amused them to terrorize Indians, who did not understand satire (there is no word in any Native American language for "chuckle") with their cornball drinking songs. The men and women who ripped their livelihood from the unforgiving black soil of the heartland knew that they were being hokey. They liked being hokey.

Nor was hokiness a uniquely rural oral tradition. Back east in the slums of New York and Baltimore, Andy Jackson's supporters would march through the streets of the infant nation in massive torchlight parades, proclaiming the virtues of Old Hickory:

> Yankee Doodle, smoke 'em out
> The proud, the banking faction—
> None but such as Hartford Feds
> Oppose the poor and Jackson.

This was Juvenal, Catullus, and Ovid all rolled into one compared to what the Whigs used to cackle during the election of 1840. Starting off with the perennial standby catcall, "Tippecanoe and Tyler Too!" the Whigs would yelp:

> Make way for Old Tip, turn out, turn out!
> 'Tis the people's decree, their choice shall be,
> So Martin Van Buren, turn out, turn out!

and follow it up with:

> Old Tip he wears a homespun coat
> He has no ruffled shirt-wirt-wirt;
> But Mat he has the golden plate
> And he's a little squirt-wirt-wirt.

During the years leading up to the Civil War, American hokiness fell on hard times, as America braced for the moment when hokey northerners would face off against hokey southerners in a war that figured to be short on laughs. But it got a real shot in the arm during the election of 1884, when the Republicans would poke fun at Democratic presidential candidate Grover Cleveland, father of a bastard, and himself a bit of a bastard, by cackling:

Ma! Ma! Where's my pa?

to which the Democrats would gleefully respond:

Gone to the White House—ha, ha, ha!

When that didn't get the opposition's goat, the Democrats would mock the shady business dealings of Democratic sleazeball and perennial presidential aspirant James G. Blaine with the words:

Blaine, Blaine, James G. Blaine,
The continental liar from the state of Maine.

Boy, did that ever make him mad.
Historians view the waning years of the nineteenth century as the Golden Age of Hoke, when people became famous for mouthing such cornball platitudes as William Jennings Bryan's "You shall not crucify mankind on a cross of gold," and politicians were referred to by such nicknames as "Old Rough 'n Ready." Foreigners found American hokiness especially grating; when Admiral Dewey sailed into Manila Harbor in 1898 and blew up the Spanish fleet, the enemy not only had to endure the humiliation of failing to inflict a single casualty on the American fleet but were also subjected to such fulsome poetry as this:

Oh, dewy was the morning
Upon the first of May,
And Dewey was the admiral,
Down in Manila Bay.
And dewy were the Spaniard's eyes,
Them orbs of black and blue,
And dew we feel discouraged?
I dew not think we dew.

The preeminent role of hokiness in the creation of the American Empire is clearly no accident. The truth about the American people is plain and simple: They like their hoke. They demand lots of sombreros and coonskin caps, not to mention ludicrous nicknames such as the Sage of Monticello, the Great Communicator, Old Fuss and Feathers, Honest Abe, Silent Cal, and Tricky Dick. They want dogs named Justice, Fala, Truelove, and Sweetlips; seafaring rabbits that attack peanut farmer presidents named Jimmy; and cute little ponies named Macaroni. They want the brother of the reigning president to be an idiot, the sons a bunch of crooks, and the wife Harriet Nelson. They want the future president of the United States to appear on *Laugh-In*, and they want the sitting vice president of the United States to appear on an episode of *Major Dad*, just to show that he's one of us.* Savvy politicians have long recognized this fact, and have worked hard to keep the populace amused with their zany antics. Indeed, one of the crowning moments in the history of American hokiness occurs every four years when each and every presidential and vice presidential candidate is required to don a stunning array of stupid hats, shapeless windbreakers, and garish aboriginal headdresses and submit to a nine-month-long ritual of abject public humiliation.

Diagnosed more scientifically, the primaries and the fall campaign are a harrowing ritual in which America literally forces candidates to answer the question: "How badly do you want this job?" But the worst part is not having your wife find out that you've been screwing Miss Sagamore on the Wabash for the past twelve years. The worst part is having to show the common touch. As noted above, most American presidents and vice presidents have been fairly wealthy men, and some have been quite educated and sophisticated. Garfield could write Greek with one hand while writing Latin with the other. Jefferson had been to France. John Kennedy's wife knew who Mozart was. How demeaning it must have been for people of this ilk to visit coal mines, kiss ethnic children with burrito stains on their cheeks, and drink Steg-

---

*One thing they don't want, however, is any goddamn poetry. In 1961, John F. Kennedy invited Robert Frost to read a poem at his inauguration; this was the first time in American history that a poet had been asked to read at such a function. Less than three years later, Kennedy was gunned down by a madman firing from a book warehouse in Dallas. It is impossible for any thinking, sentient being to believe that these events are unrelated.

maier's. No, it's no picnic. When the average parent thinks, "My son could grow up to be president of the United States," he's thinking about state dinners, parades, economic summits. What the parent is not thinking about are the pork rinds, the salsa, the Ukrainian appetizers, the interminable polka numbers.

Yet this is the gauntlet thrown down by America: *Anyone can force down a plate of pirogis. Anyone can listen to Jerry Vale. Anyone can pretend to like Cajun music. But if you really want to be president of these here United States, you're gonna have to listen to records by the Oak Ridge Boys. You're gonna have to listen to bad records by the Oak Ridge Boys. And when you're finished listening to bad records by the Oak Ridge Boys, you're gonna have to listen to bad records by Tammy Wynette. And, mister, you're gonna like it.*

———

The tradition of compelling rich and powerful people who are seeking public office to rub shoulders with the insupportable vermin who really make up most societies dates back at least to the time of the Romans. Just ask the immortal Bard. In his vastly underrated tragedy *Coriolanus*, Shakespeare depicts the rise and fall of a Roman war hero whose central character flaw is an insufficient affection for the common man. When Coriolanus is persuaded to stand for public office, he is required by Roman tradition to attire himself in "a gown of humility" and stand in the Forum chatting with the hoi polloi. His handlers implore him to be nice, to be polite, to at least try to suppress his contempt for the "rank-scented many." But Coriolanus finds this impossible. Instead, he makes snippy remarks like: "Bid them wash their faces and keep their teeth clean."

This doesn't go over very well at all. The common people thereupon make clear precisely what they expect from the candidate when they demand "the corn 'o the storehouse gratis." In demanding the corn of the storehouse, gratis, what the common people are really asking for is a little bit of hoke, a dash of the Roman *Hee-Haw* routine. But Coriolanus, a haughty, patrician type, isn't much of a cutup. Needless to say, he doesn't get the job.

The tradition of subjecting political candidates to the litmus test of hokiness comes down to us directly from this era. Indeed, quadrennial electoral hokiness is the most sacred, honored tradition in American public life. Does anyone seriously think that William Henry Harrison, a dignified old gent from Ole Virginny, actually enjoyed wearing a coonskin cap and smoking a corncob pipe? Of course not. Then why did he do it? He did it because *he wanted to be president.* Does anyone seriously think that Richard Nixon enjoyed appearing on the same dais as Sammy Davis, Jr., where he suffered permanent corneal abrasions from being exposed to that many mood rings? Of course not. Then why did he do it? He did it because *he wanted to be president.* Does anyone seriously believe that Jimmy Carter enjoyed being pushed out of the way by future-fugitive-from-justice Bowie Kuhn so that the commissioner of baseball could present the World Series trophy to a bunch of sweaty, inebriated black men who didn't seem to know who Carter was? Of course not. Why did he do it? He did it because *he wanted to keep being president.* Does anyone seriously believe that George Bush enjoys listening to Loretta Lynn records, enjoys eating pork rinds, enjoys reading *Bassmaster* magazine, enjoys shopping at Penney's? Of course not. Then why does he do it? He does it because *he wants to be president.*

Some people don't want it badly enough. The incredibly dignified Thomas Dewey (immortalized as "the man on the wedding cake") was forced while campaigning in Oregon in 1948 to subject himself to some of the most demeaning public rituals in the history of this great nation. First, he allowed himself to be abducted by seminaked Republicans clad in cavemen costumes, who then frolicked and gamboled merrily with the stunned candidate in tow. Next, he was abducted by Republicans dressed as pirates who pricked his arm and forced him to sign a buccaneer membership oath with his own blood. As if this were not enough, Dewey, once targeted for assassination by Dutch Schultz, then was compelled to wear a ten-gallon hat and a headdress left behind by the queen of Romania when she had visited the state two decades earlier. He looked like a complete idiot.

Looking like a complete idiot would have been worth it had he won the election. He did not. Instead, the luckless man suffered the most humiliating upset in the history of the presidency. Why? There are many theories explaining how Thomas Dewey managed to lose an election that virtually no one gave Harry Truman a chance of winning.

But one plausible theory is that he failed to nail a passing score on the internal hokeometer that beats in every American's breast. After having agreed to be abducted by the Republican cavemen, impaled by the Republican pirates, and bedecked in the outrageous headwear of the queen of Romania, Thomas Dewey, seemingly president-to-be, failed to pass the ultimate test. *He refused to get up on a horse.* He had been abducted by right-wing isolationists masquerading as pluralists from the Paleolithic era, had been forced to shed his own blood in a lurid postadolescent ritual, had agreed to don garish headwear once worn by a strange potentate from a mysterious Eastern European nation intimately linked with Vlad the Impaler, Count Dracula, and very possibly the Bride of Frankenstein, and had even gotten as far as donning a ten-gallon hat, a brand of eccentric headgear that makes even cowboys look ridiculous. Yet when the crucial test—mounting a stallion—presented itself, Dewey recoiled in horror.

A few months later, he was soundly repudiated by the American people in the most staggering upset in U.S. electoral history. What can we learn from all this? That if you want to be president of these here United States, *you put on that goddamn hat and you get up on that goddamn horse.* And if you want to be vice president of these here United States—or the vice president's wife—you hem those goddamn trousers, you wear that goddamn frayed dress shirt, and you drive that goddamn orange '76 Plymouth Horizon, air conditioner or no air conditioner. And, mister, you smile when you do it.

———

There are two other facets of Dan Quayle's persona that need to be discussed: his appearance and his passion for golf. It is frequently argued that Quayle was selected as George Bush's running mate because of his stunning good looks. This cynical theory, often advanced by ugly Democrats who feel that Quayle bears a remarkable resemblance to Robert Redford (to ugly Democrats, all Republicans look like Robert Redford), evolves from the belief that Lee Atwater was so calculating and sexist that he honestly believed that Quayle's looks would bring in the female vote. This is an insult to American women. Without American women, the simian rock star Mick Jagger would have had no career at all; neither would the extravagantly unattractive thespian John Malkovich. Much the same can be said of James Brown, Roy Orbison, Tom Petty, and a host of other chillingly unprepossessing men who have been elevated to the heights of stardom by American women too sophisticated to succumb to vulgar pulchriphilia.

It can be argued that the field of entertainment is different from politics, and that the same rules do not apply. In fact, they do. Since the dawn of the Republic, unbelievably hideous men—not to mention women with hatchet faces like Eleanor Roosevelt—have played a pivotal role in shaping our national destiny. George Washington was a monstrosity, the Creature from the Black Dermatological and Orthodontic Lagoon. John Adams was a beast, as was his son John Quincy Adams. James Buchanan had defective eyes that roamed all over the room; Zachary Taylor had eyes that roamed all over the state. Abraham Lincoln looked like he'd come in a distant second in an axe fight with a stegosaurus. Andrew Johnson looked like he'd come in third. Grover Cleveland had most of his jaw missing as a result of surgery to remove a tumor in his mouth. William Taft was a fat slob, Herbert Hoover a baby-faced porker, Jimmy Carter had teeth that suggested a direct genealogical descent from *la famille* Bugs Bunny, and Richard Nixon looked like Richard Nixon.

Lamentably, most American vice presidents are so obscure that it is hard to find photographs of them, but surely if Garret Hobart or Rufus King were real lookers we would have heard about it by now. On the other hand, we do know what LBJ and Nixon looked like. Thus, the coldhearted theory about the electoral appeal of Dan Quayle's good looks ignores the reality of two centuries of American life, in which the electorate has repeatedly demonstrated a noticeable, and perhaps even puzzling, enthusiasm for unattractive politicians seeking the highest office in the land.

This brings us, then, to the touchy subject of golf. From the moment he was picked by George Bush, Dan Quayle has been subjected to relentless abuse because of his passion for golf, his love affair with the links. Of course, almost all of this abuse comes from left-wing intellectuals who wouldn't know a sand wedge from a five-iron.

"If only he were a lacrosse player, he'd be home free," sighs Richard Brookhiser, an editor at *National Review* and author of *The Way of the Wasp.* "There is something about golf that the chattering classes abhor. And before they abhorred golf, they abhorred fishing."

With a handicap of seven, Quayle golfs every chance he gets at Burning Tree Country Club in Bethesda, Maryland, and every other chance he gets too. This makes a lot of people mad. As a senator, he once slipped a special tax break for foreign professional golfers into a tax corrections bill. This made a lot more people—including some conservatives—mad. In 1989, he was late for an appointment with Singapore Prime Minister Lee Kuan Yew because he stopped to play golf. This made Lee Kuan Yew mad. A couple of years ago, *Golf* magazine attacked Quayle for failing to share his umbrella with a partner and practice "golf bonding," and also accused him of being "cold" and "aloof" on the fairways. This made Quayle mad.

Quayle doesn't mince words when speaking about his passion for the fairways. "If they'd let me, I'd play every day. Wouldn't you?" he asked Reilly of *Sports Illustrated.* In the fourth installment of David Broder and Bob Woodward's massive *hommage à* Quayle, the vice president proudly admitted that he is sometimes finished with all his assignments by twelve noon and can knock off for the afternoon and play golf. "Golf is key to understanding the vice president," one of his aides told Woodward and Broder. Added Marilyn: "If you're going to play a good game of golf, everything else has to leave . . . It requires such a level of concentration that everything that's closing in on you and pounding you, it's total relief."

This is the principal difference between golf and, let's say, tort reform. To be good at golf, an individual must be capable of total concentration and focus all his energies on the matter at hand. Tort reform doesn't require anywhere near that level of concentration. Tort reform is something you can do in your spare time. So is running a secret government council that clandestinely rewrites federal regulations covering wetlands. These are things you can manage with one hand tied behind your back.

Still, Quayle's admission that he sometimes clocks out for the day at noon and spends the afternoon golfing is an astonishing admission to make in front of a pair of crusty, seasoned veterans such as Woodward and Broder. For what it seems to tell the rest of us is that the vice presidency isn't really much of a job. Mutual fund managers can't knock off at noon; the market might go into the tank and their clients would lose hundreds of millions of dollars. Software engineers can't knock off at noon; the System 386 might crash and an entire corporation would be paralyzed for the rest of the day. Policemen can't knock off for the afternoon; a talented young black director might suddenly release a powerful movie deploring racial hatred, violence, and drug sales, thus inadvertently precipitating sixteen deaths in a crowded Detroit movie lobby, and someone would need to call the fuzz. Not even managers of Burger King can knock off for the afternoon; a testy customer might try to get fifty cents knocked off the purchase price of his or her bacon double cheeseburger by inappropriately using a coupon for a Big Mac, and a person in a position of authority would be needed to mediate the dispute.

Thus, the easy, cynical way of looking at the vice president's office is to say that Dan Quayle has a less demanding job than mutual fund managers, software engineers, policemen, managers at Burger King, or just about any of us, with the possible exception of the Maytag repairman, Michael Jordan's coach, and whoever happens to be the secretary of education this week. But this contemptuous attitude overlooks the enormous symbolic value of the vice presidency, and ignores the fact that Dan Quayle deliberately and ostentatiously goes out of his way to show people that he spends a lot of time golfing, and even tells two of the nation's finest reporters that he often knocks off early for the day to get out on the links. This cannot be an accidental slip.

Quayle does this for three reasons. The first is to send a message to young Republicans, apprising them that taking an important job in Washington need not wreak havoc on one's lifestyle. This is vital to the party's future. In his illuminating book *The United States of Ambition,* Alan Ehrenhalt notes that the Republican party always has a hard time attacting talented people to politics because the hours are long and the pay is rotten. Public service is thought to be a thankless task.

But Quayle, by ostentatiously golfing at all hours of the day and night, often commandeering air force planes to do so, sends young Republicans an entirely different message, a message of hope and joy. *Look here,* he tells his young Republican cohorts, *I'm the second most powerful man on the face of the earth, yet I find lots of time to golf. You could, too. So hey, don't give up on public service.*

But that isn't the only message Quayle is sending. What Dan Quayle is also telling his adherents via his widely publicized exploits on the links is this: I am a Republican. Republicans believe in less government. Republicans believe that he governs best who governs least. Republicans believe that *he governs best who golfs most*. And that is precisely the message that Quayle sends the electorate: *Do you see what I am doing here? I am golfing. I am not governing. I am not raising your taxes. I am not crippling your businesses by imposing stringent new regulations on the use of wetlands or the recycling of perishable resources derived from paper products your company uses. I am golfing. I am not on your case. Remember that in 1996.*

But the final message he sends is the most valuable message of all. By refusing to publicly indulge in some proletarian sport such as touch football, Dan Quayle proudly proclaims: "I am an affluent American, and golfing is what affluent Americans like to do in their spare time. We like this sport, goddamn it: It's fab; it's nifty; it's boss. If you don't like it, you're probably a Democrat. Go play paddleball."

Thus, in a subtle fashion, Quayle's golfing sends an enormously powerful message to the have-nots of America. It teaches poor people—simply, directly—everything they need to know about the engine that runs American society. It teaches them the value of money. What's more, it teaches them, in a fashion they cannot possibly misunderstand, the most valuable lesson they will ever learn about money.

Get some.

INTO THE VALLEY OF TORT

In a vastly influential May 20, 1991, *Newsweek* article, political writer
Howard Fineman, in a splendid gesture of bipartisan civility, delin-
eated a plan that would enable the vice president of the United States
to improve his shabby image. Fineman had six suggestions:

1. Get nasty
2. Get out on the trail
3. Get a cause
4. Get a challenge
5. Get loose
6. Get another sport

Dan Quayle's reaction to Fineman's suggestions was decidedly mixed.
He did not get nasty. He did not get a challenge. He did not get loose.
He did not get a new sport. And since he had already been out on the
trail for three years, patting the heads of some of the finest babies in
the Lower Forty-eight, he probably wrote off Fineman's second suggestion as a fact-checker's error.

But there was one suggestion proffered by *Newsweek*'s savvy, wizened, prescient political analyst that Quayle did take to heart. Not three months after Fineman's article appeared on the newsstands, the vice president did show up in public with an issue, and, what's more, an issue he could be proud of.

Issues can be found in one of two places. They can erupt spontaneously from the breadbasket of America, as worried citizens from every walk of life cast their eyes longingly toward the nation's capital and clamor for lower taxes, safer cars, cleaner air, or better neighbors. This almost never happens.

Instead, issues are usually manufactured by tenured professors and by think tanks, which package them into influential but unreadable books that receive enthusiastic reviews from the authors' friends, who usually work for other think tanks. (Think tanks are a form of workfare for policy wonks whose writing has never been, and never will be, rewarded by the marketplace.) It is inconceivable that the American people, all by themselves, could independently arrive at the conclusion that the depletion of the ozone layer poses a dire threat to our national well-being, or that an immediate, across-the-board cut in the capital-gains tax is the only thing that stands between us and the economic abyss. The American people do not have that kind of sophistication. *They have to have help.*

And they get that help from agenda-setting conservatives such as William Kristol, Dan Quayle's Harvard-educated chief of staff, who used to work for Bill Bennett at the Department of Education during the waning years of the Reagan administration. Here he fashioned a reputation as a family-values type of guy by zealously opposing abortion, condom distribution to high school students, and other extravagant liberal practices. In 1988, he left Education to manage the campaign of a fellow neocon theorist, who was seeking a Senate seat in Maryland. The friend got massacred. A few months later, against the advice of friends who viewed the vice president's office as a political Death Valley, Kristol signed on as Quayle's domestic policy adviser, and shortly thereafter he became his chief of staff. Since 1989 it has been Kristol's job to make Dan Quayle seem smarter than he is. This is the principal difference between the vice president's office now and the vice president's office a half-century ago. When Harry Truman occupied the position, he didn't have the luxury of a large, full-time staff who would work to make him seem smarter. If Harry Truman was going to make people think he wasn't as dumb as he looked, he was going to have to do it all by himself. Fortunately for Truman, FDR died; after that, he had the staff.

For the first three years he held the job, things didn't work out so well for Kristol. Although the eager youngster stocked the office with numerous issues specialists armed with doctorates, and Quayle got on-the-job training from Henry Kissinger, Jeane Kirkpatrick, and Roger Ailes, his ratings in public opinion polls remained horrible. Attempts to enhance Quayle's image by force-feeding him biographies of Winston Churchill and Charles de Gaulle, and encouraging him to discuss Plato's *Republic* and Machiavelli's *The Prince* with influential journalists blew up in Kristol's face; once a cerebrally retrograde Hoosier starts telling reporters he's been reading Plato and Machiavelli, those heartless sons of bitches will immediately start setting traps for him, so that they can show their wiseass, know-it-all readers that Dumbo really read only the Cliff Notes version.

This is what happened to Quayle when he talked to *U.S. News & World Report*'s Michael Kramer about Plato, and was caught out by failing to identify the central image in the book, one of the most important images in all of Western literature: the shadows on the wall, in the allegory of the cave. Danny! Danny!

Here we are dealing with one of the great dangers in political life, which occurs when a public official with what is basically a Central Connecticut State intellect is surrounded by highly intelligent aides. A few weeks prior to the 1988 election, before it had made up its mind that it actually liked Quayle, *National Review* addressed this subject, remarking: "If the divide between scripted and spontaneous performance becomes too great, a lot of people might begin to assume that the men behind the scenes are telling our nation's leaders what to think, as well as how to speak."

In laymen's terms, this means: Never put any quotes from Soren Kierkegaard in a speech you're writing for a guy who went to DePauw. By and large, Dan Quayle's staff have worked hard to surgically implant words in his mouth that sound vaguely as though they might have originated in *his* brain. But there have been exceptions. In December 1989, at a gathering of Jewish leaders at New York's Yeshiva University, Quayle not only cited Albert Einstein and the Talmud but delivered a remarkable, and totally unexpected, exegesis of a passage contained in a letter that George Washington wrote to the Hebrew of Congregation in Newport way back in 1790.

There have been other embarrassing moments since then: Kristol and the gang had Quayle quote Thomas Aquinas on the subject of just wars. On another occasion Quayle "recalled" something that Stalin had said back in the 1930s about the Slavic people. This is a bit like having Bo Jackson discuss Anaxagoras's influence on Euclid. The vice president's ill-advised forays into this intellectual Mekong Delta seemed to confirm an opinion expressed by Robert Wright in *The New Republic* in July 1989: "Whatever he lacks in competence is being manufactured for him; he's surrounded by very bright aides, who gravitate toward power like moths to light, however dim the bulb."

Obviously, it was foolish of Quayle to go out and read books like *The Prince* and Plato's *Republic*. For one, those are books you're supposed to read in college; by the time you're in your forties you should be reading Frederick Hayek. Second, if you're a junior senator from Indiana who's already made it to the White House under your own steam, there's nothing left to learn from Plato or Machiavelli. Those guys should be learning from you. More to the point: Republicans don't elect people to high office because they're interested in their views about Thomas Aquinas, medieval intrigues pitting Guelphs against Ghibellines, or the meaning of the Holocaust. They elect them to cut taxes.

But there is a larger problem with jamming such inappropriate props into Quayle's hands. Kristol and his crew of Beltway Cyrano de Bergeracs believe that the function of bright unelectables like themselves is to hover around dumb electables and make them seem less dumb. In this sense, guys like Quayle are merely malleable putty.

Surrounding oneself with an entourage of wizards will sometimes reap great rewards for the politician, who can benefit from the goodwill that Beltway journalists feel toward his clever staff. This is the case with *The New Republic*'s Fred Barnes, whose coverage of Quayle, without descending to abject pandering, has been relatively accommodating. As several colleagues at *The New Republic* explain it, Barnes likes and respects Dan Quayle, but he probably likes and respects him a lot more because he's being advised by Bill Kristol. (The fact that Kristol will be a power in Washington for the next thirty years may also have something to do with Beltway reporters' increasingly congenial treatment of the veep. Outside the Beltway, reporters keep writing that Dan Quayle is as thick as two planks.)

This halo effect is amply reflected in the multipart series by David Broder and Bob Woodward, in which the veteran reporters managed to crank out 40,000 words about the vice president without ever going into much detail about the vital role of his advisers. Writing about Quayle without writing about Kristol is like writing about Bailey without once ever mentioning Barnum. Still, Kristol's presence has been successful in allaying the doubts of many Nervous Nellies throughout this great land, by reassuring them that even if Dan Quayle replaced George Bush tomorrow, the country would still be in good hands.

"Bush is smarter than Quayle, but Quayle's people are smarter than Bush's people," says Rich Vigilante, formerly a fellow at the Manhattan Institute, New York's conservative think tank. Thus, as numerous observers have pointed out, Quayle enjoys the same reflected glow of splendor and competence that another avid golfer never mistaken for Ludwig Wittgenstein enjoyed during a previous administration.

"If Quayle by some weird fluke does become president and Kristol stays on as his top deputy," wrote Fred Barnes in *The New Republic* in March 1990, "the joke will surely be told, as it was of Sherman Adams, chief of staff in Eisenhower's day: God forbid that Bill Kristol should someday die and Dan Quayle become our president."

The only difference between Sherman Adams and Bill Kristol is that every once in a while, Kristol and the boys seem to get a bit carried away with themselves. It's one thing to furtively manipulate an intellectually deficient politician in a patriotic effort to improve the national well-being. It's another matter entirely to hand him the sacred tablets from which you learned the puppeteer's art, and then tell him to read them. It's like car thieves mailing their victims *30 Days to Better Auto Heists* and expecting them to be grateful. It smacks of arrogance, condescension, and *The Wall Street Journal's* favorite transgression: *hubris.*

"There isn't anything particularly nefarious about it," says Jacob Weisberg of *The New Republic.* "It's just that this is such a part of Kristol's vocabulary that if he wants to have Quayle quoting Plato and the Talmud, he has to make sure that Quayle has at least some idea of what he's talking about. Otherwise, someday someone might call his bluff."

This is where issues come in. Books such as the *Republic* and *The Prince* are literally bursting at the seams with ideas. But books written by think-tank drones and college professors usually contain only one idea, supported by hundreds of pages of statistics defending that idea. These books are spectacularly one-dimensional, and their basic arguments can be contained on an index card (the small size, in fact). This being the case, it's hardly surprising that in the past year, Plato and the Talmud have been deep-sixed by Quayle's advisers, while public-policy issues have been brought to the fore.

In selecting an issue for the vice president, it was imperative that Quayle's staff find something that would not be incongruous, inappropriate, frivolous, or personally demeaning. This was not an easy assignment. A winnowing process had to be implemented in order to find an issue that was fully consonant with the vice president's privileged background and would not beget a jarring sense of cultural dissonance. In short, race was out.

This was unfortunate, because race continues to be an issue of major importance in the America of the 1990s. But matters of race and related issues of poverty and welfare, for example, are not the kinds of concerns that can be taken up readily by a man who spent his childhood playing forty-five holes of golf per day on the fairway that happened to be growing in his front yard, bummed his way through high school and college, ducked out of Vietnam, never worked a day at a real job in his life, and then, for all intents and purposes, got *appointed* vice president of the United States—even if his wife does still hem their son's trousers. Every time Quayle has spoken out on this issue, as he did in the wake of the 1992 Los Angeles riots, it has blown up in his face.

For obvious reasons, none of the controversial books dealing with problems in American education that have surfaced in recent years would fill the vice president's needs. An individual having as little acquaintance with the treasures of Western civilization as Dan Quayle does would certainly be in no position to champion E. D. Hirsch's *Cultural Literacy: What Every American Needs to Know,* much less Allan Bloom's *The Closing of the American Mind.* In this enormously influential 1987 book, Bloom contended that American civilization had been devastated by the 1960s, when too many young people were reading Hermann Hesse and listening to the Electric Prunes, when they should have been reading Montesquieu and listening to Giuseppe Verdi. Quayle had not read Hermann Hesse or listened to the Electric Prunes while an undergraduate at DePauw, but neither had he spent his time reading Montesquieu and listening to Verdi. He had spent his time correcting a mild slice and calibrating the mathematical likelihood of getting down in three by using a four-iron as opposed to a five-iron. For this reason, it would be difficult for Kristol & Co. to devise a matrix in which the names Allan Bloom and Dan Quayle could effectively coalesce.

No, if Quayle was going to address the educational issues of the day, it would have to be in a more indirect fashion. In the middle of 1991, he seemed to flirt briefly with the voguish issue of political correctness, which enjoyed fifteen minutes of fame when Dinesh D'Souza's laborious *Illiberal Education: The Politics of Race and Sex on Campus* appeared. But after a couple of speeches in which he mentioned the subject, the affable, fundamentally nice Hoosier dropped it like a hot potato, seemingly having decided that a former editor of the racist, anti-Semitic *Dartmouth Review* is not the kind of chap you should be chatting up with a tough reelection campaign on tap. Moreover, taking up the cudgels for an issue espoused by a person named D'Souza would have violated one of the cardinal rules of Republican political philosophy: Never borrow ideas from a person with an apostrophe in his name.

A far more enticing possibility was to attack leftist professors who have been indoctrinating our children with their dangerous Marxist ideas. This was the thesis advanced by neoconservative theorist Roger Kimball in his witty book *Tenured Radicals: How Politics Has Corrupted Our Higher Education. Tenured Radicals* was a rip-roaring yarn that skewered leftist professors for offering such courses as "Our Bodies, Our Sheep, Our Cosmos, Ourselves," and for participating in such panels as "Food and the Construction of Femininity in Drama by

Women." Though horsewhipping was never mentioned, the need for such bold measures was never far from Kimball's—or the reader's—mind.

Unfortunately, from the point of view of Dan Quayle, Kimball's cause had a number of defects. Like Bloom, Kimball had described his book as "a report from the front." But it wasn't really a report from the front: It was more like a report from the dorm. Most of *Tenured Radicals* was an attack on books that nobody reads, written by academics that nobody knows, who see each other at conventions that nobody cares about, and issue proclamations that nobody heeds. In lambasting universities for deteriorating into breeding grounds for hateful, anti-American ideas, Kimball had failed to realize that by having leftist academics on college campuses, *the rest of us have them right where we want them.*

Look at it this way: If leftist intellectuals were working at Burger King or the utility company, they might organize downtrodden laborers and bring a hungry, poorly lit nation to its knees. But by cloistering together in universities, leftists limit the subversive impact of their seditious ideas to young people between the ages of seventeen and twenty-one, many of whom do not have driver's licenses. We should accept it as a normal and healthy part of growing up for teenagers to flirt with the ideas of Karl Marx and Mao Tse-tung, knowing full well that these ideas will be banished from their consciousness forever the first time they get their quarterly earnings report from Fidelity Select Biotechnology and find out that their OTC stocks have skyrocketed 46 percent in the previous three months.

Kimball, like so many others before him, had gotten it all wrong. The way this society works is this: Leftist intellectuals with hare-brained Marxist ideas get to control Stanford, MIT, Yale, and the American Studies department at the University of Vermont. In return, the right gets IBM, DEC, Honeywell, Disney World, and the New York Stock Exchange. Leftist academics get to try out their stupid ideas on impressionable youths between seventeen and twenty-one who don't have any money or power. The right gets to try out its ideas on North America, South America, Europe, Asia, Australia, and parts of Africa, most of which take MasterCard. The left gets Harvard, Oberlin, Twyla Tharp's dance company, and Madison, Wisconsin. The right gets NASDAQ, Boeing, General Motors, Apple, McDonnell Douglas, Washington, D.C., Citicorp, Texas, Coca-Cola, General Electric, Japan, and outer space.

This seems like a fair arrangement.

———

Neoconservative, agenda-setting books have certain common characteristics. No manuscript emanating from a right-wing think tank is complete without at least one quotation from Lewis Carroll, H. L. Mencken, and Winston Churchill, plus at least one anecdote involving Franz Kafka, George Orwell, or Yogi Berra. No right-wing think-tank book is complete unless it dwells on the insidious role played by the 1960s in the ruination of our society. Finally, *all* right-wing think-tank books operate on the penumbra-of-genius principle: If you can't be funny and talented like Tom Wolfe, at the very least get someone to write a blurb saying that you are. Thus, all good right-wing think-tank books have a blurb on the back reading something like this:

"With irreverent wit, Mr. Huber does to tort law what Tom Wolfe does to New York City in *The Bonfire of the Vanities.*"

This does not work as well in reverse: "With irreverent wit, Mr. Wolfe does to New York City what Peter Huber does to tort law in *Liability: The Legal Revolution and Its Consequences*"—but never mind.

It is impossible to determine how many issues Quayle's staff delved into before settling on one that would be appropriate for the vice president. One issue that was probably reviewed but found wanting was the ugly spectacle of federal appointees resigning their posts and going to work as Japanese lobbyists. Throughout the eighties, there were periodic flurries of books attacking the Japanese for buying influence in America. One was *Agents of Influence*, by TRW executive Pat Choate, which deplored the ignoble spectacle of cabinet officers and other highly placed officials resigning from their posts after eighteen to twenty-four months, and then signing on as concubines for our inscrutable Oriental trading partners, whose cars we like but whose guts we hate. It was a powerful indictment of the American political system, but as a potential vice presidential issue, it had one major drawback: Most of the people who come to Washington, stay for eighteen to thirty-six months, and then go to work as whores for the Japanese are Republicans. That's because Republicans have held all the top posts at the Commerce and Treasury departments since 1980. Republicans counter that if Democrats had been in power since 1980, it would be Democrats that we would be chastising for hustling their asses in the Far East. Sadly, we will never know whether this argument is true, because none of us will live long enough to see another Democratic administration.

In the months following the appearance of Howard Fineman's article, there must have been many trying moments in the White House, times when it looked like Kristol and the boys would *never* find an issue suitable for the vice president. Oh, sure, there was outer space and SDI and the Competitiveness Council that Quayle headed, but outer space was old hat and SDI was Reagan-era material and Republicans get *paid* to rewrite federal regulations behind the public's back: that's what their constituents send them to Washington for. Clandestinely gutting federal regulations regarding the disposition of wetlands isn't an *issue;* gutting federal regulations regarding the disposition of wetlands is part of the vice president's job. Besides, who gives a damn about the wetlands?

Yes, there must have been many nights when Bill Kristol went home, tearing his hair out trying to find *anything* that could serve as an issue for the vice president. Not race. Not education. Not political correctness. Not the daunting power of foreign lobbyists. And then, just when all hope seemed lost, he hit upon it.

Tort reform.

Ah, reform of the torts! Here was an issue that had been quietly gathering force—like a slowly smoldering forest fire—for years. All right, all right, out there in the hinterland of America, where folks still earned money the old-fashioned way, people might not yet have heard about it, but scratch beneath the surface a bit and it was there all right. In the backs of their minds, people—blacks, whites, Asian-Americans, other—had a nagging suspicion that there was something terribly wrong with our tort system in America, something that, unless rectified quickly, could bring a once-mighty nation crashing to the ground.

Quayle's bid for tortic glory took place on August 13, 1991, when he delivered a tough, combative speech to the American Bar Association at its annual convention in Atlanta. In it, he argued that excessive litigation is costing Americans $80 billion a year. He also noted that lawyers, not their clients, receive "the lion's share of liability awards." He further argued that frivolous litigation could be minimized in this country if we would merely switch to the English system, under which losers must pay the legal costs of the winners. In addition, he proposed a cap on punitive damages, which would allow judges, rather than juries, to settle on dollar amounts. Last but not least, he proposed sharp limits on discovery, the legal procedure by which the suing party is granted virtually unlimited access to the defendant's private records— merely by bringing a lawsuit against him.

Even before giving this speech, Quayle had proposed limits on the use of expert witnesses in jury trials, arguing that this would curtail the influence of wackos and hired guns who, for a fee, would express maverick opinions not generally shared by the scientific community of which they formed a part. And Quayle had already latched on to the liability reform issue by claiming that fear of lawsuits was causing American corporations to become less competitive and less innovative. In his view, the effect of his proposals would be to discourage frivolous lawsuits, and to encourage feuding parties to settle cases before they come to trial.

Quayle's words were a shot across the bow of the *Good Ship Tort.* No sooner had the vice president unleashed his attack on the entire legal profession than he was joined at the podium by outgoing president John J. Curtin, Jr., who let him have it. It was certainly an ugly scene, one that in earlier days of the Republic might have led to a duel or a damned fine thrashing. Still, by adopting his tough stance, and by delivering his arguments in the enemy stronghold (not unlike Gary Cooper when he read the riot act to the Indians in *Northwest Mounted Police*) Quayle scored points with many Americans, who were impressed by his willingness to mix it up with the big boys.

The legal community did not take Quayle's attack lying down. Academics challenged the vice president's numbers, intimating that he had gotten them from Monte's House of Statistics, or Stats 'n' Things, and that the real cost of liability suits was only around $29 billion a year. Meanwhile, all those lawyers who earn millions by bringing frivolous lawsuits against putatively blameless corporations were outraged. This was good for Quayle. But, unfortunately for the vice president, corporate lawyers were also outraged, fearing that the vice president's proposed changes in the discovery procedure would allow competitors to gain access to corporate secrets merely by forcing the targets of lawsuits to turn over highly confidential documents. When the dust had cleared, it seemed that enthusiasm for the vice president's reforms was remarkably muted, and that Quayle had once again gotten himself into a pickle.

Still, it was a daring pickle to have gotten himself into. And where had this particular intellectual cucumber come from? Well, as luck would have it, it came from the briny barrels of Peter Huber, a fellow at the Manhattan Institute and author of the book from which Quayle's tortic passion was distilled.*

Huber, who contended that a tidal wave of lawsuits was wrecking America's competitiveness, had derived his figure from the heightened insurance premiums, legal costs, and taxes that ordinary people must pay every time some idiotic jury forks over $3 million to a policeman who'd been shot by a fellow officer (as happened in the city of South Tucson, Arizona, thus costing residents of the town $400 apiece).

In a follow-up book, *Galileo's Revenge: Junk Science in the Courtroom,* Huber had excoriated the judicial system for dishing out huge payments to alleged victims after being swayed by the testimony of quacks and crackpots. (One award, eventually overturned, provided a psychic with $1 million in damages after she claimed to have been stripped of her clairvoyant powers by a CAT scan. But that happened in Philadelphia, where anything is possible.)

---

*Quayle also borrowed a bunch of ideas from Walter Olson, also a senior fellow at the Manhattan Institute and author of *The Litigation Explosion: What Happened When America Unleashed the Lawsuit.* The premise of the book is that lawyers are ruining the country. In *Liability: The Legal Revolution and Its Consequences,* Huber had popularized the $80 billion figure Quayle was using. *Forbes* later jumped in with the festive figure of $300 billion, but that was just *Forbes* being cheeky. Moreover, another Manhattan Institute creation, Lisa Schiffren, who is now on Quayle's staff, came up with the idea of attacking Murphy Brown. Shortly thereafter, the vice president gave a speech to the Manhattan Institute regurgitating the ideas they had been paid to supply him with, and apparently doing so in a way that suggested that they were actually *his* ideas. The response to Quayle's speech was polite, but hardly overwhelming, as is only to be expected of a roomful of Geppettos suddenly confronted with an upstart Pinocchio.

A sober and serious fellow, Huber has marshaled many cunning arguments to support his thesis that the judicial system is destroying America. But he doesn't expect tort reform—if it occurs at all—to take place at the federal level. He believes that it has to take place at the state level. And he doesn't seem to have had his socks knocked off just because the vice president of the United States had gone to bat for his personal cause célèbre.

"Generally, it's nice to know that you're not working in a field that's totally irrelevant or obscure," Huber said in his self-effacing way when I asked him how it felt to be linked in the same breath as Dan Quayle. In other words: No Château Margaux 1947 for Peter Huber.

Here I would like to issue a single, personal criticism of Huber's exemplary work. Though a meticulous researcher and a powerful advocate, Huber does occasionally find himself at war with the English language. Typical Huberisms are such phrases as "Contract was just the overture to the symphony of tort," and "The Founders had labored hard to cross the high mountains of contractual language, only to find that the valley of tort below was not exactly flowing with milk and honey."

People who write this way, whatever their other virtues, cannot be said to have the common touch. They do not sound like people who are taking the Runnin' Rebels and six versus the Hoyas, or people who are camping out all night for Gloria Estefan tickets. So when Huber argues: "By now, the public senses that something is badly awry," and "The majority of Americans already recognize the need for reform," I think he may be just guessing. When I asked my mom where she ranked tort reform among the issues that were really bothering her, she said, "Joe, you're a sketch." Other mothers I consulted were similarly at sea, tortically speaking. So was the bus driver on the M12 line in Manhattan, and the guy who rents me videos at the Videophile in Tarrytown, New York. Throw in a couple of cab drivers, a guy I know at the Bureau of Labor Statistics, and a ticket-taker at a Glenn Miller Orchestra concert in Pleasantville, New York, and I think it's safe to say that the majority of Americans do not yet recognize the need for tort reform, which they equate with structural improvements in recipes for Central European desserts. As far as I can determine, the public is not nearly as worked up about tort reform as the experts would lead us to believe. As far as I can tell, the public is still stuck way up there in the high mountains of contractual language, and it'll probably be years before they come on down into the succulent Valley of Tort.

Personally, I have nothing but admiration for the vice president's stand on tort reform, and for the yeoman work that has been done by Huber and Olsen in providing him with ammunition for his speeches. But that's because I would like to see all 700,000 of the nation's lawyers disemboweled, enabling roving jackals and birds of prey to feast on their entrails, even if I had to shell out $9.95 on Pay-Per-View to see it. Nevertheless, when viewed from the cold, impersonal, economic perspective, the tort-reform clique betrays an astonishing ignorance of the way this society operates, which is thusly: Corporations steal from the public by overcharging for crappy products that aren't going to last very long, and usually aren't safe. The public steals back by lodging ridiculous product-liability lawsuits that have absolutely no merit, but that often result in hefty awards, because juries are made up of people who hate corporations. Lawyers steal from everybody by defending either side. Since everyone is stealing from everyone else, liability suits are not really sucking $29 billion or $80 billion or $300 billion a year out of the American economy. In reality, the money that frivolous plaintiffs are awarded by vindictive, irresponsible juries helps feed their children, who will one day grow up to be lawyers who will then defend major corporations against frivolous lawsuits. And so the great Mandala of Life spins and spins again.

From Quayle's perspective, it didn't matter if tort reform was going nowhere fast. All that mattered was that he had found an issue he could be comfortable with, and an issue that made him look statesman-like. Tort reform filled the bill, not only because it made him look like a man of stature and depth but also because it was an issue that would cause him minimal political fallout in the long run. Bear in mind that American political life is structured around the ostentatious public taking of seemingly courageous stands on controversial issues, when in fact the politician is risking absolutely nothing by doing so. The following chart should make this clear:

Issue	People Adversely Affected	Fallout
Tort reform	Creepy lawyers	None
Racial quotas	Poor, black Democrats	None
Cut in capital gains tax	Indigent slobs in trailer parks	None
Cutting down rain forest	Eco-Smurfs, subscribers to *The Utne Reader*, Ben & Jerry types, owners of 8 Paul Winter Consort CDs, aboriginals	None
Single motherhood	Poor, single mothers	None

With torts, Quayle was on perfectly safe ground.

In a sense, it was inevitable that Quayle's personal cause should be a legal matter. Back in the early 1980s, the future vice president had gotten his first big-time political coaching from a D.C. media consultant named Don Ringe. A transcription of one of the legendary Ringe-Quayle elocution sessions appeared in Sidney Blumenthal's *Pledging Allegiance*, where, during a disarmingly moronic exchange between the youthful senator and his baffled handler, Quayle explained his attitude toward the law:

> I've always wanted to have a law background. Thought maybe a lawyer, interested in laws. Laws affect people. And it's a good background for anything, whether you become a full-time lawyer or become a businessman or whether you get into government or whatever you're going to do. I've always wanted to be a lawyer, to have a law background. And political science, political science is the, ah, best type of major most people say for going into law.

With these words in mind, we may come to a fuller understanding of how the vice president and his staff persuaded themselves that tort reform was an issue burning gaping, searing holes in the bosom of America. On August 13, 1991, Dan Quayle, a lawyer, got up in front of a bunch of lawyers to blame lawyers for everything that is wrong with this country. He probably got the idea for attacking lawyers from his press secretary, David Beckwith, a lawyer who was formerly the managing editor of *Legal Times*, a magazine for lawyers. Or he may have gotten it from Alan Hubbard, his deputy chief of staff, who is a lawyer. On the other hand, it might have been suggested to him by David McIntosh, deputy director of the Competitiveness Council, who is a lawyer, or by deputy counsel John Howard, a lawyer. Whoever suggested that Quayle adopt the issue probably got the idea from reading *Liability: The Legal Revolution and Its Consequences*, which was written by Peter Huber, a lawyer who used to work for Sandra Day O'Connor, a lawyer who is now a judge.

After the president of the American Bar Association, a lawyer, jumped up to denounce the vice president, a lawyer, *The Wall Street Journal*, which is filled with alumni of *American Lawyer*, a magazine for lawyers, published an editorial defending him. The editorial was written by L. Gordon Crovitz, a lawyer. This probably made Quayle, a lawyer, feel good when he went home to see his wife, Marilyn, a lawyer, whom he met when they were both young law students rewriting Indiana's death penalty.

In a universe as hermetically sealed as this one, it's not surprising that tort reform—as opposed to health insurance or unemployment or crime or education or AIDS or breast cancer or air pollution or the plight of the hapless Tamils or an immediate, federally mandated reduction in the number of Los Angeles waitresses named Trish who insist on telling you the house specials—should surge to the top of Quayle's consciousness. Remember, out of forty-one presidents, only seventeen have not been lawyers, and out of forty-four vice presidents, only a dozen have failed to stand for the bar.

So it's understandable if these people occasionally overestimate the intensity of the average American's concern about this issue. These guys aren't going out of their way to bust our national chops. *They can't help themselves.* Ordinary people like you and me are still stuck way up there in the mountains of contractual language. But Quayle, Kristol, Huber, Olson, Marilyn, et al. have already passed into the Valley of Tort.

X I
THE LINE OF SUCCESSION

I don't want to be vice president. I bet I can go down the street
and stop the first ten men I see and that they can't tell me the
names of two of the last ten vice presidents of the United States.

—HARRY TRUMAN

t is has long been assumed that the vice presidency of the United States
is the special preserve of second-rate politicians. This is only part of the
story. The office is actually the province of third-rate lawyers. Whereas
twenty-four of our forty-one presidents have been members of the bar,
a whopping thirty-two of our forty-four vice presidents have held law
degrees of some sort. And that's not counting Teddy Roosevelt, who
started out studying law, quit, but would have still become the thirty-
third veep/attorney had he proceeded with his original intention of
studying for the bar exam during all the free time he expected to have
as vice president. Instead, McKinley was assassinated shortly after his
second inauguration, and Roosevelt had to shelve the law books forever.

In Dan and Marilyn Quayle, the nation finds itself menaced by the
first double-barreled barristerial vice presidency in history, the first
pairing in which both partners are lawyers, and a presidency dominated by Hoosier lawyers is only a heartbeat away. Were Quayle to
snare the 1996 GOP nomination and face a Bill Clinton (whose wife
is a lawyer) or a Tom Harkin (whose wife is a lawyer) or a Paul
Tsongas (whose wife is a lawyer), the Republic for the first time would
be guaranteed both a president and a First Lady with law degrees, no

matter which party won. This would be a fitting way to close what is shaping up as a fairly grim decade, what has been a fairly depressing century, and what in truth has been a pretty awful millennium.

Like most of his predecessors in the office, Quayle is not much of a lawyer. He puttered around for a few years out in Hoosierland before entering politics at the age of twenty-nine. This *legalischen putter-jahren* is a time-honored American tradition. Veeps as varied as the unnecessary William Almon Wheeler (1877–1881) and the justifiably forgotten James Schoolcraft Sherman (1909–1912) used their law degrees as springboards to influential political positions, but there is no indication that either of these men—or the dozen who resemble them—thereby deprived their profession of future lords of the bar. The same may be said of Quayle.

In many ways, Quayle's career eerily parallels that of his fellow Hoosier Thomas Andrews Hendricks, who operated an unimportant law practice in the unimportant town of Shelbyville, Indiana, before being elected to an unimportant position in the Indiana Assembly at age twenty-nine, from which he wheedled his way into the most supremely unimportant job of them all: vice president. Hendricks has left no real mark on American history other than a tiny vice presidential asterisk: Eight years before being elected vice president on a ticket with Grover Cleveland, he was rooked out of the very same office while running on a ticket with Samuel Tilden. Eighteen seventy-six was the year that he and Tilden won the popular vote, but failed to achieve a majority, and were shafted out of the two highest offices in the land when the election was decided in the GOP-dominated House of Representatives.

Hendricks is, therefore, the only man in the history of the United States to get jobbed out of the vice presidency in one administration, then serve as vice president in another one. He is also the only vice presidential candidate in history to run both with a man who got rooked out of the presidency and with a man who became the only president to win election to nonconsecutive terms (Cleveland). These are records that are unlikely to be broken. They are also the kinds of arcane trivia that afford such nebishes their only chance to claw their way into the history books.

If the expression "motley crew" did not exist, it would have to be invented to describe our vice presidents. In the depressing history of America's zaniest public office, there have been drunks (Cactus Jack Garner, Andrew Johnson); lechers (Richard Johnson); crooks (Spiro Agnew, Schuyler Colfax); shady characters (Richard Nixon, Chester Arthur); pinko mystics (Henry Wallace); secessionists (John Calhoun, John Tyler); bozos (Gerald Ford); layabouts (Thomas Marshall); hypochondriacs (William Wheeler); and traitors (Aaron Burr, John Breckinridge).

And some of these characters were the veritable crème de la crème compared to other people who have held the office. For in compiling this list of lechers, drunks, crooks, traitors, and whoremasters, we have overlooked doddering old farts (Rufus King, Elbridge Gerry, George Clinton); schlemiels (Millard Fillmore, Garret A. Hobart); and hopeless clowns (Daniel Tompkins and Adlai Stevenson). Several of our vice presidents were cadavers-in-waiting when elected; Elbridge Gerry and Rufus King were already at death's door when they took office, and George Clinton was so worn out by his sixty-five years that he used to doze off during Senate debates. One day he got so tuckered out that he slipped this mortal coil forever.

No, the ranks of the vice presidents have not been filled with names that ring down through the ages. Typical is the parvenu shoemaker Henry Wilson, whose exploits have been chronicled in the book *Cobbler in Congress: The Life of Henry Wilson*, or the hypochondriac mope William Wheeler, who lied to Rutherford B. Hayes about attending the funeral of a brother-in-law who did not even exist just so he could get out of attending an official function. Not at all out of place in this legion of numbskulls is Daniel Tompkins, who used to have his salary garnisheed because he owed the federal government money from back when he was governor of New York. Also fitting right in with this galaxy of screwballs is Richard Johnson, who used to run around waving a bloodied shirt that he claimed to have torn from the corpse of the fallen Indian warrior Tecumseh (the opposition party said it was a lucky shot). Johnson, a tavern operator, was known to have sired a daunting number of mulatto children by his black slave girlfriends. Taking note of this fact, a Washington magazine warned that if Martin Van Buren died and was replaced by Johnson, it would precipitate "an African jubilee throughout the country." Of course that was back in the days when the United States was still a racist society, before David Duke and Pat Buchanan.

Say what you will about the rakish Johnson, at least he'd killed a few thieving redskins (make that, acquisitive Native Americans) in his time and thus possessed solid credentials to hold public office. Not so the steady stream of complete and utter nobodies who occupied the office for the remainder of the nineteenth century. Here, pride of place must be given to Garret A. Hobart, the Pride of Paterson, New Jersey, who had never held public office outside his state when he was selected as William McKinley's running mate in 1896.

According to Leslie W. Dunlap's electrifyingly interesting book *Our Vice Presidents and Second Ladies:* "When the news of Garret Hobart's nomination reached Paterson in the evening of June 18, 1896, the city became delirious with joy." June 18, 1896, was the last time on record that the city of Paterson, New Jersey, was reported as being delirious with joy.

It does no disservice to the office of the vice president to say that, with a handful of notable exceptions, our veeps have generally been inconsequential men whose careers had little effect on the course of American history. This fact is reflected in the somber books written about them: *George Mifflin Dallas: Jacksonian Patrician* and *The Life and Times of Hannibal Hamlin.* Whereas Lincoln left behind the Gettysburg Address, Madison *The Federalist Papers,* and Jefferson the Declaration of Independence, our vice presidents have generally bequeathed us such treasures as *Recollections of Thomas Marshall, Vice President and Hoosier Philosopher; A Hoosier Salad;* and *Go Quietly . . . Or Else* by Spiro T. Agnew. It hasn't been an easy two centuries.

As any schoolchild—and most members of Congress—can tell you, the vice presidency has been an out-and-out joke almost from the moment it was originally dreamed up by an apparently inebriated group of Founding Fathers. Yet we must not forget that the office has become a colossal joke with the active assistance of many of its occupants, some of whom have gone out of their way to treat the job with contempt and derision. George Dallas (1845–1849) moonlighted as a lawyer throughout his single term because he felt his salary was too low. John C. Calhoun (1825–1832), one of only two men—Clinton was the other—to serve as vice president under two chief executives (both of whom hated his guts), resigned the vice presidency in 1832 so that he could go back to having a real job in the Senate. John Breckinridge (1857–1861), having served four years under James Buchanan, immediately decided to betray his country, interviewing for and landing a job as a general with the Confederate States of America.

Moreover, the most memorable wisecracks about the office are not the ones coined by pundits and wits but the ones coined by occupants of the office themselves. John Adams, no cut-up, made fun of the office. So did Thomas Jefferson. Thomas Marshall, Woodrow Wilson's rotten, cowardly vice president (but a good after-dinner speaker), is probably most famous for his line about America's needing a good five-cent cigar. But he is also responsible for the anecdote about the woman with two sons; for the description of a vice president as "a man in a cataleptic fit," who is aware of everything going on around him but can't do anything about it; and for the remark that the vice president's position as head of the Smithsonian Institution was an appropriate one because it gave him a chance to compare himself with other fossils.

Cactus Jack Garner was a very famous man in his time (Speaker of the House in 1931), but when his name appears in the history books today it is usually because of his comment that the vice presidency was not worth a bucket of warm piss (sometimes reported as "spit"). And when Calvin Coolidge learned that he had been selected as Warren Harding's running mate in 1920, his wife supposedly said, "You aren't going to take it, are you?"

Given the torrent of abuse that occupants of the office themselves have directed at the vice presidency, it is hardly surprising that historians and political scientists have treated the position with such disdain. When Clinton Rossiter wrote his 248-page book *The American Presidency* in 1956, he devoted just seven pages to the vice presidency and begged the reader's indulgence for suggesting that the office deserved even that much attention. Woodrow Wilson said much the same thing in *Congressional Government*, published in 1885, twenty-eight years before he would take office with the pointless Marshall, when he wrote, "The chief embarrassment in discussing his office is, that in explaining how little there is to be said about it, one has evidently said all there is to say."

Perhaps the sharpest criticism of the office again comes from Rossiter, who pointed out that "there have been fifteen occasions in the history of the republic, a total of more than 36 years, when we had no Vice-President and never knew the difference." And that's not counting the four months that the intellectual colossus Gerald Ford straddled the Republic alone, before soliciting the strong, silent support of veteran bridesmaid Nelson A. Rockefeller.

With very few exceptions—most of these at the dawn of the Republic—the men who have occupied the office have been fitting targets for Rossiter's contempt. "The Vice Presidency is a hollow shell of an office, an uncomfortable heir apparency sought by practically no one we should like to see as President," he wrote in 1956. "It has perked up noticeably in the years since 1948, but fundamentally it remains a disappointment in the American constitutional system." This, of course, was written before the Age of Agnew and the Age of Quayle. Adds Joel K. Goldstein in *The Modern American Vice Presidency: The Transformation of a Political Institution:* "The history of the office is rich in Washington folklore, but poor in solid accomplishment."

———

Generally speaking, the Founding Fathers did a magnificent job in setting up this country, bequeathing us such a wonderful system of laws, courts, and traditions that not even a complete idiot could screw it up. However, dozens have tried.

In the early days, the Founding Fathers assumed that the presidency would always be filled by a spectacularly talented leader, and the vice presidency by a man just a few notches below him in talent and experience. That's because the Founding Fathers were the political equivalent of the Boston Celtics, so deep and so talented that the Thomas Jeffersons and James Monroes and James Madisons—the John Havliceks and Kevin McHales of their day—had to ride the bench and wait for a chance to break into the starting lineup. (Hell, John Jay and Benjamin Franklin never even got to play.) The Founding Fathers had no inkling that two hundred years later Washington would be run by a bunch of guys named Jimmy, Jodie, Andy, Ed, Lyn, and Sununu. They also had no inkling that the vice presidency—originally awarded to the runner-up in the electoral college balloting—would degenerate into the virtually exclusive domain of cretins, layabouts, pinheads, and Hoosiers.

The vice presidency is the only place that the Founding Fathers screwed up royally. Some historians believe that the office of the vice president was only an afterthought in the first place. Others, such as Rossiter, feel that Jefferson and the boys had three good reasons for setting it up, but paid insufficient attention to the grave risks that were inherent in the institution.

The reasons were: Because it would provide a president of the Senate who would not be aligned with any particular state and would be able to cast tie-breaking votes; because it would provide a successor to the chief executive in the event of his death; and because it would help in the election of the president. Of the three, the third seems to be the most plausible claim; as Goldstein points out, the framers of the Constitution were concerned that the electors would all vote for men from their own states, so they gave them the option of casting two votes, with the candidate garnering the most votes becoming president and the runner-up becoming vice president. This was fine in the very beginning when everybody sort of liked one another because George Washington was still running things, but by the time Washington went home to Mount Vernon in 1797, the rise of political parties was already making the system unworkable. The first two vice presidents—John Adams and Thomas Jefferson—spent most of their terms bellyaching about how much they hated the job while waiting to springboard to the presidency from it. But it wasn't doing the infant country any good to have a president whose heir apparent was his direst political enemy, which was certainly the case with Adams and Jefferson, and then with Jefferson and Aaron Burr.

"Presidents must have suspected the motives of men who would accept an office whose sole appeal depended on their own death," writes Goldstein.

The wheels on the wagon started to fall off in 1801 after President Adams lost his job to his own vice president, Jefferson. The badly flawed electoral system, under which the man with the second highest vote total became vice president, ended in a tie between Jefferson and Burr, even though it was clear to just about everyone that Jefferson had been the presidential candidate of his party. But Burr refused to throw in the towel, and the election was finally thrown into the House of Representatives, where after thirty-five ballots Alexander Hamilton signed his own death warrant by throwing his support to Jefferson, whom he hated only slightly less than Burr.

Burr served four years as a disgruntled veep, then killed Hamilton in a duel he had provoked. This pissed off everyone, since Hamilton was the savviest financial expert of his time, sort of a David Stockman with brains. Fearing for his life, Burr vamoosed to the western frontier, where he apparently hoped to set up his own country. His dreams of a Western Empire came to naught, however, and he was eventually seized and tried for treason. But in sterling American judicial tradition, this complete and utter scoundrel beat the rap because he knew the right people, including John Marshall, the chief justice of the Supreme Court. All the same, Burr's political career lay in ruins, his dreams of immortality ashes in the dust. Penniless and despised, he did the only thing a complete and utter scoundrel could do: He returned to New York and resumed his career as a lawyer.

Anxious to avoid a reprise of the Burr affair, Congress in 1804 passed the Twelfth Amendment, which provided for the separate election of presidents and vice presidents, virtually ensuring that the president would serve with a vice president who had run on the same ticket. But this had the unintended effect of making the office *completely* meaningless, and resulted in the vice presidencies of the hoary, impotent George Clinton, the cadaverous, incompetent Daniel Tompkins, and Elbridge Gerry, a debt-ridden Methuselah. With the exception of John Calhoun (whom Andy Jackson wanted to hang) and Martin Van Buren, the office was occupied for the remainder of the nineteenth century by an unending stream of men who had no business being anywhere near the White House. Six of them died in office, and of the four who replaced dead presidents (Tyler, Fillmore, Johnson, Arthur), not one was rewarded with his party's renomination to the office he already held. (Teddy Roosevelt was the first vice president to win election to the White House on his own merits after taking over for an expired chief executive.)

The plain truth is: The vice presidency has been scaring the hell out of Americans for almost two centuries. On just about all of the nine occasions that a vice president has been called upon to step into the shoes of a fallen chief executive, the nation has had to hold its breath, often for several years. The nine caddies (Tyler, Fillmore, Johnson,

Arthur, Teddy Roosevelt, Coolidge, Truman, Johnson, Ford) have served as president for more than twenty-six years as replacements, but if we throw in the terms served by vice presidents who later became president (Adams, Jefferson, Van Buren, Roosevelt, Coolidge, Truman, Johnson, Nixon, Bush), the nation has been ruled for sixty-four years—roughly one-third of our history—by men who were once vice president. *Scary.*

The first transcontinental cardiac seizure occurred in 1841 when William Henry Harrison caught a bad case of the sniffles at his inauguration and died thirty-one days later. A forerunner of the smarmy Jimmy Carter, Harrison was known as an obsequious consumer, purchasing his own groceries while president. As Barbara Holland points out in *Hail to the Chiefs,* many historians have scratched their heads trying to figure out what the hell a man dying of pneumonia was doing buying his own groceries when he should have been in bed. History provides us with no conclusive answer; it seldom does. Tragically, this is where the parallel with Carter ends; the morose peanut farmer did not give a two-hour address in a driving rainstorm, did not die thirty-one days into his first term, and, in any event, antibiotics had been invented by 1977.

Harrison's second-in-command was John Tyler, who supposedly received the news of the president's death while playing marbles on the floor of his Virginia home. This immediately created a host of problems (not the marbles, but the news). For starters, no one was sure that the Constitution actually made the vice president the chief of state. But that wasn't the biggest problem: Tyler, a Democrat at heart, had only been put on the ticket with Harrison, a Whig, for electoral balance. He thus had no political allies and could not rule effectively. After assuming office, he immediately locked horns with Whig leader Henry Clay (one of several immortal Americans who never held the highest office in the land) and vetoed just about every bill that was brought to him.

This was a terrific way to resolve the constitutional crisis questioning the power invested in the executive office, but a rotten way to run a country. As a result, Tyler's entire cabinet walked out on him, with the exception of Daniel Webster (the second greatest American never to hold the highest office in the land). Tyler was thrown out of the

Whig party, and the United States was ruled for the next four years by a president who was viewed by both the Democrats *and* the Whigs as a double-crossing traitor. Tyler rounded out a long career of eccentric political maneuvering by accepting a seat in the Confederate House of Representatives, but died in January 1862 before the treasonous assembly could convene. He was not missed.

Not a whole lot got done between 1841 and 1845, and what did get done was the work of Daniel Webster, not John Tyler. Yet the Republic survived. This was to become the dominant theme throughout the remainder of American history whenever the highest office in the land was suddenly occupied by a dimwit vice president: Things might get a bit hairy, but the Republic carried on. For instance, the Republic had no trouble surviving the presidency of Millard Fillmore, who stepped in for Zachary Taylor, a war hero who didn't even belong to a political party, had never voted before taking office, and didn't find out he had been nominated until several weeks after the convention because he refused to pay the postage due on the letter that contained the big news.

Taylor attended a Fourth of July picnic on a scalding afternoon during his second year in office, larded up with a vat of cold milk and a bucket of cherries, and busted a gut. A theory that he had been assassinated was put to rest in 1991 when his remains were exhumed by a group of roving Oliver Stone protégés masquerading as historians; it is now generally agreed that Taylor died not because of some labyrinthine White House intrigue but because he was a pig.

Taylor was succeeded by the Prometheanally inept Millard Fillmore, one of many presidents who claimed to have been born in a log cabin. Fillmore had been picked by the Whigs because he was *a handsome man with lovely blue eyes who could probably carry his own state.* His term was undistinguished, and after being dumped by his own party in 1852, he headed the ticket of the shameful Know-Nothing party in 1856. Unlike god-awful presidents such as Franklin Pierce and James Buchanan, whom history has forgotten, Millard Fillmore is remembered to this very day. But he is remembered for only one thing: being a god-awful president.

The Republic survived a far greater crisis, perhaps its greatest crisis ever, when the coarse Andrew Johnson stepped in for the martyred Abraham Lincoln in 1865. Like Tyler a quarter of a century earlier,

Andrew Johnson was a political oddity, a Democrat holding the second highest office in the land under a Republican president because Lincoln had decided in 1864 that he needed to attract votes from disgruntled members of the opposition party, and because he'd also decided that running for reelection with a guy from Maine named Hannibal Hamlin might be tempting fate.

Andrew Johnson was treated more disgracefully than any political figure in American history. Falsely accused of having conspired to kill Lincoln, he escaped impeachment in the Senate by a single vote. A personally courageous man, whose opposition to slavery nearly cost him his life back in Tennessee where he was once dragged from a train and very nearly hanged, Johnson left Washington after one term, but in a magnificent, in-your-face gesture, he was reelected to the Senate in 1875, where he got to exchange pleasantries with dozens of corrupt Republicans who had attempted to railroad him a decade before. All this notwithstanding, Johnson's was one of the worst administrations ever.

A tailor whose wife taught him to read when he was already in his twenties, Johnson was the poorest, least eloquent, and possibly least educated vice president to ever hold the office, though all of those educational records have since been eclipsed by Dan Quayle. His personal life was a shambles: Two of his sons were drunks, a third was a Confederate, and his wife came downstairs only twice in the four years that he was president, both times to complain. Johnson, who was actually born in a log cabin, was the only senator from the eleven Confederate states to remain in the Senate after the Civil War erupted. Although he enjoyed a brief honeymoon after Lincoln's assassination, largely because he pledged to unsheath the North's terrible swift sword in the South, Johnson's conciliatory attitude toward the defeated Confederacy caused him to run afoul of the Republicans who had put him in office. There are many theories as to why Johnson would adopt a namby-pamby attitude toward the rebels he had deserted just five years earlier. One theory is that he genuinely hated blacks. Another is that he liked forcing southern aristocrats to accept favors from a humble, semiliterate tailor. Whatever the reason, Johnson fell afoul of the wrong people, suffered the consequences, and the American people had to endure four more years of hell.

And yet the Republic survived.

The Republic dodged another bullet when sleazeball chunkster Chester Arthur stepped in for the murdered James Garfield in 1881. Garfield was an interesting, well-educated youngster (forty-eight) who might have made a good president, whereas Arthur was the quintessential political stooge, a creature of New York political lowlifes. Before his election as vice president, Arthur had served as the Collector of Customs at the Port of New York, a position from which he was dismissed by Rutherford B. Hayes due to rampant corruption. Although he surprised everyone by leaving the silverware behind at the end of his single term in the White House, Arthur was probably the least qualified man to ever hold the office.

And yet the Republic survived.

The Republic also survived the deeply troubled presidency of Woodrow Wilson. When Wilson succumbed to a massive stroke in September 1919, it was the duty of Vice President Thomas Marshall to assume the reins of office or at least to talk to somebody important about doing so. But Marshall, an ambitionless Hoosier, wanted no part of such a demanding job, so he allowed Wilson's wife Edith to run the country for the remaining seventeen months of his term, during which time she even forged her husband's signature on important documents.

And yet the Republic survived.

―――

Throughout much of our history, the vice president was a political hack rammed down the throat of the presidential nominee by the party itself. Vice presidents were usually chosen to add geographical balance to the ticket, explaining the preponderance of mediocrities from New York and Indiana. Known as the "Mother of Vice Presidents," the Hoosier state landed eleven of its native sons on presidential ballots between 1868 and 1916, ten for vice president, one—Benjamin Harrison—for the number-one slot. These included such successful vice presidential candidates as Schuyler Colfax (a crook); Thomas Hendricks (a hypochondriac liar); Charles Fairbanks (a nobody); and Thomas Marshall (a spineless wimp who once said that any Americans killed by German U-boats while traveling through hostile waters probably deserved what they got).

But vice presidential candidates were also chosen to add ideological balance to the ticket or because everyone at the convention was so drunk after the thirty-sixth ballot that they settled on whoever happened to be lying around who would offend the smallest number of people. Thus, when it was suggested to Rutherford B. Hayes that he run on a ticket with William A. Wheeler, he had to ask who Wheeler was.

Since 1901, Goldstein observes, presidential nominees gradually have tried to assert more influence over the vice presidential selection process. This is a good idea because presidents and vice presidents have not always seen eye to eye. Adams and Jefferson hated each other. So did Garfield and Arthur. Clinton refused to go to Madison's inauguration, and Jackson said he had only two regrets when he left office: that he had not shot Henry Clay and that he had not hanged John C. Calhoun. Calhoun was his first vice president.

Just the same, as FDR's experiences with his three sidekicks illustrate, no matter who ends up being vice president, an awful lot of people are going to be pissed off and start complaining that a moron is but a heartbeat away from the most important political office in the world, and that society is going to hell in a handbasket. This is precisely what happened when Nixon bypassed more moderate, more qualified running mates such as George Romney and Charles Percy and John Lindsay and instead chose Spiro Agnew. Of course, Agnew *was* a moron, and society *was* going to hell in a handbasket. But never mind.

Instead, let us consider the vice presidential vexations confronted by the greatest American president since Lincoln. Before settling on Harry Truman, FDR spent the bulk of his first three administrations saddled with vice presidents who caused him nothing but trouble. Cactus Jack Garner had been Speaker of the House before accepting the number-two slot on the Democratic ticket in 1932, and lived to regret taking the office. Garner spent eight years trying to undermine Roosevelt's New Deal before finally running for the White House himself in 1940, challenging his own president. Garner was a nasty old son of a bitch once described by the famous union leader John L. Lewis as "a labor-baiting, poker-playing, whisky-drinking, evil old man." There is no evidence that FDR disagreed with this description.

Being the coarse buffoon that he was, Garner appeared to have everything going for him as an American presidential candidate, and as late as the spring of 1940, it seemed that he had a decent shot of taking his boss's job right out from under him, something that hadn't occurred since Jefferson unseated Adams in 1800. But then the Germans invaded Denmark; everyone got nervous; and Garner got thrashed in the primaries. This is the only time in American history that a military disaster occurring in the general vicinity of Jutland has exerted a direct influence on the American electoral process.

With this rum-soaked albatross out of his way, Roosevelt ran for an unprecedented third term with the lefty mystic Henry Wallace, whose qualifications for office were a lengthy tenure as editor of a celebrated Iowa farming magazine and eight years as secretary of agriculture. A certifiable "parlor pinko" (to use Harry Truman's elegant term), who had delved into mysticism, Buddhism, and Confucianism, this intellectual forebear of Jerry Brown was deemed too liberal, too intellectual, and too wacky by the Democratic powers-that-be, who arranged for his demotion from heir-apparent to secretary of commerce in 1944. But before long he was forced out of even that largely ceremonial post after giving a speech at Madison Square Garden in which he manifested an affection for the Soviet Union that was not shared by most of his countrymen, and certainly not by Truman.

Two years later, the increasingly preposterous Wallace ran as the presidential candidate of the Communist-backed Progressive Party and got his head handed to him. One thing that really hurt was a series of "Guru Letters" he had written in the 1930s to an enigmatic cult figure named Nicholas Roerich. Roerich was a White Russian painter, poet, and mystic who had a long, flowing white beard, and had written books with titles such as *Fiery Stronghold* and *Flame in Chalice*. He was also founder of the Himalayan Research Institute in Nagara, India, and the Roerich Museum, which even had its own flag. (Yes, the museum was located in New York City, and yes, the flag was red.) The letters, which Wallace did not deny writing, began with the salutation "My Dear Guru" and invoked such obvious non-Republican personalities as "The Dark Ones," "The Steadfast Ones," and "The Dugpas." *America didn't need any of that.* So Wallace was politically ostracized, banished to a job in which he could do little further damage to the nation. He became the editor of *The New Republic*.

Manifestly, the dump-Wallace movement of 1944 had been a wise decision; there can be no doubt that the Republic had dodged a bullet in putting this dangerous fruitcake out to pasture. Steven Ambrose, author of a three-volume biography of Richard Nixon, feels that the Wallace vice presidency was the greatest threat ever posed to this society by that misbegotten office, even though just about nobody can remember all the details today.

"It was absolutely essential to get Wallace off the ticket in '44," says Ambrose. "It was one of the scariest what-ifs? in American history, and, in fact, in world history, if that man had been president of the United States at the beginning of the Cold War."

How did Wallace's political decapitation take place? Says Ambrose: "The top officials in the Democratic party came to FDR and they said, 'Look, you're dying, you can't do this to us. You can't stick us with Henry Wallace.'"

And that was that.

Wallace was succeeded by the now legendary Harry Truman, who has come down in history as a fine, courageous, colorful president, but who was certainly hated by a good portion of the American public throughout much of his term in the White House, and even people who liked him recognized that his resemblance to Pericles of Athens was slight indeed. Before entering politics, Truman had been a complete washout, having failed in the oil and mining business before becoming a haberdasher in his mid-thirties and failing at that. Throughout his career, he wore terrible shirts, played poker with a future stooge for BCCI, and threatened to beat up music critics who made fun of his daughter's sub-par operatic singing. Truman-bashers to this very day stress that he was still living with his mom at the age of thirty-three, but then again, so was Jesus Christ, another late bloomer. In short, at no time before moving into the White House did Harry Truman seem like the kind of guy a troubled nation would want to entrust with the serious job of dropping nuclear weapons on hundreds of thousands of Japanese civilians.

It is important, as the English historian A. J. P. Taylor has written, to always bear in mind that events that were once very far in the future are now very far in the past. This is a roundabout way of saying that although we now know that Harry Truman was the right man for the job in 1945 when FDR died, people certainly did not know it then. As Michael Barone notes in *Our Country: The Shaping of America from Roosevelt to Reagan*, when Truman became vice president, he was an inconsequential back-bencher slated for oblivion, a second-tier senator who was probably going to lose his seat in the 1946 election. During the eighty-two days of his final administration, FDR refused to have anything to do with his new vice president, a machine creation through and through, and Truman seemed content to party up a storm in Washington.

At the time he took office, Truman did not even know of the existence of the atomic bomb. That's how much confidence FDR had in him. In the weeks and months immediately after taking office— before the Japanese surrender in August 1945—Truman literally sent chills down the spines of his countrymen, continuing to dine in the Senate cafeteria as if he were still a humble legislator, rather than the most powerful man on earth. Eventually, Truman snapped out of it, shaped up, won the greatest upset in history by beating Thomas Dewey in 1948, and lived on to humiliate General Douglas MacArthur in 1951. But it is important to remember that at the time he took office in 1945, Harry Truman seemed like a guy who was still living with his parents.

The exploits of Richard Nixon will be treated in a later chapter, which brings us to LBJ and Gerald Ford. Few vice presidents were better prepared to lead their country than Johnson, yet look what happened to him! Vietnam. Watts. Two Robert Caro books that completely slander his memory—and Caro has only gotten up to 1948.

Contrast this with the experiences of Gerald Ford. After decades of futilely toiling in the worst job on earth—Republican congressman— Ford was getting ready to retire in 1974. Instead, the man once described by LBJ as "too dumb to fart and chew gum at the same time" became the only man in American history to serve as both vice president and president without being elected to either office, and today is widely credited by his countrymen with shepherding the nation through a difficult period, serving as a pleasant sort of *scherzo* between the tortuous *largo* of Richard Nixon and the *opéra bouffe* of Jimmy Carter. Proving once again how fundamentally resilient this society is. Yes, the vice presidency is a complete disaster as an office—a walking time bomb, an accident waiting to happen, a tip of the executive iceberg waiting to sink the ship of state. Yet vice presidential disasters and all, the land of the free and the home of the brave always seems to come out of things relatively unscathed. Leading us to the Ur-truth about the American system of government: It takes a licking, but it keeps on ticking. If twenty-four lawyer presidents and thirty-two lawyer vice presidents couldn't destroy it during its first two centuries of existence, nothing can.

X I I

FROM GENGHIS KHAN TO WARREN G. HARDING

I do not propose to be buried until I am really dead.

—DANIEL WEBSTER, turning down the
vice presidential nomination in 1848

Our brief history of the vice presidency reveals it to be a flawed and perhaps imbecilic institution that has more often than not been occupied by poltroons, varlets, dimwits, and, yes, the occasional moron.

But there is another, larger issue. At no point should our relentless criticism of the vice presidency deceive us into thinking that it is the world's *most* moronic political institution, or even that it is among the top ten. As moronic institutions go, the vice presidency is one of the better ones. This fact becomes clear from even a cursory examination of lines of succession established by other societies throughout the course of human history.

Down through the ages otherwise sane, respectable, *well-liked* nations have seen all their best efforts go awry because of their inability to devise a suitable line of succession. For example, at the very same moment that the United States was coming into being, the French were experimenting with such extreme political innovations as serial decapitation, which satisfied just about no one. At the same time, the British Empire found itself dominated by George III, an out-and-out moron, who reigned for sixty years. No moron has ever reigned more than eight years in the history of this country; Gerald Ford reigned barely two. And this Republic has *never* been saddled beneath the yoke of a moronic ex–vice president for more than four years; this during the single-term administration of the harmless cretin Millard Fillmore. Clearly, this system, whatever its faults, could be far, far worse.

Those who do not believe this should turn again to the annals of history for illumination. The decline of the Roman Empire was hastened by the rise of the Praetorian Guards, which was literally a private army, stationed in Rome, that was powerful enough to auction off the throne to the highest bidder. Not thirteen years after the beloved sage Marcus Aurelius died, the Praetorians marched into the imperial palace, lopped off the head of the kindly old Pertinax, who had ruled as emperor just eighty-six days, and stuck the unappetizing grayish red object on a lance. Shortly thereafter, they fenced the empire to a senator named Didius Julianus, who bought it for 6,250 drachmas (he may have overpaid). Didius didn't last long—fifty-four days. Neither did Elagabalus, murdered in 222 after less than four years on the throne, or Philip, massacred in 249, or any of the other interim emperors the Praetorian Guards decided to get rid of when the mood struck them. This was not a workable system.

Similarly, English history has been besmirched by a number of horrid incidents in which bloodthirsty villains with distant claims to the throne hacked their way to the top by butchering lovable tykes and then blaming the deaths on wayfaring strangers, demented serfs, itinerant cutpurses, or migrant stout yeomen. This was the case with Richard III. Many people unfamiliar with the warp and woof of English history mistakenly believe that Richard III was a complete interloper, a usurper who had no legitimate claim to the throne. This is not true. By the time Richard became king of England in 1453, his claim to the throne was the strongest of any man alive. True, he had established this claim by murdering one brother, two nephews, and the king of England—in short, everyone who would otherwise have had a stronger claim than his—but technically he was within the letter of the law in declaring himself king. Clearly, the American line of succession is a vast improvement over *that.*

The vice presidency, as it has evolved, is designed to ensure that the office will not be held by a blackguard, a scoundrel, an ambitious upstart who would undermine the policies of his president, or a gnomish infanticide. With the exception of Richard Nixon, this system has worked rather well. Yes, it is a horribly flawed system that relies on the goodwill of presidential nominees and their political parties to refrain from picking idiots like Millard Fillmore and sons of bitches like Andrew Johnson, but it is better than no system at all.

Still not convinced? Fine; let's talk Mongols. It is an unchallenged historical fact that the only reason Western Europeans—and, by extension, Americans—do not all speak Urdu today, and have names like Mangku and Genghis and Kubilai instead of Aileen, Shawon, Jordan, and Brittany is because of the cretinously unsophisticated rules of succession adhered to by the Mongols in the thirteenth century.

The Mongols, easily the worst race of people the world has ever known (this is Bertrand Russell's opinion, not mine) had a lot of time on their hands early in the thirteenth century, so in 1219 they set out to conquer the planet. Atavistic horsemen with plenty of pep, the Mongols by the year 1241 had burned down most of Asia and eastern Europe and were poised on the banks of the Danube, ready to annihilate the paltry squadrons of German infantry that were all that stood between them and the prostrate duchies of France and Italy. By this point, detachments of the Golden Horde had already appeared as far west and south as the outer suburbs of Venice. With Russia, Poland, and Hungary already in ruins, nothing on earth could have prevented the fiendish Mongols from putting Christendom to the torch.

What happened? What saved Western Europe from the Mongol sword? Not God, you can bet your bottom dollar on that. It was pure luck. As the conquest of the West proceeded, tensions over authority mounted between Batu (a grandson of Genghis Khan, who happened to be the greatest Mongol warrior of the time), and Kuyuk, the eldest son of the reigning Emperor Ogedei. Under pressure from Kuyuk, Ogedei ordered the invasion of the West halted. This was one of the worst mistakes in history, and, as with most of the worst mistakes in history, substance abuse was involved. Ogedei, a stinking, whoring boozehound, had been ordered by his brother Chagatai to cut back on his juicing, to consume no more than a fixed number of cups per day.

He agreed to the quota system—sort of. According to Luc Kwanten's *Imperial Nomads*, Ogedei did not disobey his brother's order; he merely changed the size of the cup. This made life impossible for the hapless juice-monitor that Chagatai had appointed to keep tabs on his brother's drinking. Ogedei's subsequent death, Kwanten reports, "was the result of his excessive wine consumption at one of his celebrations." Sounds a bit like Franklin Pierce.

As James Chambers makes clear in *The Devil's Horsemen,* it was Ogedei's death that saved the West from annihilation. According to Mongol custom, whenever the reigning khan bought the farm, all of his sons and grandsons were required to return to Karakorum, the capital of Mongolia, and vote for his successor. (Karakorum is just south of Lake Baikal, not far from present-day Ulan Bator. For best results, make a left at the River Lena and then ask.) Mongolia is a long, long way from the banks of the Danube; in fact, it's a long, long way from anywhere. By the time a new khan had been elected, the momentum the Mongols had built up over twenty-three years of uninterrupted rape and murder had dissipated, and they never seriously threatened the West again.

The point of all this should be obvious: Don't ever say that the American vice presidency is the stupidest political institution in the history of mankind. If the Mongols had had a second-in-command who could have stepped into Ogedei's shoes, all the fish-and-chips places in London would serve braised yak entrails and the finest restaurant in Paris would be La Tour de Kulchuk or Chez Jemuga.

We have already alluded to the Turkish system of confining potential heirs to the throne in a "cage." This curious setup was devised at the beginning of the seventeenth century after the maverick Sultan Mehmet III had all nineteen of his brothers strangled upon his ascension to the throne, and even the most jaded political observers realized that *the system was not working.* The system required all trainee sultans to be confined in a "cage"—actually a series of buildings hidden away inside the imperial palace—until the sultan died. "There they went, with their mothers, their women, and their slaves, to live a life of gilded imprisonment, from which they emerged only to die or to reign," writes Bernard Lewis in *Istanbul and the Civilization of the Ottoman Empire.* "With such a system, it is not surprising that the Sultans who emerged to rule over the Empire during the seventeenth and eighteenth centuries were for the most part feeble in mind and body, sometimes dangerous degenerates."

They were certainly in a foul mood when they emerged from imprisonment after thirty or forty years. Robert Liddell, author of *Byzantium and Istanbul,* reports that the "neckless hunchback" Osman III was so fed up with women after spending fifty years in his cage that when he became sultan in 1754 he prohibited *any* woman from going out on the street on Sunday, Thursday, or Friday. But even the sultans who had spent only a few years in prison emerged from the experience with serious personality disorders. Murad IV had 50,000 people executed during the last seven years he spent on the planet, and this was after spending an entire lifetime doing things like murdering deaf people who took too long to get out of his way when he strolled down the streets of Istanbul.

The Ottoman cage system had little to recommend it, but even this was superior to the horrors brought on by the dreaded palace eunuchs. Palace eunuchs have popped up all over the place down through the ages, their shadowy hegemony ranging from the imperial palaces of Rome to the sultry harems of Istanbul to the dank, dark dungeons of better forbidden cities everywhere. Eunuch power arose directly from the inability of various civilizations to work out a suitable line of succession. Consider the problems that developed in China during the First Empire. During this era, which lasted from around 200 B.C. until A.D. 600, the emperor was required to go outside his family when seeking a spouse, to pick a wife from a family that had a different last name than his own. Otherwise, people would start marrying their sisters and first cousins, and children would end up looking the way they do in the Ozarks.

The problem with the Chinese system was that it immediately made the emperor's new in-laws the second most powerful family in the kingdom, and, worse still, it made them the family that would become *the* most powerful once the emperor died. Intrigue abounded. Before long, the empress's relatives were seizing all the good jobs, preparing for the moment when the emperor died and his family would become second in importance to hers. Emperors tried many solutions to this problem: One was to marry into obscure, unambitious families that would pose no threat to his own. These were hard to find. Another was to marry into wealthy families, which would not be excessively hungry for power because they already had some. These were even harder to find.

Only one emperor ever hit upon a solution to this thorny dilemma. The mighty Emperor Wu, who reigned from 140 B.C. until 86 B.C. Wu prevented his wife's family from intriguing against him by having them all murdered. This certainly resolved the succession problem to everyone's satisfaction, but there are some indications that tensions would periodically flare up between the emperor and the empress, particularly around the holidays. Lamentably, Wu's successors did not follow in his footsteps, paving the way for the rise of the eunuchs. Initially, eunuchs were chatty, capable advisers who came from obscure families, and thus had no power at court. Being eunuchs, they could not found powerful families, which encouraged several of the late Han Dynasty emperors to grant them a great deal of power. But this backfired in the end because ambitious eunuchs would take advantage of weak emperors and attempt to seize power for themselves or for the miscreants they represented.

"Had the Emperors been strong rulers," writes C. P. Fitzgerald in *A Concise History of East Asia,* "they could have checked the growth of eunuch power. But in the thirty years between A.D. 159 and A.D. 189, the throne was occupied by foolish or weak sovereigns who simply relied on their eunuch advisers in all things and let them have their way. The eunuchs abused their power in every way. They sold public appointments, promoted men for bribes, had those who did not satisfy their demands dismissed, and thus corrupted the civil service and weakened the army." The most famous of the eunuchs was the legendary Sun Nu-Nu.

What can we learn from the machinations of these dysfunctional castrati? A whole lot, *if* we are willing to listen. People often complain that after two full centuries, the American political system is still flawed by a troubled line of succession. But the Chinese wasted 1,700 years trying to come up with a solution to the palace eunuch problem and ended up right back where they started. Given that the palace eunuchs were running wild all the way back in the second century A.D., you would have thought that by the time the Pilgrims landed at Plymouth Rock, the Chinese people would have deep-sixed them for good. But no, when the Ming Dynasty collapsed in 1640, it was the palace eunuchs who precipitated the disaster, by betraying the hapless emperor. And when T'ung Chih, the last legitimate *adult* emperor in the history of China, died of smallpox in 1875, the evidence indicates

that his physical condition had been seriously weakened by his notorious cavorting with eunuchs, the nineteenth-century Oriental equivalent of today's groupies: the Plaster Casters of Peking, if you will.

This roistering with eunuchs set in motion the final collapse of the
Manchu Dynasty. After the death of T'ung Chih (a dissolute youth),
his mother the Empress Dowager (a right-wing hooker) forced the
Council of Princes (spineless punks) and High Ministers (cowardly
windbags) to illegally put her nephew Kuang Hsu (a callow infant) on
the throne. When he was old enough to assume the throne, Kuang Hsu
(now a callow youth) set in motion a series of reforms suggested by
K'ang Yu'wei (a forward-looking scholar), which enraged his aunt (still
a right-wing hooker), who persuaded General Yuan Shih-k'ai (a feck-
less traitor) to depose the emperor and replace him with Hsuan T'ung
(a baby who would later be the subject of an extremely long but
visually opulent movie by Bernardo Bertolucci). Exhausted by centuries of murder, corruption, sexual depravity, and extremely confusing
name changes, the Chinese people opted to part company with their
beloved imperial form of government and instead turned over the reins
of power to gangsters and mass murderers.

This brings us to an important point: Although the American vice
presidency is stupid, it cannot be accused of being complicated. It's not
byzantinely stupid, like Australian Rules football; it's flat-out stupid,
like ice hockey. Every child, and every secretary of state, save one,
knows that when the president of the United States is incapacitated,
the role of governing falls to the vice president. Consider what an
improvement this is over many other forms of government. Let us
consider, for example, the incomprehensibly complex system that arose
in the waning years of Japan's Kamakura Shogunate (1185–1333). The
whole problem arose because of a dynastic dispute between two different branches of the imperial family. In these times, Japan had a series
of retired emperors who, in Fitzgerald's words, "ruled but did not
reign." First there was the Emperor Go Saga, who was born in 1220,
assumed the throne in 1242, reigned for four years, and abdicated in
1246. After that, he became the éminence grise who secretly dominated the court for the next twenty-six years, until his death in 1272.
Go Saga had two sons—Go Fukakusa and (No-Go) Kameyama—both
of whom occupied the throne for a short time, and both of whom

ultimately abdicated. When Go Saga died, the question arose of whether the power behind the power should pass to Go Fukakusa, the older son, or Kameyama, whom dad always liked best; in short, which of the two men's sons got to be a puppet? The controversy took more than a century and many civil wars to resolve, at the conclusion of which a completely different family seized power, and the rest of the country went back to work.

Go figure.

———

The preceding thumbnail sketch of the entire history of mankind should convince even the most cynical observer that the American vice presidency, tragically flawed though it may be, is still an improvement over many other arrangements. It stands somewhere in the middle between a parliamentary form of government (as in France, Germany, or England), where the heir apparent is always a political heavyweight, and outright anarchy (as in every country whose name ends in "ala," "guay," or "dor"), where it's every man for himself. In this sense, the vice presidency should be thought of as the political equivalent of Romania: not nearly as attractive as Hungary, but a whole lot more appealing than Albania.

One thing that can be said with absolute certainty about the modern vice presidency is that although many of the men who have held the office have seemed like cadavers, the office itself is no longer the political graveyard it was in the nineteenth century. Seven of the last ten vice presidents ended up running for the White House (Bush, Mondale, Nixon, Humphrey, Johnson, Ford, Truman), and five of them made it (Truman, Ford, Nixon, Johnson, Bush). Four of the last six presidents (Nixon, Ford, Johnson, Bush) and five of the last nine (add Truman) were vice president first, not to mention Franklin Delano Roosevelt, who ran as a vice presidential candidate in 1920. The only election in the past thirty-two years in which neither party nominated a presidential candidate who had once been vice president was 1980 (Reagan-Bush versus Carter-Mondale), and even there both Mondale and Bush wound up running for the White House the next time the job opened up.

In the ninety-one years since Teddy Roosevelt became the first vice president to succeed a fallen chief executive and then win reelection on his own merits, most occupants of the office have recognized that the position really does give them the inside track on the nation's top job. When *The Modern American Vice Presidency* was published in 1982, Joel Goldstein observed that, of the seventeen men who had held the job between 1901 and 1976, "thirteen later sought the presidency or received consideration for the nomination near the time of the convention." To their numbers can now be added Fritz Mondale and George Bush, and very possibly Dan Quayle.

Goldstein further points out that of the other four veeps who did not seek the presidency, Agnew would have been the frontrunner in 1976 had he not been forced to resign, and Rockefeller would have sought the presidency in 1976 had Ford not chosen to run again; and he further believes that James Sherman (who died during his reelection campaign in 1912) and Charles Curtis (who was defeated in 1932 and died in February 1936) might also have sought the presidency.

The importance of the office is illustrated by the number of men who have actually campaigned for the vice presidential nomination. Nixon went after it in 1952 in his trademark underhanded fashion; four years later JFK went after it in more direct, aboveboard style; and, if Bob Woodward and David Broder are to be believed, Quayle also mounted a surreptitious campaign for the number-two position in the months leading up to George Bush's nomination in 1988. According to James Reston, Jr., when Spiro Agnew resigned from office in disgrace in 1973, John Connally was so sure he had the job that he booked a hotel suite in the capital and started offering people positions on his staff. (Like George Romney, Charles Percy, John Lindsay, Gary Hart, and many other "glamor boys," Connally is one of those quixotic figures who drift across the American political landscape from time to time, enjoy a brief period of renown during which their accession to the highest office in the land takes on an aura of inevitability, then wander off into obscurity, death, Mexico, bankruptcy court, or jail.)

The growing importance of the office is also illustrated by the occasions on which the vice presidential nominee may have cost his running mate the election. This may have been the case in 1968, when Humphrey narrowly lost to Richard Nixon after running with Edmund Muskie, a Democratic warhorse who, unfortunately, came from the same politically insignificant state as Hannibal Hamlin: Maine. And many people believe that with a kinder, gentler running mate at his side instead of the poker-faced hitman Robert Dole, Jerry Ford might have kept his job in 1976. Of course, Ford probably figured that it would look bad unless somebody on the GOP ticket had a brain.

The importance of the office is also illustrated by the fact that it's, well, important. "During 20 of the first 38 presidencies," Goldstein wrote in 1982, "the Chief Executive either left office prematurely or completed his term only after surviving some threat to his incumbency." These crises ranged from assassination attempts (Jackson, FDR, Truman, Ford, Reagan); to surgery (Cleveland, Ike, LBJ, Reagan, Bush); to the time Madison was in danger of being captured by the British. It is an institution fraught with significance, even though it is still basically a stupid one.

Throughout our history, there have been more than two dozen attempts to improve the office of vice president. The improvements are usually the brainchildren of disgruntled intellectuals, journalists with time on their hands, or moping barflies, and have rarely been taken seriously. More than thirty years ago, Clinton Rossiter said, "It must be recognized . . . that no permanent solution to the problem has been worked out, and I doubt very much that it can be." Rossiter lamented that most ranking politicians would still rather be speaker of the house or secretary of state or a senator rather than accept the number-two slot. This being the case, the historian sadly concluded, a vice president should "make whatever can be made of this disappointing office."

Over the years, those who still believe that the office can be salvaged have proposed a number of structural improvements. One is to make the veep the president's chief executive assistant. Another is to make him a cabinet officer. Another is to select vice presidents through a primary system. (Great—even more debates from even dowdier town halls in even tinier towns in New Hampshire, and all brought to you live on CNN!) Still another is to require the presidential nominee to present his party's convention with a list of three or four names, so that the delegates can vote on it the next day, when they're sober.

Still another proposal would require the president-elect to submit his choice to Congress and let that august body decide the issue. This is the approach favored by Jules Witcover in *Crapshoot: Rolling the*

Dice on the Vice Presidency. Terrific, a Republican president, duly elected in a landslide by his fellow Americans, then has to go over to Capitol Hill with hat in hand and let people like Joe Biden and Teddy Kennedy decide whether his vice presidential choice meets with *their* approval. (Gee, weren't there some problems a while back with a guy named Bork? A guy named Thomas?) Under these circumstances, what chance would a Republican president have of getting a conservative vice president—even a smart conservative president—approved by a Congress likely to be dominated by Democrats for the next 400 years?

But the wackiest Witcoverism of all is his homage to Fritz Mondale in the chapter entitled "Good Process, Good Result." For more than a decade now, Mondale has been held up to the rest of us as the paragon of vice presidential excellence, as perhaps the best vice president of them all. Gee, I don't know. Sober, serious, thoughtful, and courageous, Mondale was a splendid American senator in his time. But his four years as Jimmy Carter's caddy provide pretty solid evidence that Mondale, with that imperceptible "Norwegian charisma" his wife once spoke about, was woefully out of step with the values of his countrymen, and was guilty of astonishing political naïveté. When you spend four years on the threshold of omnipotence, as Mondale did, you're supposed to come away from the experience intellectually transformed, imbued with a profound insight into the soul of the American people. But after spending four years poised on the very threshold of power, and then spending four years trying to nail down his party's presidential nomination, Mondale went on national television in front of 220 million Americans and told them that his first act as chief executive would be to raise their taxes.

And people call Dan Quayle dumb.

———

Ill-informed journalists must also be held partially responsible for the erroneous notion that the White House has always, or even usually, been occupied by men who were playing with a full deck. Nothing could be further from the truth. Honest Abe frequently claimed to have seen ghosts flitting around the bedroom he shared with his insane wife. Grant had persuaded himself that he was descended from William the Conqueror. James Buchanan suffered from dizzy spells, and is the only man ever to hold the highest office in the land after a fiancée committed suicide. Nine years after being voted out of office, William Taft told reporters that he had no recollection of having ever been president. (He made these comments while serving as chief justice of the Supreme Court.) Ronald Reagan believed in life on other planets, did not know that deceased SS officers had once been affiliated, however tenuously, with the Nazi party, was convinced that Armageddon was nigh, thought that supply-side economics would work, and was married to Nancy.

Furthermore, there is the question of moral character. Today we all know that John Kennedy was scoring babes by the bushel when he should have been acting as a sentinel for the arsenal of democracy. Well, JFK may have been the most promiscuous chief executive, but he certainly wasn't the first to have trouble keeping his pecker in his pants. Jefferson had a mistress, as did Ike and FDR. Andrew Jackson was a bigamist. Grover Cleveland had a bastard child while he was serving as sheriff of Erie County in northern New York, earning him the nickname the "Beast of Buffalo." And a jilted girlfriend of Warren Harding's published a bestselling book after his death detailing her amorous adventures with the late president. Dan Quayle is at least as morally upstanding as any of those guys.

The truth is, if a vice president is merely breathing, he is already one of the twenty most qualified men to ever hold the office, and is already assured of finishing no lower than thirtieth in the ranks of our presidents. Dan Quayle would have to put in twenty-two-hour days of full-time, abject ineptitude to be as bad as Harding, Grant, Fillmore, Buchanan, or Pierce, and would have to work at least twenty hours a day, seven days a week to get as little done as Benjamin Harrison, Rutherford B. Hayes, or William Taft. He would have to work twenty-four-hour days to get as many of his fellow Americans as pissed off at him as Herbert Hoover or Jimmy Carter managed to do. Yes, it is true that, of the presidents considered to be great by historians, only one (Thomas Jefferson) held the office of vice president first. But there have been several good presidents (Van Buren, Teddy Roosevelt, Truman); several adequate presidents (Arthur, Ford); and several presidents who exerted a major influence on the future course of American history (Nixon and the two Johnsons) who were vice presidents first.

And then there is Calvin Coolidge, whom liberal historians deride as a nonentity, but whom conservatives extol as the most successful president of the twentieth century. Of all the vice presidents who succeeded their running mates, the only out-and-out disaster was John Tyler. And even he was a lot better than Buchanan, Pierce, Grant, Harding, and Hoover.

Finally, in fairness to our vice presidents, we should always bear one thing in mind. They could be worse. Yes, most of them are obscure. Yes, most of them are goofy footnotes in the musty appendix of American history. But when you really think about it, the most pitiful figures aren't the men who got elected vice president and were never heard from again. The most pitiful ones are the men who ran for vice president and lost. Men with names like William H. English and William O. Butler and William E. Miller. Men with names like John W. Kern and Joseph Robinson and Theodore Frelinghuysen. Far better to have been an Alben W. Barkley than a B. Gratz Brown. Far better to have been an Elbridge Gerry than a Whitelaw Reid. Far better to have been a Hannibal Hamlin than a Sargent Shriver.

Well, *slightly* better.

XIII
HOW TO WRITE A POSITIVE DAN QUAYLE ARTICLE

1. Concede that Dan Quayle is a rotten public speaker, but note that eight of our last ten presidents were also rotten public speakers. Mention Thomas Jefferson's speech defect. Quote liberally from Ted Kennedy. Don't mention that you would like a job in the State Department if Dan Quayle becomes our next president.
2. Stress that Dan Quayle is a Republican, a conservative, a fundamentalist, and a Hoosier. So even if he were Copernicus or Max Planck's brother-in-law, everybody at *Time* magazine would still hate him.
3. Don't mention Marilyn.
4. Admit that Quayle used influence to get into the National Guard. But describe it as a late-sixties forerunner of eighties "networking."
5. Point out that nobody else in the administration cares about the plight of the valiant Kurds. Act like *you* do.
6. Refer to the fact that Quayle cosponsored the Job Training Partnership Act (JTPA) with Ted Kennedy in 1982. Cite this as a sign

of his enviable ability to reach across the aisle, put enmity aside, and build lasting, bipartisan coalitions. If anyone writes in to ask what the hell the Job Training Partnership Act (JTPA) is, tell them to go to the library or do a NEXIS search, or something.

7. Point out that until he squared off against Dan Rather, George Bush was thought of as an inarticulate, wimpy jerk who didn't know his ass from third base, and look at him now.

8. Get out Harry Truman's and Gerald Ford's old SAT scores.

9. Concede that Dan Quayle's father, Jim, joined the John Birch Society in the 1950s. But draw attention to the fact that American history is filled with famous politicians whose fathers were scoundrels, ne'er-do-wells, or crooks, and that it is just not American to blame a son for the sins of his father. Note that Ronald Reagan's father was an alkie, Jimmy Carter's father a segregationist, John F. Kennedy's father a bootlegger. Mention that Franklin Pierce's father couldn't spell the word "but." If really backed into a corner, remind the reader that John Quincy Adams's father was the closest thing this country has ever had to an out-and-out fascist. And John Quincy Adams's father was the second president of the United States. So there.

10. Attribute Quayle-bashing to "cultural condescension": the snooty, East Coast perception that Goldwater was nuts, Nixon vulgar, Ford stupid, and Reagan all of the above. Don't go into too many details.

11. Mention John Zaccaro.

12. Use sentences like "Dan Quayle is from what you might call the heartland gentry."

13. Don't mention Marilyn.

14. Explain that Dan Quayle is no anomaly to those who are steeped in Hoosier lore.

15. Stress that Dan Quayle has never had shock therapy.

16. When asked to explain such direct Quayle quotations as:

The western part of Pennsylvania is very, uh, midwestern. Midwestern. And the eastern part is more east. Uh, the Midwest, uh, Pennsylvania is a very important state, a big state, we've done well there in the past. The western part is—Pennsylvania is a divided state, like Tennessee is divided into three parts, Pennsylvania is divided into two parts. You have western Pennsylvania and then you have eastern Pennsylvania. And that's the way you campaign there.

or:

The Holocaust was an obscene period in our nation's history.

or:

potatoe

wonder aloud whether these gaffes really are proof of incompetence or stupidity, or merely are a sign of youthful inexperience and inarticulateness that can be outgrown and overcome, given the fullness of time. Mention Thomas Jefferson's speech defect.

17. Wax eloquent about Sargent Shriver.
18. Note that, although the stories about the Samoan happy campers and Pogo Pogo and the anatomically correct doll are all true, the story about Quayle's thinking that people speak Latin in Latin America is not.
19. Insist that Quayle is worth only about a million, not $600 million. Don't mention the trust fund.
20. Don't mention Marilyn.

XIV

CLEANING UP ON QUAYLE

I really hope that I'm not in this business for too long.

— STEVE ANDERSON, a Chilean-based marketer
of anatomically correct Dan Quayle dolls, with
huge red penises that spring out when pressure is
exerted on the head

One wintry evening about two years ago, I found myself sitting behind a two-way mirror in the offices of a New York market research company watching eight members of a focus group chomping on what they had been led to believe were "bunnyburgers." Bunnyburgers, they had been told, were burgers made from helpless little cottontails that had been slaughtered by a Japanese-backed franchise that planned to open twenty-six outlets in the United States within the next six months. The bunnyburgers were packaged in ecologically repugnant Styrofoam containers and had lurid pink plastic ears sticking out of them. They were really quite revolting.

The focus group had been convened as the second phase of a prank for a *Spy* magazine TV special. The first phase was to send nine New York public relations firms a bogus bunnyburgers business plan and invite them to bid for the account. Out went nine press kits; in came nine positive responses, from which four finalists were chosen. Of the four PR firms that came to meet us at the Ritz-Carlton Hotel, only one was less than enthusiastic about bunnyburgers' chances for success. "Americans like things that are chic" was a typical accolade. How true.

A few nights later, it was the focus group's turn to tell us what they thought of bunnyburgers. Those of us behind the mirror—writers, producers, sound engineers, hangers-on—were hoping that the unsuspecting consumers munching on the fake bunnyburgers (they were actually made from ground turkey meat) would say that they were appalled by the very notion of wolfing down Thumper. We were hoping for this response because this would make our flack victims seem even more money-grubbing and foolish. We were not disappointed.

It was while watching the eight disoriented focus group members try to force down those vile bunnyburgers that the true genius of the capitalist system dawned on me. The group members were eating disgusting—or what they thought to be disgusting—fast food, but were getting $50 an hour to do so. The leader was wasting his time, but he was being paid a handsome fee by his company to do so. The caterer who had prepared the fake bunnyburgers was earning a nice piece of change for the evening, as was her assistant. And that didn't include the TV producers, the writers, the researchers, the audio guys, the hangers-on, plus me, all of whom were bringing home a more than adequate slab of bacon in exchange for an easy night's work. Turning to a friend, I remarked that this was the basic difference between the United States and, say, Poland: that in that tiny room twenty-two different people were making money by participating in something that was preposterously stupid, whereas in Poland people had to do preposterously stupid things for free.

This very same thought occurred to me when I started paging through the irreverent newsletter *The Quayle Quarterly*. As I studied the catchy ads that appeared in the pages of this three-year-old publication devoted entirely to ridiculing Vice President Dan Quayle, I realized that dozens, and perhaps even hundreds, of ordinary people, both in this country and abroad, derive a substantial portion of their income from Quayle's status as a national punching bag. Here, I am speaking not only of Jay Leno, David Letterman, and Arsenio Hall; I am referring to far less renowned entertainers. In 1991, Collier Books sold 260,000 copies of *Where's Dan Quayle?*, a parody of the extremely popular *Where's Waldo?* series of children's books, written by a trio of complete unknowns. Shortly thereafter, Carroll & Graf published a compendium of Quayle jokes, anecdotes, and cartoons entitled *Quayle*

Hunting. Even before that, Little Brown had brought out a lunkheaded affair called *The Dan Quayle Quiz Book,* which sold quite handily.

And that's just the printed material. What about all the "humorous" Quayle items: the T-shirts, the watches, the bumper stickers, the anatomically correct dolls. All over America, and even in such geographically disparate locales as southern Chile and mainland China, people earn their daily bread by manufacturing, carving, or hawking satirical items that remorselessly poke fun at the vice president. This is as fine a vindication of Adam Smith's system as I have ever seen; how can anyone deny that the free enterprise system truly works when even those who most despise it—wiseass liberal Democrats—make a killing by satirizing one of its most fulsome progeny?

"Quayle is always good for the comedy business because he has different edges to him," says Jim Aidala, technical director of the Capitol Steps, one of those dreaded, Tom Lehrerian satirical ensembles that seem to flourish only in rube-fraught hellholes like Washington, where they amass the wealth of Croesus by belting out such numbers as "Stand by Your Dan" or this mutilated version of "Has Anybody Seen My Gal?":

> Five-foot-ten, hair like Ken
> Looks like TV weathermen,
> Yes, Danny Quayle is my Ken Doll.
> Teeth of white, very bright,
> Twice as smart as Vanna White.

"Quayle will continue to be good until he leaves office forever," says Aidala. "What you live in dire fear of is quiet competency. Michael Dukakis or Sam Nunn is our equivalent of a recession."

The Quayle industry is a wondrously diverse affair, whose marketing mix ranges from clever, inexpensive T-shirts to fancy, overpriced watches to uninspiring doormats that are priced right about where they should be. In Alexandria, Virginia, a mail-order house called PDQ Productions sells a T-shirt with the words PRESIDENT QUAYLE framing the Edvard Munch painting *The Scream* for $15. In Lenexa, Kansas, the President's Prayer Club sells T-shirts ($12.95), sweatshirts ($19.95), and bumper stickers ($1.50) depicting the vice president above the logos "Keep George Healthy." (Add $2 and $3, respectively, for sweats and T-shirts in sizes XXL and XXXL.)*

Out in Livermore, California, a company called Healy's sells a J. Danforth Quayle original "America's Second-Hand Watch" for $250 (*Quayle Quarterly* subscribers can get it for $199 plus $4.50 shipping; California residents please add 7% sales tax). In fact, there are several companies that sell some type of Dan Quayle watch, ranging from one depicting Quayle beside the Pillsbury Doughboy to one where the numbers are in the wrong order. These watches tend to be in the $30 range—and of dubious quality.

And that's not even mentioning the scores of foreigners whose livelihood depends on veep-bashing: the Chinese factory workers who crank out Dan Quayle watches for a whole plethora of American outfits, the local artisans in southern Chile who handcraft mildly Dan Quayleized replicas of the anatomically correct doll the veep bought on his trip to Santiago in 1990: a squat, totemistic object with a Dan Quayle head that when yanked on triggers a big red cock.

Several of these businesses are doing quite well. Walt Sullivan, owner of PDQ Productions, estimates that he has "easily" sold more than a thousand of his Edvard Munch T-shirts, with requests coming from as far away as Norway. Kay Healy, who sells the upscale Dan Quayle watches, expects to have no trouble unloading the 300 items she has already produced. She notes that Spiro Agnew watches, which ran $29 when Agnew was in office, are now worth ten times that price.

Because the Agnew watches were crude and cheap—not unlike the man who inspired them—and were turned out in the thousands, there are still plenty of them around, holding down their long-term value as collectibles. Healy, who is in the political collectibles business, says that her watches are deliberately designed as a limited-edition collector's

---

*This practice of charging extra for jumbo sizes is a clear case of discrimination against the avoirdupoidally challenged. Up in Fairfield, Connecticut, a firm called Deecken Studios has been marketing T-shirts with a picture of Dan Quayle's head atop James Dean's body above the legend "Rebel Without a Clue." The shirts run $14, plus $2 postage, for regular sizes, $2 extra for XXL. But Connecticut residents must toss in $1.12 for sales tax, thanks to Lowell Weicker, who looks like an XXL himself. In other words, if you're a short, skinny, pasty-faced liberal from Vermont, you can get the shirt for $16, but if you're a fat, pinko action hog from Hartford or New Haven, you have to shell out a whopping $19.12 for the very same shirt. And Democrats have the nerve to talk about the fairness issue.

item (she is setting some aside for herself, convinced that their value would skyrocket should Quayle ever become president). In fact, Healy says that after Agnew received his complimentary watch (every other living ex–vice president got one, too) he ordered several others as gifts, as did Fritz Mondale. Healy, who is, to my knowledge, the only conservative Republican active in the Quayle industry, says that her watch, though amusing, was not intended to show disrespect to the vice president.

This is not the case with most other purveyors of Quayleiana. These folks make no secret of the fact that they despise the vice president, and would be quite happy to be forced out of the Quayle-bashing business forever if it would ensure his disappearance from the political arena.

"Unfortunately, Dan Quayle has created a cottage industry of people like me," says Sullivan, the manufacturer of the "Scream" shirts, who does not sound like he voted for Goldwater or Reagan. And even though Steve Anderson of the Patagonian Trading Company figures he can make a 50 percent markup on the 1,200 anatomically correct Dan Quayle dolls he hopes to sell this year, he is plagued by the paradox of it all. "I really hope I'm out of business by November."

Although some of the Quayle-bashing companies are doing quite well, it would be a mistake to think that every business enterprise depending on Dan Quayle for its livelihood is booming at this moment. As recently as the Summer/Fall 1991 issue of the *The Quayle Quarterly*, Radar World of Wheeling, Illinois, was running ads for its $29.90 Dan Quayle watch (add $4.90 for shipping and handling), but by February of 1992, the 800-number had been disconnected. When I contacted Bean Avenue Publishing of Tucson, Arizona, in the early spring of 1992, company head Bruce Kaplan said that Quayle-bashing had probably subsided, explaining why sales of *No Exit*, a book with flip art depicting Dan Quayle eating a Twinkie "could be better." When I called Bold Concepts, a New York button manufacturer, the proprietor gave no indication that Quayle buttons were flying out the doors. Steve Messina, owner of Manhattan's Revenge & Guilt, told me that he'd sold around 350 of his Dan Quayle/Bart Simpson T-shirts, but moaned that satirical T-shirts are one of the first luxuries consumers cut back on during a recession. And Anderson said that the Washingtonian he hired to peddle his *Indio picoro* dolls "was not the right guy."

In exhilarating news for the vice president, some people are getting out of the Quayle-thrashing racket entirely. When I called him on Super Bowl Sunday, 1992, Jay Leno said that he was cutting back on the Dan Quayle jokes because they were becoming "redundant." He added, "You can't use the *Tonight* show as a bully pulpit." The *Where's Dan Quayle?* creators also think that Quayle-bashing may be on the decline. Andy Mayer, one of the three men from Washington state who dreamed up the project, feels that "market saturation has been reached," and that the next project he and his partners launch—also a political parody—will lay off the vice president. The mood was pretty much the same in Lenexa, Kansas, when I spoke with John Wade, owner of the President's Prayer Club. "Frankly," Wade explained, "I'm tired of picking on the guy. I'm out here in Kansas, and in Kansas we've got a saying, 'It takes a good man to build a good barn, but any ole mule can kick it in.' "

Not being from Kansas, or from anyplace that even vaguely resembles it, I had no idea what the hell Wade was talking about. Still, his decision to get out of the Quayle-creaming business was not entirely motivated by altruism; he admitted that sales had steadily dwindled since 1989, and although he had sold 3,000 shirts all told, he had noticed a gradual leveling-off in the public's enthusiasm. "I probably broke even on the deal; no more," he reported.

Wade's experiences illustrate the hidden perils of the political satire industry. To an unsophisticated outsider, the idea of going into the Quayle-excoriating business probably sounds like fun and games. But Sullivan says that business is business, and that any successful enterprise is going to invite competition from pirates: His Edvard Munch shirt has been so successful that it had inspired illegal knockoffs all over the country.

Sullivan is also the victim of a cruel paradox: A Democratic administration would be much more likely to step up regulation of the satirical T-shirt industry, but if the Democrats were to dislodge Bush and Quayle from office, he would lose the market for his shirts.

Gary Cohn knows how tough the Quayle-bashing industry can be. The Wheeling, Illinois, entrepreneur, who used to sell Dan Quayle watches direct-mail through Radar World, is also founder of the immensely popular Dan Quayle 900 Bloopers & Jokes Line ($2 for the first minute; 99 cents per minute thereafter; a free Dan Quayle watch to every fiftieth caller).

"We had the Joke Line where people could hear jokes and Quayle bloopers or leave their own jokes," Cohn recalls. "We also had Fax-a-Quayle, where we'd send you a one-page sheet of jokes. And we had an electronic shopping market where people could order all the different Quayle products from other companies. I used to be in the picture-phone business—there are about ten to twenty thousand of those things out there—so we had things hooked up so you could get a picture of the different Quayle products online."

But then the bottom fell out, as it has for so many other Quaylerific entrepreneurs. To hear Cohn tell it, he's *never* surprised when a Quayle-bashing business goes belly-up; he's convinced that anyone who makes fun of the vice president ultimately falls prey to the "Quayle curse."

As proof, he says that he was audited by the Internal Revenue Service "right after we started selling the watches." Still, it was not the government that caused 1-900-USA-DANNY to go under; it was his own business partners.

"The phone company went bankrupt," Cohn explains. "They got involved with a lot of 1-900 porn lines, and they paid the porn guys but they never paid us. So first I made a lot of money, and then I lost a lot of money. Scumbags."

Cohn claims to have sold thousands of his Dan Quayle watches until he started running into quality-control problems with the Chinese manufacturers he was using.

"With the first model, you used a pen to turn a thing on the side and then the hands just started spinning around," he explains. "People loved them. But then we started having problems with the later shipments; we had a 25 percent defective rate, and that was just not acceptable."

As for the IRS audit, Cohn says that the government inspector spent "two or three weeks around here digging up any dirt on us he could find, but he got nothing. He was a real dork, too; he would sit around all day reading his model railroad magazine, ordering parts for his train set."

Still, the mere threat of an IRS audit was enough to put the fear of

God into a number of other entrepreneurs toying with the idea of getting into the bash-Quayle racket.

"I had a guy in California who was going to promote my phone line, but when he found out it was about Quayle he backed out," recalls Cohn. "He said that a few years earlier he'd made fun of George Bush and had gotten audited twice. There seems to be an unwritten rule that anybody who goes after the government gets audited."

Cohn says that he has now decided to "lay off the guy for a while. I'm turning into more of an environmental-type person. I want to promote solar heating and electric vehicles. I want to get away from making fun of people who shouldn't be in public office in the first place."

As with bunnyburgers, Cohn's experiences redound to the credit of the capitalist system, demonstrating that even left-wing satirists based in Wheeling, Illinois, can reap huge economic benefits from heaping interactive and fax-aided scorn on the man occupying the second highest office in the land. It is a further testimony to the unfettered progress of Adam Smith's remarkable system that peasants in rural China should earn their daily bread by assembling inexpensive watches poking fun at the vice president of a distant land in their pathetic little factories. But the demise of Radar World is a powerful cautionary tale, warning us that there is still much to be done; it was, after all, the shoddy workmanship of all those Third World pinkos that led to the collapse of Cohn's enterprise. Maybe Cohn should have had the watches assembled in the good old U.S.A.

The only Quayle-basher I was not successful in tracking down is Dr. Joe Waldbaum, a New York physician so incensed by the vice president's ascent to the penumbra of omnipotence that he has abandoned his practice and become a folk singer. Waldbaum, whose fusion of Hippocratic and Pete Seegerian talents makes him sound like one of the most sinister threats the Republic has ever faced, has been advertising an album called *The Ballad of Dan Quayle* in *The Quayle Quarterly*. His badly punctuated ad notes that the album of "comedy and topical songs" contains numbers such as "Where's Dan Quayle?" and can be bought by sending $10 to: Dr. Joe Waldbaum, Apartment J, 139 East 35, NYC, NY 10016.

But when I called Waldbaum's number, an extremely curt receptionist said that the doctor was not in.

"Well, where is he?"

"He's out on the road, playing his music," she replied.

"Look, I'm writing a book about Dan Quayle and I'm sure he would like to be in it."

"Well, I just told you, he's out on the road playing his music."

"Yeah, but where out on the road?"

"*Out* on the road."

I finally laid my hands on some lyrics by Dr. Joe, printed in *The Quayle Quarterly*. They ran like this:

> Danny had good luck
> That kind of thing can happen
> When Daddy's got big bucks.

Stay out on the road, Joe. You belong there.

———

The heliocentric orb in the Quayle-bashing universe is, of course, the three-year-old *Quayle Quarterly*. This spiteful newsletter, published by two ordinary Americans just like you and me from Connecticut, is a twenty-page hodgepodge of press clippings, article reprints, original material, and cartoons involving Dan Quayle, plus lots of ads for the various Quayle-related products. Launched in 1990 by Deborah Werksman (a mother who works at home) and Jeff Yoder, a computer programmer, the *Quarterly* once had a circulation of 16,000, but has now subsided slightly to around 14,000. It costs $14.95 a year, or $3.95 per issue; while back issues can be had for $3.95 apiece.

As with most amateur publications, the quality of the newsletter is uneven. Though it does contain good, well-written stories, these tend to be reprints from *The New Republic*, *Spy*, or *Harper's*. (Notable exceptions are an interview with Arthur Schlesinger, Jr., and a staff-written article about Marilyn Quayle's troubling relationship with the church of Robert Thieme, Jr.) The staff-written material is mostly generic, lefty sarcasm, much of it supplied by Jefferson Morley, a dour alumnus of *The New Republic* and *The Nation.*

The best parts of the *Quarterly* are the ads, the oddities (a photograph of a pumpkin in the shape of Quayle's head), and the letters, many of them from God-fearing Republicans who are probably working on their fifth tumbler of Dewar's. The worst parts are the cartoons and the volunteer poems, works of such breathtaking idiocy that the authors would seem to be spiritual kinsmen of the man they seek to ridicule. "The Love Song of J. Danforth Quaylefrock" is a typical abomination, though the "Battle Hymn of the Republicans" is far worse. Here is the final verse:

> But if perchance our thousand points of hate get people sore;
> Our recourse will be simple,
> We'll just start another war.
> Few eyes are clear when they're suffused with patriotic gore.
> Our hype will win once more.

Beneath the work of most contributors, the *Quarterly* usually lists their current residences. But in the case of the poets, the newsletter doesn't even mention what state they live in. Probably for their own safety.

Early issues of the *Quarterly* tended to be funnier, with lots of reports of Quayle's legendary gaffes: his United Negro College Fund remarks; his "happy camper" comments in Samoa; his idiotic statement that Czech hero Alexander Dubcek had "invited" Soviet tanks into his country back in 1968. The tone of the newsletter got Quayle so mad that when its publishers appeared on the *Phil Donahue Show* on June 1, 1990, the White House sent out its siege guns: media wizard Roger Ailes, Quayle press secretary David Beckwith, and conservative think-tank kingpin Mitch Daniels, Jr. After that, subscriptions went through the roof.

But in the past two years, as Quayle himself has become moderately less gaffe-prone and more confrontational (witness his *Murphy Brown* comments), the *Quarterly*'s attacks have become less personal and more ideological. Where once the *Quarterly* ridiculed the vice president as a person, it now ridicules him as a Republican. The more it tries to be sophisticated and analytical, the less funny it is. Since things that aren't particularly funny are my stock-in-trade, I decided it was high time I moseyed on over to Connecticut and paid a visit on the *Quayle Quarterly* people.

Litchfield, Connecticut, Litchfield, Connecticut. Nestled in the copses and woodlands watered by the mighty Housatonic, this slumbering village would seem to be the very apotheosis of traditional Republican values: community, frugality, civility, gin. With its manicured lawns; its colonnaded churches; its neat-as-a-pin crafts shops; and its dough-boy-era tank, poised like a sentinel in the village square, Litchfield is the sort of self-parodying Yankee hamlet where all of the residents seem to have been issued a Shetland sweater and a collie at birth and told never to go out in public without them. It would thus seem a fairly odd home for a muckraking, left-wing, Thomas Payne–like publication such as *The Quayle Quarterly*.

And, of course, *The Quayle Quarterly* isn't located in charming, affluent Litchfield, but around thirty-five miles to the east and south in cruddy, run-down Bridgeport. Bridgeport, a dump that sits just to the north of trendy, posh Westport, has rarely been in the news in recent years, but when it has, the news has usually dealt with the municipality's dire financial condition (it declared bankruptcy in 1991). With its sad little clapboard houses, its empty stores, and its hardscrabble streets, it is the perfect home for a sneering, nose-thumb-ing, Republican-bashing, grass-roots newsletter.

Founders Deborah Werksman and Jeff Yoder are an earnest pair of Ben & Jerry Democrats who look exactly as you would expect them to, only more so. Indeed, Werksman and Yoder are so letter-perfect for their roles as Quayleophobes that I briefly suspected that the Republi-can National Committee had broken into their clapboard house the day I arrived for the interview, abducted them, and replaced them with people who are even more stereotypically liberal.

Yoder is a tall, thin, late-thirtyish man who speaks in a soft-spoken voice from behind a neatly trimmed beard and wire-rimmed glasses. You have seen him at many benefits to save the imperiled manatee. Werksman is tougher, more strident, more earthy, and exudes that aura of glib righteousness, moral superiority, and overall sanctity that easily costs the Democratic party 20 million fence-riding voters every election year. Werksman, a northern Connecticut St. Theresa of Avila, uses expressions like "lack of vision," "lack of compassion," "deep fault lines in our society," "too much selfishness," "heading the country in the wrong direction," "our democracy is breaking down," and my personal favorite, that old standby: "He's an emperor without clothes."

As is the case with Marilyn Quayle, their props are impeccable. When they offer me coffee, and I ask for milk, I am told "We only have soy milk." *Well, of course.* When I use the bathroom, I am not surprised to find the usual periodical suspects: *The Utne Reader, Mother Jones.* (For those unfamiliar with *The Utne Reader,* it is a left-wing *Reader's Digest* that specializes in reprinting articles from obscure publications that even devotees of obscure publications may not have seen. Last year, *The Quayle Quarterly* was nominated for Best New Title by *The Utne Reader.* One of the other entries in this category was a magazine called *Snake Power.*) As I am leaving at the end of our two-hour interview, the Peach Blossoms Diaper Service pulls into the driveway. "1-800-PEACHIE" reads the emblem emblazoned on the side of the vehicle.

Caring for our children
Caring for their world

Grrr.

Werksman and Yoder say they have no affiliation with the Democratic National Committee, that they launched the newsletter all by themselves after the Quayle-Bentsen debate because Quayle "was just so much fun at the time."

But then things turned a tad more serious.

"We're concerned citizens," says Werksman. "We have looked at our political leaders and said, 'The emperor has no clothes on. Quick! Rush this to the press.' "

To Werksman's best knowledge, *The Quayle Quarterly* is the first satirical newsletter in the history of the United States devoted entirely to a sitting vice president. But the absence of a *Mondale Monthly,* a *Wallace Weekly,* a *Bush Bi-Annual,* or an *Adams Chronicle* is less an indication of our forebears' underdeveloped sense of humor than a reflection of technological advances that occurred in the past decade.

"It's a function of desktop publishing, and that's a function of technology," says Werksman. "Whereas we have no experience in journalism or politics, what we do have is a computer system with the capability to turn out a twenty-page newsletter camera-ready." (Technical Note for Burgeoning Satirists: *The Quayle Quarterly* use both an IBM PC and an Apple.) "Without desktop publishing, we couldn't do this."

Although supporters of Dan Quayle do not see it this way, Werksman and Yoder insist that their publication is not just a bunch of Dan Quayle jokes, that it has a more serious purpose. "It's always been mostly political," says Yoder. "We've never done Quayle jokes. We don't do the David Letterman thing. We've always been fairly serious-minded." Werksman says this contention is supported by the fact that many Republicans buy the magazine. (*The Quayle Quarterly* is too small to be ABC-audited, so readers will have to take such nebulous demographic suppositions on faith.)

"A lot of our original subscribers were Republicans," she says. "We'd get letters from people who would say, 'I've voted a straight Republican ticket for the last thirty years, but I think Dan Quayle is appalling.' A lot of people buy it as gifts for their Republican fathers-in-law. And then their Republican fathers-in-law renew it." Nevertheless, admits Werksman, the newsletter is vigorously partisan. "We are not attempting to be fair and balanced," she says.

Certainly not. Werksman and Yoder are ungrudgingly contemptuous of the vice president, whom they view as an out-and-out piffle-skull who has no business being anywhere near the White House. They hate him for being rich. They hate him for being a rotten student. They hate him for being the "darling of the right." And they hate him for golfing, even though Werksman admits that her own parents golf (the fiends!). Although they concede that Quayle's public performances have improved a mite since 1988, Werksman and Yoder don't think that says much for him.

"Now he just looks like a marionette," she says. "He's not putting his foot in his mouth quite as much, but neither is he looking like a leader." She elaborates, "He has a staff with seven Ph.D.s* on it. Quayle knows that he needs to surround himself with people who have

---

*At the time of our interview, Werksman was unaware that Carnes Lord had been told to take his two Ph.D.s and stick them where the sun don't shine.

the credentials to appear smarter than he is. His staff's credentials are to make up for his lack thereof."

Told that Quayle's TV ratings are good, that talk-show hosts like to have him as a guest, Werksman sneers, "That's partly because people tune in to see if he's going to make a mistake. When Dan was on *Face the Nation*—was it *Face the Nation* where he said that stuff about Kuwait not being another Vietnam because you've got sand? No, *Nightline*. I think Lesley Stahl asked him, 'Are we getting into another Vietnam?' And he said, 'Oh no, this is nothing like Vietnam. In Vietnam it's a jungle; in Saudi Arabia and Kuwait you've got sand.'"

I try to explain that Quayle was obviously talking about the strategic differences between fighting in a jungle, where the enemy has cover from air attack, and fighting in a desert, where he does not. But Werksman was having none of it.

"What Quayle is trying to get across is that terrain is a very large part of military strategy, and that it makes it a whole different scenario," says Werksman. "But what comes out of his mouth is: 'Vietnam is a jungle, Kuwait is sand.' That is as far as he is able to absorb what twenty people have spent all night telling him: 'Dan, when they ask you about Vietnam, talk about the terrain.'"

Every once in a while, Werksman takes a breather from pillorying Quayle to tee off on his wife.

"Marilyn has no hesitation about taking her daughter horseback riding in Manassas State Park the weekend that the whole country's national parks are closed," she fumes. "I mean, you have to say, 'Who do you think you are, Princess Di or something?'"

Werksman also expresses immense irritation that Marilyn, against her staff's wishes, opted to appear in full riding gear in *Vogue*. And she is furious about Marilyn's use of taxpayers' money to fix up the vice president's mansion.

"They raised $390,000 in private funds and got Congress to appropriate another $200,000," she seethes. "They also ended up with an Olympic-size swimming pool and a thirty-by-thirty putting green. This is at a time that most Americans can't afford to buy a $200,000 house. I get a sense from Marilyn of a certain imperial delusion, a delusion of grandeur."

Little by little, it becomes clear the Werksman and Yoder don't really have a beef with Quayle so much as they have a beef with everything he stands for. What he stands for is conservatism, and they just don't like conservatives. This being the case, I ask them what in particular they have to fear from Quayle. Viewed from the standpoint of a liberal Democrat, how could Quayle possibly be any worse than Ronald Reagan, Richard Nixon, Barry Goldwater, Patrick Buchanan, or, for that matter, Warren Harding?

"He doesn't scare me any more than Ronald Reagan, but Ronald Reagan is pretty scary," Werksman says. But the magic word "Reagan" makes her turn wistful. "I think Ronald Reagan has done damage to this country that it's going to take . . . that Kayla will pay for." (Kayla is *The Quayle Quarterly* daughter, a lovable tyke who scampers all around the living room throughout the interview.) It is probably true that Ronald Reagan has done irreparable damage to this country, and that Kayla will have to pay for it. But most Republicans I know think that kids unlucky enough to be born to parents who name them Kayla *should* have to pay for it.

"What I fear is that we're not getting any better, that we're just mired, that there's no growth, in an organic way, in a human way," Werksman explains. As she philosophizes, I think back to something John O'Sullivan, the sharp-tongued editor of *National Review,* told me about the difference between Ronald Reagan and George Bush: "People like George Bush think that the entire country would vote for them if they could only find the right issues," said O'Sullivan. "But Reagan realized that there are certain people in this country who will never vote for you, no matter what you do. So Reagan would go on the offensive and attack those people again and again and again."

Deborah Werksman and Jeff Yoder *are* those people.

———

For a publication that has as much fun attacking Dan Quayle's gaffes, misstatements, and incoherent remarks, *The Quayle Quarterly* folks are a bit incoherent themselves. On the one hand, Werksman views Quayle as a chowderhead who "lacks the breadth and knowledge to run this country." But then she says, "We definitely perceive him as being very shrewd politically. You can see it in the discussion he had with Richard Fenno, when he talked about which committees he wanted to be on when he joined the Senate. He didn't want to be on Judiciary, because they were going to deal with a lot of controversial things like abortion and busing, and he didn't want to be anywhere near that stuff."

Werksman dismisses Quayle as a creation of his advisers, as a "marionette." Still, she says he is calculating enough to pick all those think-tank policy wonks for the express purpose of enhancing his own image. She argues that Quayle's "whole constituency" is the fire-breathing, brain-dead Jesse Helms and Pat Robertson wing of the Republican party. This being the case, she refuses to believe that mainstream Republicans will ever vote Quayle into the White House, confidently citing polls showing that Quayle remains unbelievably unpopular with a large segment of the American populace. But then she turns around and says not only that she has detected a pro-Quayle backlash in recent months, as more and more readers write in to demand why they are picking on him, but that she expects him to be our next president. Yes, in breathtakingly good news for Quayle and his crew, even Yoder and Werksman are convinced that the Humble Hoosier has a bright political future.

"He's going to be our next president," sighs Werksman. "By ninety-six, the guy is going to be a household word."

"You really think he's going to be president?" I ask.

"I really do. I think that people are going to be stupid enough to elect him. By ninety-six Quayle will have moved enough to the center that he'll pick up the people who are going to lose Bush because he can't run for a third term."

"And everybody else will go back to watching television," Yoder chimes in.

This brings us to the central contradiction in the credo of all full-time Quayle bashers. To people on the left, Quayle is deemed both stupid and shrewd, cretinous and calculating, impotent and imperial, daft and dangerous. He is, they assure us, quite remarkably unpopular, yet in the same breath they would have us believe that he will be voted into the White House by a majority of the American people—you know, the ones who think he's an idiot—after George Bush fulfills his second term in office. For the life of me, I cannot follow this argument.

Anyone who can provide information enabling me to resolve this mystery, please call and claim your $50 reward.

———

It must be an immense relief to Dan Quayle and his staff to know that even the editors of *The Quayle Quarterly* view him as the odds-on favorite to succeed George Bush in 1996. Conversely, it must be reassuring to both Deborah Werksman and Jeff Yoder to know that they could be making a few bucks off Dan Quayle's foibles for perhaps another twelve years to come, by which time Tucker will be old enough to run for the White House, hemmed trousers or no hemmed trousers. With 4,000 subscribers and approximately 10,000 readers who buy the publication at newsstands, the *Quarterly* is already profitable, and as the possibility of a Quayle presidency grows, those numbers and profit margins could grow to truly staggering proportions.

Yet it isn't just Werksman and Yoder who find themselves ensnared in an ambivalent financial relationship with the vice president. In recent years, the city of Bridgeport has fallen on hard times indeed. A dwindling tax base, a decaying downtown, and escalating crime finally brought the city to its knees in June 1991, when it was forced to file for bankruptcy. The same year, the city got clobbered with a huge, national public-relations black eye when the University of Bridgeport unsuccessfully tried to auction itself off to the Moonies for $50 million. This year, it got a bigger black eye: They closed the deal.

This is a city whose industrial infrastructure has withered. This is a city whose corporate citizens have departed. This is a city whose most talented young people have fled to the outlying suburbs. This is a city with a stagnant cultural life. This is a city with no future. In a blighted municipality such as Bridgeport, Connecticut, there is every possibility that *The Quayle Quarterly*, with its 14,000 subscribers, may be the city's largest, most successful industry, its only going concern. In a blighted municipality such as Bridgeport, Connecticut, there is every possibility that *The Quayle Quarterly*, with its two employees, may even be the largest employer. Which makes it all the more imperative that Dan Quayle continue to function as a national punching bag, as a figure of mirth, as the Republic's designated whipping boy. For should Dan Quayle ever be voted out of office or—God forbid—stop being perceived as a dimwit, *The Quayle Quarterly* would have no further reason to exist. Which would be bad for Deborah Werksman, bad for Jeff Yoder, and bad for little Kayla, but which would be even worse for their 142,000 neighbors in Bridgeport. Because when Dan Quayle goes, *The Quayle Quarterly* goes, too. And when *The Quayle Quarterly* goes, Bridgeport, Connecticut, is going with it.*

---

*Obviously, when Dan Quayle goes, his wife Marilyn and her sister Nancy T. Northcott are going to have to look for another line of work; it's hard to imagine much demand for *Return of Embrace the Serpent* or *The Silence of the Hoosiers* co-written by an *ex*–vice president's wife and her sibling.

X V

THE FAIR CHAPTER

> The democratic principle holds that the business of state can be
> conducted by ordinary men, subject to the ordinary failures of
> character as well as to the moments of ordinary courage and
> intelligence.—LEWIS LAPHAM, *Imperial Masquerade*

As vice president, Dan Quayle must be commended for refusing to go
quietly. Unlike his invisible predecessor, George Bush, whose most
memorable accomplishments during his eight years in office were (1)
writing a report on terrorism at a time when the Reagan administration was trading arms for hostages and hiding guns in Iranian birthday
cakes, and (2) heading an anti-drug task force that accomplished
absolutely nothing, Quayle has been active, bold, and visible. He has
piped up at White House meetings, even when his input is neither
desired nor heeded, and has pressured the president to oppose tax
increases, racial quotas, reductions in the defense budget, and selling
the Kurds down the river. He has been an extremely popular fund-
raiser for the Republican party, has traveled the low road—à la Nixon
and Agnew, when asked to do so—and has generally avoided complaining about all the personal abuse he has had to put up with, even
going so far as to pen thank-you notes to the authors of the *Where's
Dan Quayle?* children's book. Unlike most of his predecessors in this
horrendous office, Quayle does not think of himself as a political
cadaver approaching the end of his career. When Dan Quayle leaves
public office, he will leave it kicking and screaming.

It is undeniable that Dan Quayle has been consistently underestimated by his opponents. His biographer Richard Fenno notes that he trailed eight-term incumbent Ed Roush by thirty-four points in 1976 and beat him. He trailed eighteen-year incumbent senator and one-time presidential hopeful Birch Bayh by forty points in 1980 and beat him. He won reelection in 1986 by the widest margin in the history of Indiana (he was not, however, running against Franklin Delano Roosevelt). Although he is a poor public speaker, he debated Roush five times and Bayh once, and won each time, largely because they refused to take him seriously. For a guy who can't put two sentences together, he manages.

———

On the other side of the ledger, there have been many, many lapses, faux pas, misstatements, and verbal gaffes since Quayle became vice president. It is true that he once said:

Hawaii has always been a very pivotal role in the Pacific. It is in the Pacific. It is part of the United States that is an island that is right here.

It is true that he once told a gathering of Samoans:

You all look like happy campers to me. Happy campers you are, happy campers you have been, and, as far as I'm concerned, happy campers you will always be.

It is also true that he once told guests at a United Negro College Fund luncheon:

And you take the UNCF model that what a waste it is to lose one's mind, or not to have a mind is being very wasteful. How true that is.

This remark has been included in the latest edition of *Bartlett's Familiar Quotations.*

It is true that Quayle pronounced Pago Pago "Pogo Pogo," true that he eulogized the victims of the 1989 San Francisco earthquake by saying: "The loss of life will be irreplaceable." It is true that he was known in the Senate as "Florida's third senator" because of his passion for golf; that he once proposed a tax break for visiting foreign golf pros; that he once protested a Democratic moratorium on anti-satellite-weapons testing because these weapons had been instrumental in helping us defeat the Russians in Tom Clancy's novel *Red Storm Rising.*

But he said and did most of these things in the early months of his vice presidency when he was still a hopeless basket case, before Bill Kristol and the boys lent him Plato and Machiavelli, and Francis Fukayama. Moreover, nothing in *Red Storm Rising* is anywhere near as insane as the stuff in his wife's book, *Embrace the Serpent.* And anyway, Hawaii *is* an island in the Pacific, and, as far as I'm concerned, Samoans *are* happy campers, *have been* happy campers, and *will continue* to be happy campers for time immemorial. If anyone has heard otherwise, please let the rest of us know before we start planning our summer vacations.

One other thing: The *next* time Dan Quayle loses an election will be the *first* time he loses an election.

XVI

HANDICAPPING QUAYLE

If he has any handicap, it is his lack of sophistication.

—Richard Nixon's faculty adviser in a note
accompanying his application to law school

"Had my husband been elected to the highest office in the land in 1988," wrote Kitty Dukakis in her 1990 autobiography, *Now You Know,* "it could have been very dangerous for me. I was addicted to alcohol."

Had Kitty Dukakis's husband been elected to the highest office in the land in 1988, it could have been very dangerous for *all* of us: We would all have been addicted to alcohol. Which just goes to show that we are not taking this stuff very seriously. For the past four years, as we sit here locked in dread terror of the moment that Dan Quayle takes over, we ignore how much worse things could have been. Imagine Kitty Dukakis and Boris Yeltsin breaking into the medicine cabinet at three in the morning after the Mateus rosé is all gone, both of them knowing the access codes to those little black attaché cases. Think about it.

American history is God's way of saying: Next time, read your Santayana more carefully. Yet, even though we must be chided for ignoring the overused but underheeded words, "Those who cannot remember the past are condemned to repeat it," there *have* been mitigating circumstances. Who wants to remember a past that includes George Wallace, Joe McCarthy, and Herbert Hoover? Looking on the bright side, it's nice to know that no matter how bad things get, they were at least as bad a half-dozen times in the past. Before the corrupt

Harding, there was the corrupt Grant; before the dithering Carter, the dithering Hoover; before the useless, fatuous Coolidge, the useless, fatuous Hayes, the useless, fatuous Harrison, the useless, fatuous Buchanan, etc., etc.

This is equally true of the vice presidency; before the hopelessly unqualified Dan Quayle, there was the completely unqualified Spiro Agnew and the ludicrously unqualified Henry Wallace, etc. Europeans and other thoughtful people sit and marvel at our system, wondering how to size up a country that ridicules a Dan Quayle but lionizes a Geraldine Ferraro, the textbook political hack, complete with matching accessories—a sleazeball husband and a drug-dealing son. Is it possible to argue that the names Spiro Agnew, Thomas Eagleton, or William Miller inspire more confidence than the name Dan Quayle? How can a people be taken seriously who flirt with the idea of entrusting their destiny to a socialist from South Dakota and a man named Sargent?

No, it is intellectually dishonest for people to keep harping that with Dan Quayle American public life has finally hit rock bottom. American political life has hit rock bottom dozens of times before. In a sense, having bad vice presidents serves as a helpful reminder that we all have to die, and that when we die we'll probably leave behind a mess. As P. J. O'Rourke remarked in *Republican Party Reptile:* "America was founded on danger. How many lifeboat drills were held on the *Mayflower?* Where were the smoke detectors in the Lincoln Family cabin? Who checked to see whether Indian war paint was made with Red Dye No. 2? . . . America is a dangerous country. Safety has no place here."

Were Dan Quayle to assume office sometime between now and 1996, the common wisdom is that he would have a tough time running the country because he would face a Democrat-dominated Congress and a bunch of Republican adversaries for the 1996 nomination who would be only too happy to see him caricatured as an idiot by Jay Leno. He would be very dependent on his philosopher-king buddies like Bill Kristol, and they would have to come up with much better issues to run on than tort reform and Murphy Brown's pernicious influence on American motherhood. His predicament would immediately invite comparisons with all the other second- and third-rate vice presidents who took office upon the death of the president, but would probably not invite comparisons with all of our third- and fourth-rate presidents. That's too bad, because it is these comparisons that are most relevant, most instructive, and, in a sense, most reassuring.

The first comparison is with Franklin Pierce, elected in 1852. Pierce came along at a time when many of the seminal figures in nineteenth-century politics were dead. Like Quayle, he was the youngest senator of his era. (He was thirty-two when first elected; Quayle was thirty-three.)

Like Quayle he had an odd, unpleasant wife, and a son named Benjamin. Like Quayle, he had a military stain on his record; he was accused of having fainted during the Mexican War (his foes even published a book called *The Military Services of General Pierce* during the campaign; it was one-inch high and a half-inch thick). He was selected on the forty-ninth ballot at the 1852 convention because he was less hated than anyone else, because it was getting kind of late, and because everyone was drunk.

Pierce was a dreadful president who served just one term and was then sent packing by his own party. He is one of only two presidents to have ever been arrested while in office (Grant, of course, was the other), apprehended after trampling an old woman while riding his horse, probably after having a snootful. "There's nothing left to do but get drunk," he said when asked what he would do after being president, and, in fact, he did drink himself to death. Dan Quayle would have a hard time being a worse president than Franklin Pierce. Anyone would.

Quayle would also have a hard time being a worse president than Warren Harding. Harding, who presided over the second most corrupt administration in history, was a card-playing lush who was totally in the back pocket of crooked businessmen. A colossal nonentity, he was chosen by his party because no one could dig up anything dirty on him, because it was getting late, and because everyone was drunk.

As with Franklin Pierce, Quayle's resemblance to Warren Harding is quite stunning. Harding was a spectacularly chipper fellow, with beautiful, striking eyes, who had previously worked in the newspaper business as a publisher. A bit on the dumb side, he once expressed his dismay that he could not find a particular book that would provide him with all the answers to his political problems. (Lamentably, he did not have Bill

Kristol to lend him Plato or Machiavelli or Francis Fukayama). "His mind was vague and fuzzy," wrote Frederick Lewis Allen in *Only Yesterday*. "Its quality was revealed in the clogged style of his public addresses, in his choice of turgid and maladroit language . . . and in his frequent attacks of suffix trouble."

Yes, like Quayle, Harding was mystified by the secret workings of the English language. H. L. Mencken said of his speeches: "It reminds me of a string of wet sponges, it reminds me of tattered washing on the line; it reminds me of stale bean soup, of college yells, of dogs barking idiotically through endless nights. It is so bad that a sort of grandeur creeps into it. It drags itself out of a dark abysm (I was about to write abcess!) of pish, and crawls insanely up the topmost pinnacle of posh. It is rumble and bumble, it is flap and doodle. It is balder and dash."

All sorts of people from Harding's administration went to jail; he himself succumbed to a heart attack brought on by the pressure of being a national disgrace, though some suspect that his wife murdered him. Quayle would have a hard time being a worse president than Harding. Anyone would.

There are many other awful presidents Quayle resembles whom he would have a hard time being worse than. Benjamin Harrison was a hack lawyer from the Hoosier state with a strange wife and a famous grandfather (William Henry Harrison). Before taking office, John Tyler was thought to be a simpleton, after which he was thought to be, well, a simpleton. Millard Fillmore grew up in a house that only had one book, just slightly more than the Quayle household.

There are also strong parallels between Dan Quayle and Ulysses S. Grant (excepting, of course, the National Guard business). After two scandal-plagued terms, Grant's handlers sent him on an image-enhancing tour of the Continent, where he got to meet the crowned heads of Europe. According to Thomas C. Reeves, author of *Gentleman Boss: The Life of Chester A. Arthur*, Grant's Republican supporters were "convinced that he had been broadened and deepened by his sojourn, that he had absorbed knowledge and insight, and was at last prepared to become the tower of enlightened statesmanship he had promised to be in 1868. After all, it was said, he had talked with kings and skilled diplomats, he had studied a variety of political systems, and had scrutinized mankind's highest cultural achievements."

But, Reeves laments, "such enchantment was fabricated out of hope." Grant was an idiot. He spent his whole time in Europe complaining about having to look at too many cathedrals, paintings, sculptures, and museums. One friend in Rome took him to see a statue of Marcus Aurelius because, as he remarked later, "I thought he would like the horse." Grant's most memorable comment throughout the trip was that Venice would be vastly improved if the streets were drained. Despite the best efforts of his handlers, the truth could not be withheld from the public. The guy was a dunce.

This did not automatically disqualify him from serving a third term as president of the United States. By the time campaign season got underway in 1879, Grant was, in Reeves's words, "probably the most popular man in the country." As Harry Truman later wrote: "Ulysses Simpson Grant's period in office seems to prove the theory that we can coast along for eight years without a President."

For a while there in the summer of 1880, it looked like Grant might get the nomination again. But then, after much bickering among supporters of Grant, whose administration had been infested with crooks, and supporters of James G. Blaine, who was a crook, the convention settled on James Garfield, who was accused of being a crook. Just to make sure there were enough alleged crooks on the ticket—for geographical and ethical balance—the convention chose the crooked Chester Arthur, whose patron, the crook Roscoe Conkling, was the mortal enemy of Blaine. People who were not crooked (five milkmaids in Delaware and a couple of Shaker housewives from Hancock, Massachusetts) were outraged when Arthur was nominated to be vice president, but the frenzy passed quickly, because, as one wit smirked, "There is no place in which his powers of mischief will be as small as in the vice presidency."

Chester Arthur was the Alfonse D'Amato of his time, a sleazeball who was clever enough to surround himself with other, bigger sleazeballs. He had enriched himself at the taxpayers' expense while serving as collector of New York's customhouse, the highest office he ever held before being elected vice president. (There were rumors that he was born in Canada, future home of the Vancouver and Calgary Stock Exchanges, which would explain his dishonesty.)

In 1877, he was removed from his post, charged with corruption, by order of Rutherford B. Hayes, no St. Francis of Assisi himself.

Although many people were outraged when Arthur, who had never been elected to public office in his life, was chosen as Garfield's running mate, Republican apologists said: (1) Don't worry, the vice presidency isn't important; (2) Garfield is only forty-eight; it isn't like he's going to die in office or anything. Hey, lighten up.

Instead, just six months into his administration, Garfield was shot by an Arthur supporter named Charles Guiteau. (Guiteau joins a long list of presidential assassins or would-be assassins with weird names—John Wilkes Booth, Leon Czolgosz, Lee Harvey Oswald, Squeaky Fromme; Arthur joins a long list of presidents suspected of having conspired in the murder of their predecessors.)

Although Chester Arthur was basically a scoundrel who never belonged anywhere near the White House, he was not an abysmal president. He was just another nobody. "Surely no more lonely and pathetic figure was ever seen assuming the powers of government," said Secretary of War Elihu Root in 1899 when a statue was erected in Arthur's honor. Another commentator noted that no one ever entered the White House as "profoundly and widely mistrusted" and no one had left the office as widely respected. This is not quite true; at the end of his four years in office, Arthur was told by his own party, the Republicans, to get out and stay out.

Some historians believe that Arthur's greatest mistake was not becoming the mountebank everyone expected him to become, in which case he would have at least gone down in history as the worst president the country ever had. As Albert Weinberg put it: "Had Arthur only fulfilled the sensational pessimism of his initial critics—that is, proved a bad president—he doubtless would have had greater fame." Whoever Albert Weinberg is.

This leads us to a subject of such immense unpleasantness that I have deliberately put off discussing for more than fifteen chapters. No, I am not talking about Dwight D. Eisenhower, the bland, affable sort who golfed away his eight years in office. Parallels with Quayle are tenuous at best, for although both men can fairly be described as intellectual superflyweights, Ike sort of had a resumé and a reputation when he took office; he had won the Second World War with the help of guys like Bob Dole and George Bush back when these things still mattered. He was also one of the most beloved men in U.S. history, a fact often attributed to the fact that he wasn't a lawyer, and he wasn't a politician.

Nor are tantalizing comparisons with Ronald Reagan appropriate. Even the roughly 40 percent of the American people who despise the Great Communicator must admit that Reagan grew up in the school of hard knocks, and had a genuine career before entering politics: first as a sportscaster, and then as an actor who was not nearly as bad as people believe. Reagan has extraordinary personal charisma (imperceptible to those who dislike him), is a talented speaker, and held a real job before entering the White House—governor of California. Except for the fact that he is a handsome, dumb conservative who came from a midwestern state beginning with *I*, went to a nothing college, never fired a shot in anger, and was surrounded by advisers who thought they were smarter than he was, and is married to a mean-spirited spendthrift everybody hates who ended up writing an incredibly stupid book, Reagan has nothing in common with Quayle.

No, it is not Eisenhower or Reagan that we will be discussing here, but a far more macabre figure from recent American history. Yes, it is now time to lock horns with the most obvious American political figure with whom Dan Quayle can be compared: Tricky Dick.

In many ways, Dan Quayle is simply a dumber, nicer version of Richard Nixon. Both men got on the GOP ticket to keep the Republican right happy. Both men are scorned by intellectuals. Both men are political Houdinis, surviving one death-defying feat after the other. During his two terms as Ike's veep, Nixon was a figure of mirth, the object of public derision, an impotent clown the press poked fun at for saying that he was dropping by the White House "to see if there are any loose ends I can take care of." Ike treated him with contempt throughout his two terms, having nothing to do with him socially; Garry Wills says that when Nixon was elected president in 1968, he had trouble finding his way around the White House. When asked during the 1960 campaign to name a single important policy decision that Nixon had helped him make, Ike sneered, "If you gave me a week I might think of one." And Ike was a nice guy.

One thing Nixon was good at was climbing out of the grave. He was dead in 1952, when Eisenhower wanted him off the ticket after accusations that Nixon was living high on the hog from a secret businessmen's fund. But Nixon gave the Checkers speech and he survived. He was dead in 1956 when Eisenhower wanted him off the ticket. But Nixon got the boys in the back room to read Eisenhower the riot act, and he survived. Nixon was dead in the late 1950s until he got into a debate with Nikita Khrushchev in a Moscow kitchen; dead in 1960 after his makeup ran in his first debate against JFK; dead after his 1962 gubernatorial loss to Pat Brown; and has been listed as dead numerous times since Watergate. But he has always gotten up off the tarmac.

"There were many attempts to 'dump Nixon' over the years," writes Wills in *Nixon Agonistes,* "but he would not bow out gracefully, leave well enough alone, disappear. That gaucheness of a man lingering on when he is no longer wanted becomes, at a certain point, the crazy proof of his importance. He survived."

Stephen Ambrose knows as much about Richard Nixon as any man alive. The director of the Eisenhower Center at the University of New Orleans, he is the author of a three-volume biography of the only president ever forced to resign. And Ambrose doesn't think that drawing comparisons between Nixon and Quayle is an entirely fruitless exercise.

"There is a very strong parallel in the way their vice presidential careers started," says Ambrose. "There were a lot of calls to dump Nixon; Quayle's case is nowhere near as dramatic as Nixon's was when he made the Checkers speech."

Here, Ambrose makes an interesting point. Many writers, Wills among them, view the Checkers speech as a masterpiece that showed Nixon at his Machiavellian best, wheedling his way into the bosom of his countrymen by sniveling that the only gift his family had ever accepted from political supporters was a little dog named Checkers. But Ambrose does not view the Checkers speech as a stroke of genius.

"The Checkers speech probably hurt him as much as it helped him, because a lot of people thought: *This is pure corn.* It exacerbated the already very negative view of him that a lot of people had. Checkers has become a standing joke in American political humor; it's part of American folklore. And Nixon never shed that image. Quayle handled his difficulties more adroitly. He does not appear to have rubbed more salt into the wound."

Ambrose also finds strong parallels in the careers of the two men in their ability to survive attempts to dump them from the ticket the second time around.

"There was a very strong movement to dump Nixon in '56," says the historian. "Ike *did* want to get rid of him in the worst way. But the Republican establishment—the congressmen, the governors, the mayors, the party officials—came back to him and said, 'You are not going to get rid of this guy. He has been the most loyal vice president in history, and after all that Nixon has done for you, you just can't do it.' "

Sound familiar?

Of course, Ambrose stresses that there are many important differences between the two men. "Nixon was already a national figure in 1952, because of the '46 and '48 campaigns, but primarily because of Alger Hiss," says Ambrose. "He had become unprecedently well known as a freshman congressman, and Quayle had not. Quayle became a national figure after the 1988 campaign. But both men seem to have known their way around the Republican party pretty well. Nixon was unopposed in 1948, so he went on a national speaking campaign, beginning that process of piling up chits, which he's always done, which he's still doing today. My impression is that Quayle is pretty good at that too. I know he's a good fund-raiser."

Actually, the most difficult thing about being Dan Quayle is that the vice president has grown up almost entirely in public. There is no Quayle mythology; everything we will ever know about him we already know. This is a great disadvantage for a politician. Richard Johnson, vice president under Martin Van Buren, milked the claim that he had slain the mighty Indian warrior Tecumseh for all it was worth politically; LBJ cooked up engaging if untrue stories about his military service; it now appears that JFK's war-hero stature was almost entirely manufactured by Camelot Industries. Ronald Reagan believed that he had helped liberate Jewish prisoners at a Nazi death camp, and many of his supporters may have believed the same thing. Many of his supporters may have believed that they were there with him. But everything Quayle has done he has done right out there in public. And he hasn't done a whole lot.

Still, he has certain things going for him. Nixon, LBJ, and Bush all served in the shadow of popular, powerful presidents. But George Bush himself casts no shadow. Quayle is held in contempt by Democrats, but he is not hated and feared the way Spiro Agnew was. And one great thing he has in his favor is that he lives in a country where people seem to go out of their way to hand over power to bizarre presidents.

"It always amazes me what sort of people become president of the United States," says Alan Ehrenhalt, author of *The United States of Ambition.* "In 1920, Harry Truman was a thirty-six-year-old man who was running a failing men's store in Kansas City. Can you imagine what his reaction would have been if you had walked up to him and said, 'In twenty-five years, you're going to be president of the United States'? Can you imagine? I'm sure that when he was very old, Truman must have found himself sitting out there on the porch saying, 'Did that really happen? Was that really me? Was I really president of the United States?' "

Also working in Quayle's favor is that he has been, and will continue to be, the beneficiary of a peculiar form of upward intellectual paternalism. As Wills said of Nixon a generation ago: "Those who support him . . . make virtues of every deficiency; he will not feed the people on movie-star dreams, as Jack and Jackie did. If Nixon is lacking in stature and all too human, that will teach the country that it must be great on its own, not vicariously, not leaning on its ruler's strength. A great country will be great no matter who comes and goes in the White House."

For at least eighteen months, certain members of the press have been preparing the public for the moment they first hear the words "President Quayle." At first, it was the right that did the heavy lifting. In 1991, William F. Buckley wrote an enthusiastic revisionist piece, noting that Nixon was only thirty-nine when he became veep (Quayle was forty-one), "but they both had the same capacity to grow." Said Buckley: "The public finds it hard to think of any non-president as President—until it actually happens. On a Wednesday morning early in November 1960, a hundred reporters who had treated their subject like a brother, in some cases a kid brother, were waiting for him to come into the large room at Hyannis Port. Suddenly he entered, and overnight he had become the President-elect. They all stood up. And they'll do that for Quayle, should it happen to him."

In an odd way, that's just how a number of left-wing commentators look at the Quayle situation. Some think the process of standing up for the president-to-be has already occurred. In April 1990, Christopher Hitchens wrote an article in *Harper's* entitled "The Repackaging of Dan Quayle," which was perhaps the first serious attempt to broach the subject of a Quayle presidency. (Hitchens even said that for a guy who's grown up surrounded by as many screwballs as Quayle has—Dad, Mom, Marilyn, the Tucker clan—the vice president is surprisingly "calm and reflective.") Today, Hitchens feels that the "he's-grown-in-office" efforts of Broder and Woodward have gone a long way toward laying straight the path for Quayle in 1996.

"There is a consensus in Washington that it is vaguely unacceptable that a person with a strong actuarial sense of becoming president should be a clown," says Hitchens. "It's just no good if everybody thinks that ipso facto Quayle must be a fool. So the spin physicians and the masters of consensus will be able to narrow the gap between what he really is and what they want us all to think he is."

It should be borne in mind that, with the exception of a few nice words by Fred Barnes here and there in 1989 and 1990, plus the statutory *Saturday Evening Post* puff pieces, Quayle was not taken seriously by the media until the spring of 1991. Then, suddenly as if on cue, *The New York Times* columnist A. M. Rosenthal said he was doing a good job; *Time* logged in with some kudos about his diplomatic skills; and the *Los Angeles Times* and the *Washington Post* abruptly began treating him with civility. Surveying this turnabout for *The Columbia Journalism Review* in October 1991, William Boot remarked: "Many Washington journalists revere power. They understand that it is the ultimate commodity in this city, and have learned by long experience that power transforms what it touches. Thus, anyone who has a lot of power, or is close to having it, simply cannot be dull-witted; if they were, how could they ever have gotten as far as they did? Once many reporters accepted the reality that Quayle was, indeed, a heartbeat away from the presidency (and it took Bush's own heartbeat scare to drive this point home) they could not help but observe the president in a new light. They could not help but discover new dimensions in the man."

Shortly thereafter, the Broder-Woodward *hommage à* Quayle appeared, and the rehabilitation of the man was in high gear. "They seemed to treat his ability to eat with a fork and walk upright as a refutation of everything that had been said about him," hisses Rick Hertzberg, former editor of *The New Republic,* who once asked his readers: "How long can a great nation afford to have silly leaders?"

"Dog bites man *is* the story," says Victor Navasky, editor of *The Nation.* "But even with a person as shallow as Quayle, there is a demonization that is a natural part of the process. The establishment media view it as one of their functions to provide these internal correctives."

The establishment media also gets a bit nervous about covering a story—DAN QUAYLE IS A MORON—that they, with considerable assistance from Dan Quayle, created. "There is an ambivalence in our press about covering a story when the press is part of the story," says Susan Estrich, who managed Mike Dukakis's unsuccessful presidential campaign in 1988. "The press does a much better job covering eastern Europe than it does covering Washington."

Hitchens also feels that the press worries so much about the unfairness charge that they fail to adequately report the news. Thus, journalists will avoid drawing the seemingly unavoidable conclusion from George Bush's "train-wreck" sentences that the man speaking them is a piffle-skulled mushmouth. No, Bush's grammatical *Lusitania*s must be the result of fatigue, flu, Halcion. Says Hitchens, "People hear Bush talk like an idiot, but they say to themselves, 'That can't be true, because he's the president.' "

Even though Hitchens says that Quayle looks like "the tailor's dummy," is "intellectually tenth rate," and is "a sort of global village idiot," he still thinks Quayle has a number of things going for him. He is certainly no dumber than Reagan, and probably no dumber than Joe Biden or Jesse Jackson. Like Nixon, he has been successful in accumulating IOUs inside the party. Like Nixon and Reagan, he can run against the media, which, he believes, will fall all over itself in an effort to be fair. A sign of that effort to be fair are articles such as the Woodward-Broder series, which went out of their way to avoid mentioning Quayle's deficient intellect, his odd delivery, his serious problems with the English language.

Hitchens also feels that at a certain point Republicans of all stripes will have so much invested in a Quayle candidacy that the barbs about his intellect will be dismissed as liberal hyperbole. "People were unwilling to believe things about Iran-Contra because they had invested a great deal of themselves in Ronald Reagan. At a certain point, they will hear Quayle being attacked and they'll say, 'Excuse me, but that's my vice president you're talking about.'"

Martin Anderson, chief domestic policy adviser during Reagan's first term, does not share Hitchens's low opinion of the veep. He feels that Quayle has a very good chance of winning in 1996, provided he can survive the primaries.

"If you look at where he's been on a lot of issues, you have to be impressed," says Anderson. "He opposed Bush's cave-in on taxes in 1990. He supported the Persian Gulf War. He's been in the leadership on Star Wars. Those are the positions that matter to Republicans. It's always the economy and national security; it's not crime, it's not gun control, it's not abortion. The economy and national security are what matter to Republicans."

Anderson also argues that Pat Buchanan's insurgency in the early months of 1992 pulled the Republican party to the right—but he is convinced that this benefits Quayle more than Buchanan.

"Quayle is a sitting vice president and a conservative, who has the support of the Republican establishment. When a guy has been elected a senator or a governor, and then has been reelected senator or governor, you should never underestimate him. The same thing about calling someone a dummy. My attitude when people say that stuff is, 'Hey, you go out and do it.' Back in 1975, when I said I was going to work for Ronald Reagan I had people hooting and hollering at me. It didn't matter to them that he'd been governor."

"I still think that he's the odds-on favorite in 1996, and I'm a lifelong yellow-dog Democrat," says Ken DeCell, a senior editor at the *Washingtonian* and co-author, with Allan J. Lichtman, of an intriguing book called *The 13 Keys to the Presidency*. In it, the authors argue that there are thirteen separate factors that determine who wins the presidency, only one of which can be controlled by the challenger. Dismissing the widely held belief that the Willie Horton ads played a major role in the 1988 election, DeCell and Lichtman contend that presidential campaigns are largely meaningless, that the factors determining who wins or loses are decided at least six months before the election. DeCell likes to point out that at a time when most polls showed

Dukakis comfortably ahead of Bush in 1988, he and his partner were already declaring Bush the winner.

The "keys"—too numerous and too complex to explain here—suggest that if the economy is in reasonably good condition in 1996, and if the administration has not been embroiled in any scandals, social upheaval, or disastrous foreign wars, Dan Quayle will have an extremely good shot at the White House, despite his "slight political stature." And with each passing day, DeCell is less and less sure how slight that stature is.

"Dan Quayle draws huge crowds, he raises a lot of money, and he's very ambitious," says DeCell. "He had the audacity to run for the House at the age of twenty-nine, for the Senate at the age of thirty-three, and for the vice presidency at the age of forty-one. That doesn't happen in the ether. There is real ambition there, and there is a real base."

DeCell continues, "Dan Quayle has been out there doing a yeoman job. Name anybody you want—Buchanan, Baker, Gramm, Bennett—none of these guys have laid the groundwork for 1996. The worst thing that Quayle has against him is George Bush's second term." Noting that Quayle is extremely popular with state chairmen, and that Jack Kennedy and Richard Nixon both campaigned for the vice presidency early in their careers, DeCell says, "Dan Quayle is a lot like Jack Kennedy. Ambitionwise, they're identical. This is a guy who has run early, he has run often, and he has won."

Also in Quayle's favor is the fact that he is a relatively congenial person who does not hold grudges, a big advantage in a country that tends to punish candidates perceived as being nasty (Bob Dole, Lyndon Johnson, John Connally) or arrogant (Alexander Haig, Nelson Rockefeller). Newt Gingrich is smart, but he's also mean and arrogant. Bill Bennett is smart, but he's mean and arrogant. Phil Gramm is smart, but he's really mean and really arrogant. Quayle is not in a league with these men intellectually, but he's a genuinely nice person. Sunniness counts.

Could he get the nomination against this crew? Jacob Weisberg, of *The New Republic*, feels that Quayle would have a hard time getting through the primaries, but might be aided by the GOP loyalty issue.

"There are still a lot of Republican National Committee types who believe in being rewarded for service and waiting your turn to get your shot at it," says Weisberg.

"Republicans are royalists," adds Richard Brookhiser of *National Review*. "That's why Bush won it. Republicans believe that these are the people who put in their time, and took the piano lessons, and now it's their turn. That's why they supported Richard Nixon."

Brookhiser sees much of this from a purely cultural perspective. In *The Way of the Wasp: How It Made America and How It Can Save It . . . So to Speak,*" he argues that "the WASP character is the American character. It is the mold, the template, the archetype, the set of axes along which the crystal has grown." He adds: "For a decade—for a century, in some cases—Americans have been turning away from WASP ways of thinking and behaving, with disastrous results."

Brookhiser says that the six basic WASP traits are conscience, antisensuality, use, industry, success, and civic-mindedness. He does not include ingenuity, or, for that matter, intelligence in his list, these not being traditional WASP values. And of these six vital traits, Dan Quayle possesses four and a half. Moreover, in Quayle's defense, Brookhiser stresses that intellectuals usually make rotten politicians. He further notes that the Republic has often been served well by dumb aristocrats such as Averell Harriman. And he cautions against confusing the WASP *refusal* to cerebrate with an *inability* to cerebrate.

"Wasps only think when they have to," he says. "They're not like Germans in Thomas Mann's novels, who are thinking all the time—and look what happened to Germany. They do all their thinking in bursts. And when they do, they think really well. Then the crisis is over, and they go back to dealing with normal things: making the nut, etc." ("Making the nut" means "bringing home the bacon" in WASP.)

Quayle himself has always recognized that election results have less to do with the talents of the candidates than with the values they share with the electorate. As he told an Ellis Island audience in a September 5, 1988, speech: "Our elections are also about values—our values—and they are fundamentally about the kind of leadership which promotes those values. The people of America want to know the kinds of values that underscore our beliefs, and George Bush and I proudly, unapologetically, embrace the values embodied in the Pledge of Allegiance. To us, they are not hokey, or cornball, or passé."

But is that cultural bond with one segment of the nation enough to get him elected on his own merits? The verdicts are mixed.

"I still have enough confidence in my fellow Americans to believe that will not happen," says Michael Kinsley of *Crossfire* and *The New Republic.* "Quayle is slightly more mediocre than most people in the United States Senate, but he is significantly more mediocre than most people who run for president. But if you took all of the five billion people in the world and had to decide which one has the best chance of being the next president of the United States, he is certainly one of those people."

Says Navasky, "Of course he could be elected. Richard Nixon had a far worse reputation than Quayle had when he was vice president, after the Helen Gahagan Douglas campaign, after the loan scandal, after the Checkers speech, and he survived." Navasky says the biggest question is whether Americans would prefer a "dumb conservative" like Quayle or a "brilliant reactionary" like Bennett or Buchanan.

Says Rich Vigilante, former fellow at The Manhattan Institute, "I think that a lot of inside-the-Beltway conservatives are thinking that Quayle will be president. Quayle has the best people; Kristol is incredibly smart and quite principled. And Quayle is not going to spend his second term as a joke. Issues get tired; no one is going to bring it up. People like him better; he's four years older. He's not going to have to spend the next four years proving that he's qualified to be vice president."

Alan Abelson, editor of *Barron's,* has always felt that Quayle has a shot at the highest office, if only because of the nature of the vice presidency.

"Quayle is like that old brown armchair in the corner," says Abelson. "At first, you want to throw it out. But the longer it sits there, the more you get used to it. The more it seems to belong there."

"Old furniture is just what Quayle needs to be," counters Vigilante. "Not because old furniture is such a great thing, but because old furniture is the opposite of what he came in as."

Not all conservatives would welcome a Quayle presidency. Warren Rudman, the New Hampshire senator who ditched his job out of frustration with the political process, once said that Quayle lacked the "moral authority" needed to run the country. Senator Dan Coats, the man who took Quayle's seat in 1988, has described his fellow Hoosier as "out of it." Many neoconservatives view Quayle, the nation's most influential conservative, as another wasted opportunity for the right.

One neocon writer starts off with the generic rationalization—"It's not so important who he is but who he appoints"—but then admits, "This guy doesn't have it in him to be a mensch; he's not going to grow. He's good in small circles; he's not a complete idiot, but he has no capacity for statesmanship. He belongs to some kind of ruling class, but he just doesn't get it; a normal person would have figured it out by now. The guy just kind of lacks something. It's such a depressing subject; the number of lies you have to live with just grows astronomically."

Adds conservative theorist George Gilder, "I'll say what I said in 1988: At least he's better than Bush. But I have an intuition that he's not quite a conservative, just the way Bush was too plush. Bush has never associated with conservatives in real life. His closest friend is Nicholas Brady, who's right up there with William Kuntsler in my book. Nicholas Brady is an upper-class wimp with a feminist wife and feminist daughters, and there isn't anything conservative about any of them. Quayle is a little like that: Waspy upper class. Totally unreliable politically. I don't trust them across the street politically."

John O'Sullivan, editor of *National Review*, says that he still thinks it "very unlikely" that Quayle will ever be elected president. Were Quayle to run in 1996, O'Sullivan remarks, "We would look kindly on a Quayle candidacy, but I doubt that we would support it in the primaries.

"Our view has never changed," he elaborates. "He's better than his media picture: He's bright, but not brilliant, and he's surrounded himself with good people. But I also think that he does not have the quality of authority. Bill Bennett instills confidence in his audiences. Dick Cheney knows how to stand up to the opposition. Bennett looks like a stevedore, only slightly out of kilter. That's very valuable in a Republican." But in O'Sullivan's view, Quayle does not have that aura of authority and toughness. "It's a quality of personality quite unrelated to class or background," he says. "Either you have it or you don't."

Wladyslaw Pleszczynski, managing editor of *The American Spectator*, doesn't think he has it.

"Quayle would never be in a position to be the conservative standard bearer, and moderates already think that he's too conservative," he says. "He's always going to let you down and disappoint you. He doesn't have the spine. What makes Bennett and Buchanan effective is that right away you get a sense that a mind is at work. But with Quayle, there's no way he can communicate any kind of authenticity to the voting public." He adds, "The best people don't seem to be going into politics anymore. It's like NBA expansion; we're starting to get CBA politicians. He plays the game well enough, but the level of competition has fallen."

Rick Hertzberg shares Pleszczynski's doubts about the unlikelihood of a Quayle presidency. Well . . . sort of.

"What I can't believe is that the rest of the Republican party is just going to sit around and let him get the nomination," says Hertzberg. "Bush was the kind of grown-up, Establishment figure that Gramm and Kemp weren't going to mess with. But Quayle isn't like that."

Still, he says, "It's conceivable that he could be nominated. Just demographically, you'd have to say that he's capable of being elected. All it would take would be a really bad Democratic candidate."

Now, where would we get one of those?

X V I I

ROAD TRIP

Q: What's the difference between Dan Quayle and Jane Fonda?

A: Jane Fonda went to Vietnam.

The people who own the country ought to govern it.

— Famous remark BY JOHN JAY that is usually
taken woefully out of context, as it is here

Journalists, some of them well-meaning Canadians like Robert MacNeil and Peter Jennings, are forever telling the American public that gutter journalism and negative political advertising have gotten completely out of hand, and are somehow a tawdry departure from gallant American traditions. Balderdash. The idea that negative ads are new or unseemly is pure balderdash that these guys learned from Bill Moyers and Fred Friendly and Walter Cronkite. All the expression "negative campaigning" means is accusing your opponent of doing things that he wishes he hadn't done *then* and doesn't want to talk about *now*. Grover Cleveland was accused of fathering a bastard. He *did* father a bastard. Barry Goldwater was accused of not playing with a full deck. Well? Michael Dukakis was accused of authorizing a prison furlough program that allowed a convicted murderer to obtain a weekend pass so he could go out and rape a harmless old woman and beat up her husband. He *did* authorize a furlough program that allowed a convicted murderer to go out and rape a harmless old woman and beat up her husband.

When John Quincy Adams ran against Andrew Jackson in 1828, his supporters accused Old Hickory of being a murderer, an adulterer, and a sleazeball. It was horribly tasteless to say these things in public, but none of them was untrue. Jackson is known to have killed at least one man in the hundred duels he supposedly fought. (Most of them had something to do with nasty comments about his wife; good thing Quayle's no duelist.) He was, technically, a bigamist; he did steal another man's wife; and he did have sleazy business associates: Yes, the allegations killed his wife, and ruined his life, but nobody ever said life was fair.

The same is true of the media's treatment of our presidents and vice presidents throughout American history. Washington was treated like scum by the press. Adams was called "blind, crippled, and toothless." Lincoln was vilified in the most extravagantly simian terms. Andrew Johnson was called " a low sot" who "defiled our council chamber with the spewings of a drunken boor." Henry Adams said that the life of Ulysses S. Grant proved that Charles Darwin's theory of evolution was completely wrong. Nastiness in the news media is as American as apple pie.

I raise these issues because the whole time I was writing this book I knew that I would eventually have to get down into the gutter, too. No, I am not talking about the unfounded rumors that surfaced a few weeks after Bush picked Quayle as his running mate that the Humble Hoosier had committed plagiarism while an undergraduate at DePauw University. I am not even talking about the Paula Parkinson incident; I have always accepted Quayle's explanation that when he went on that golfing weekend with two other congressmen and a lobbyist who later posed nude for *Playboy*, he slept in another room, and that it was all very innocent. And I have always accepted Marilyn Quayle's spirited defense of her husband, who deflated the rumors by saying, "Anybody who knows Dan Quayle knows he would rather play golf than have sex any day."

Still, in the interests of journalistic thoroughness, I decided to see if other wives, placed in a similar situation, would be so absolving. I asked my wife if she would mind if I went to Florida for the weekend and stayed in a vacation house with two buddies and a gorgeous, unmarried female, provided I slept on the couch in the living room. I don't know any gorgeous Washington lobbyists who have posed, or will one day pose, nude for *Playboy*, and I'm not much of a golfer, so I asked if I could go on a weekend basketball junket with two friends and a positively gorgeous New York publicist I know.

"Sure," my wife said, barely looking up. "Anybody who knows you knows you would rather play basketball than have sex any day."

No, what I'm really talking about when I use the word "gutter" are the recurrent charges that Quayle used to buy marijuana from an Indianapolis drug dealer named Brett Kimberlin in the early 1970s, and that during his first Senate term Quayle was investigated by the Drug Enforcement Agency.

Less than two weeks before the election, Kimberlin, who went by the moniker "The Speedway Bomber" because he had been convicted of planting bombs near the site of the Indianapolis 500 racetrack, began making collect phone calls to reporters from his home at a prison in El Reno, Oklahoma. Kimberlin, a wayward Hoosier doing fifty-one years in federal prison for various malfeasances, said that he had met Quayle at an Indiana University frat party in 1971, and that for the next eighteen months, Quayle would come to a fast-food outlet in Indianapolis to buy dope. According to *The New Republic*, Kimberlin said that he had given Quayle an ounce of Afghan hashish as a wedding present in 1972.

In the beginning, Kimberlin did not want to go into too many details; he was up for a review by his parole board and probably realized that spreading drug rumors about a man on the verge of being elected vice president of the United States was not a good way to impress people. But eventually he decided to talk, and the ensuing excitement was so great that the prison warden scheduled a press conference for the Friday before the election. But before the press conference could occur, Kimberlin was tossed into solitary confinement on the orders of the Director of the Board of Prisons, J. Michael Quinlan. The press conference was canceled.

Kimberlin was released from solitary confinement the next day, but when he announced his plans to hold a telephone press conference, he was thrown back into the hole. On November 14, four days after the election, he was informed that the National Parole Commission had just added five more years to his sentence. He subsequently sued the government for violating his First Amendment rights, in a case that is still pending.

While all this was going on, a number of newspapers investigated Kimberlin's allegations and found them without foundation. When reporters asked Kimberlin for the names of people who could corroborate his story, the Speedway Bomber said he had told the story years earlier to James Lewis, the Tylenol extortionist. Hmm.

Kimberlin's charges resurfaced in 1991 when political satirist Garry Trudeau drew a two-week-long *Doonesbury* strip describing the prisoner's travails. What interested Trudeau was not so much the original allegations of drug use, as the lengths to which the White House—which had seemingly leaned on the Board of Prisons to ream Kimberlin—went to keep the prisoner under wraps. Moreover, Trudeau felt that the real threat posed by Kimberlin was not his claim to have sold Quayle marijuana but his charge that early in his Senate career, Quayle had been investigated for drug use by the DEA, and that a DEA file on Quayle did actually exist, even if nothing was in it. Trudeau accuses the White House of engaging in a politically motivated cover-up of the DEA investigation, and of treating Kimberlin as a political prisoner.

"I can't make the case that Kimberlin sold Quayle marijuana," says Trudeau. "What I can say is that there was a huge effort by the Bush people to keep the DEA story under wraps."

Quayle's office, predictably, went ballistic when the cartoons appeared late in the summer of 1991, raging that the charges had been thoroughly investigated three years earlier and found to be groundless. Numerous newspapers refused to run the strips, and some that did—including *The Philadelphia Inquirer*—did so only by printing a pious disclaimer above the strip: "Allegations that then-Sen. Dan Quayle purchased cocaine have been investigated by the DEA and news organizations, including *The Inquirer*, and found unsubstantiated. This sequence in *Doonesbury* is satire of this incident." Then *The Wall Street Journal* logged in with the truly heinous allegation—borrowed from *Entertainment Weekly*—that Trudeau did not draw his own cartoons, but had them drawn by a Kansas City artist named Don Carlton, and was thus guilty of premeditated Milli-Vannilyism. Imagine.

Trudeau finds all this fairly ridiculous. He still can't figure out why the government would go to such lengths to muzzle a convicted per-jurer, drug dealer, and fire bomber with serious credibility problems. He feels that slapping Kimberlin in solitary only strengthened the suspicion in the minds of Quayle's foes that there was merit in the charges. And he still thinks the press has missed the bigger story.

"What they've checked is whether or not Quayle used drugs, not what's in that DEA file," says Trudeau.

In the end, Trudeau seems to have been performing a public service: The DEA was forced, reluctantly, to admit that there was a file on Quayle, although it said there was nothing of substance in it. The rest of us will never know; its contents were revealed, in Trudeau's term, "selectively," to the *Indianapolis Star*. The *Star* is part of Quayle's grandpappy's empire.

As for Kimberlin, tough times seemed to lie ahead. "I'm getting screwed," he told me in a March 3, 1992, collect phone call from the Memphis, Tennessee, prison where he now finds himself. "I'm being held for purely political purposes." He adds, "I was just a little pot dealer." Brett, to use the single most popular cliché of the 1992 campaign season, just doesn't get it.

———

The big question remains: Does Quayle have a chance in 1996? It is a tough question to answer, though by this point, I realized that I had spent too much time talking to people from fancy Washington maga-zines and influential New York newspapers and well-regarded Tennes-see penitentiaries. I had spent too much time talking to the likes of Susan Estrich and Stephen Ambrose and Michael Kinsley, and had neglected the most valuable resource a reporter can have. I had made the cardinal mistake in journalism. *I had neglected to talk to the people.*

Talking to the people is the worst part of a journalist's job. The people dress badly, smoke stinky cigars, and force you to buy them drinks. They blame you for everything from Jesse Jackson's rise to Gary Hart's fall, and they don't want to give you their last names because the boss might find out. They own way too many Barbara Mandrell records, and they have hair growing everywhere. That's why I waited until the very last chapter to go out and talk to them. But sooner or later, I knew that moment of truth would arrive.

I decided to start off nice and easy, by blindly telephoning people who were obviously Democrats or obviously Republicans, and seeing what *they* thought about Quayle's chances in 1996. I decided to begin with a Democrat. I dialed Hot Wild Live Girls at a 900-number and asked "Lauren" if she'd given any thought to Quayle in '96. She hung up on me. Then I called Valley Pharmacy in Valley, Nebraska, and asked the owner what he made of Quayle in 1996.

"To tell you the truth, I hadn't thought about it," he replied.

"But I would have to assume that it's not inconceivable that you would vote for Dan Quayle in 1996?"

"That's right."

I next called Bad Bad Girls Live and asked "Michelle" if she was going to vote for Quayle. She hung up. So I called the Labrador Retriever Club in Boise, Idaho. The answering machine gave me a number in Tallahassee. When I dialed it I reached club secretary John W. McAssey. He told me that Dan Quayle and his wife were not yet members of the club "because no one has sponsored them."

"Would you vote for Dan Quayle in 1996?"

"You bet."

"So you think he's a credible candidate?"

"I sure do."

I was getting ready to hang up when McAssey added, "If you talk to him, tell him that I'd be happy to propose his name for membership."

"I'll do that."

Next I called an entrepreneur who had taken out this intriguing advertisement in a New York newspaper:

Vacation. My Massage Table. Scott.

I was pretty sure Scott was a Democrat, so I called to see how he thought the '96 election was likely to shape up.

"How did you get my number?" he inquired testily.

"It was in the Personals, right near 'Story of O—Live It!'—and 'Naturopathic Tongue Reader.' I'm looking for Democrats and I figured . . ."

"I'm going to start a session in about one minute," he replied tartly. "I can't talk to you right now."

Click.

One thing I found truly fascinating was that the obvious Republicans had no hesitation in talking about Quayle, whereas the subject seemed to make obvious Democrats nervous. I called pharmacists in Sioux Falls, Wichita, and Salinas, and they were all right there with Quayle in '96. But when I called an ostensibly Democratic number in the suburbs of Philadelphia, I immediately detected a certain frostiness.

"Who would vote for *him?*" demanded the proprietress of the Cross Dresser Service, which, according to its ads in *Philadelphia Magazine,* was "distinctly different from the rest," offering instruction in "Make-up Application, dressing-up, shopping outings and feminization lessons" for aspiring transvestites living on or near the Jewel of the Schuykill. The owner of this fine concern could not believe the nature of the call. "I just don't think that he's equal to the task of running the country," she said. "No one's going to vote for him."

Now I figured I should get the pulse of the criminal community, so I called Richard Nixon's office and tried to set up an interview. He never called back. Then I decided to check in with the imperceptibly charismatic Norwegian-American community, so I called Fritz Mondale's law office in Minneapolis. He never called back, either. I came very close to calling Jimmy Carter, but figured he was probably busy installing the plumbing in some Lower East Side tenement—*Carmelita! The man with those helicopters in Iran is here!*—and wouldn't want to be disturbed.

Since I was having so much trouble getting real-live ex-presidents and vice presidents to take my calls, I decided to track down some of the scores of less widely known third-party candidates who had run for the White House in recent years. I found their names in a book by Glenn Day called *Minor Presidential Candidates and Parties of 1988* that I had reviewed four years ago. Weren't they a richly variegated bunch! Roy James Clendenan of Parma, Ohio, had run on a platform demanding Internal Revenue Service audits of dentists and orthodontists, mandatory reduction in law school enrollment, and free deliveries of milk, flour, sugar, and tea to any American family with dependents at home. Clendenan also favored mandatory correspondence courses for doctors so that they would learn more about the side effects of drugs, and federal legislation compelling dentists to advertise the price of false teeth. Unfortunately for me, the orthodontophobic ex-candidate's number was unlisted. He was probably tired of taking calls from Phil Donahue.

Roger Lee Huddleston of Hot Springs, Arkansas, had run on a similar populist platform in '88. Huddleston was convinced that urban schoolchildren would be a whole lot safer if the federal government positioned gigantic blimps in the skies above our cities to make sure the kids got home safely from school each day. But that wasn't the half of Huddleston's message; he also felt that he could put his finger on the single moral failing most responsible for the decline of the United States in the last quarter of the twentieth century.

Pettifoggery.

"Pettifoggery seems to be prevalent in this country," the Hot Springs candidate declared in *Minor Presidential Candidates*. "Action should be taken to insure against pettifoggery of image or vocal introduction to honest citizens and loyal subjects of this country, which concern the national defense, rather than a practice session for unleadership-like influences."

I tried to track down Clendenan and get his views on Quayle's chances in 1996, but the anti-pettifoggery candidate had dropped out of sight. So had many of the other picaresque candidates of 1988. Actually, one of the most interesting side effects of Dan Quayle's ascendancy has been to discourage many of the more colorful characters in American politics from seeking high national office. For example, in 1988 Harold Lawrence Poland, of Alexandria, Virginia, ran for the White House on the ticket of the Christian-Charity-Federalist Independent Democratic Party. At the time, Poland was campaigning on a platform that, according to Day's book, would support "the complete elimination of money so that people could get what they want without having to worry about paying for it."

Since Poland's platform was virtually identical to that of every Democratic presidential candidate since George McGovern, it was not entirely surprising that he had polled so few votes. But Poland had also inserted a plank in his platform declaring: "Everybody would work except the elderly, handicapped and children. If they didn't, they would go to jail."

Since this sounded an awful lot like Dan Quayle's position on workfare, I decided to phone Poland and see what he thought of the job the vice president had been doing. But when I dialed chez Poland, he refused to come to the phone.

"He's not running this year," said a woman I took to be his daughter-in-law. "He's not interested."

"But surely as a previous candidate for the highest office in the land, he'd be interested in commenting upon the job that the current vice president's doing."

She vanished for a second, then came back on the phone.

"He's busy right now. Call back later."

Other candidates were simply impossible to track down. For example, Michael J. Frei, of Oscoda, Michigan, had made a run for the White House in 1988 under the banner "Get Straight by '88," claiming to have been run out of the air force by a cabal of gay aviators. But when I tried to contact him in 1992, his phone had been disconnected. (Citizens daring enough to challenge the dark forces of the gay aviation community have to keep on the move.)

One candidate who had not been discouraged by his 1988 electoral experiences was Kip Lee of Redding, California. In 1988, Lee ran on a platform that would have eliminated the monetary system and replaced it with a global barter setup. In order to ensure the success of this system, Lee had vowed to eliminate the hated Trilateral Commission and the equally sinister Council on Foreign Relations. And it goes without saying that he would have also invited extraterrestrials to appear in a special session before Congress.

"What we know as UFOs are real people from other planets," Lee told Day. "They have a high love for this planet and its inhabitants. They are called the Ashtar Command, and they want us back in their Alliance."

When I phoned Lee early in 1992, he was already busily preparing his 1992 presidential campaign. Again, the Trilateral Commission and cheerful extraterrestrials would figure heavily in his platform, but this time he wouldn't have to worry about being upstaged by Pat Robertson.

"I want all space people to come down to the surface of this planet and share the benefits of their technology with us," explained Lee. "For example, they can cure cancer."

I asked Lee what he thought of the job Dan Quayle had been doing since taking office in 1988.

"I don't think he's too well in touch with the people," said Lee. "*I think he's up there in the ether.*"

Much as I appreciated the input I was getting through transtelephonic intercourse with Them the People, I knew that the time had come to lace up my brogans and pound the pavement. What I had in mind was gumshoeing a locality where I could really tap into the primal feelings of the American people. Here in New York, we get such a skewed view of things, and sometimes it takes a real jolt to shake us out of our complacency. Just look at our attitude toward popular music. In 1991, a new computerized record-scanning system dreamed up by a company called Soundscan was installed in record stores. Under the old system, *Billboard* magazine simply asked record store employees what was selling, a system that encouraged immensely subjective remarks, not to mention bribery by record companies. But the Soundscan system simply measures store sales. The week after the system was introduced, *Billboard* stunned the record world with its demographically riveting findings. Overnight, culturally elite people like me who thought they were living in a country dominated by Metallica and Madonna and Mötley Crüe woke up and found out that we were living in a country dominated by people named Garth and Reba. Garth and Reba were Dan Quayle's kind of people, and it was my duty to go out and talk to them.

But I wanted to do it on my own terms. I didn't want to visit Appalachia and end up like Ned Beatty in *Deliverance*. And I ruled out Mount Rushmore because it was fourteen degrees below zero out there in South Dakota. The Alamo was a nice, middle-American place, but I generally try to stay out of states where desperate loners kill twenty-two people at a time. Disney World was too obvious; Niagara Falls was still in New York; and the Washington Monument, even though it was a quintessentially middle-American shrine, was still inside the Beltway.

And then it hit me. There was one place in the United States that fulfilled all my criteria, one locale that was conservative, middle-American, and packed to the rafters with people of the Garthic and Rebaish persuasion. It was a place that had anointed every single president of the United States going all the way back to 1952, a place that had emerged as a mysterious bellwether of American politics over the years, a sacred hearth in the chimney of democracy that every four years lit a small but powerful fire under the Franklin Furnace of our civic aspirations. It was the birthplace of the perpetually loaded Franklin Pierce and the freeloading John Sununu, not to mention Horace Greeley, whoever he was. It was New Hampshire, the Granite State, where people lived free or they died.

It was time to head north to Manchester.

New Hampshire was not always the perfectly calibrated bellwether of American political sentiment that it is today. When James Monroe beat John Quincy Adams in 1820, 231 members of the Electoral College voted for Monroe. The one guy who voted for Adams came from New Hampshire.

The easiest way to get from New York to New Hampshire is to drive northeast across Connecticut and Massachusetts. Massachusetts is the state that sent Gerry Studds to Congress, and then, after it was revealed that he had slept with an underaged male page, sent him back over and over again in a series of landslides. Massachusetts is the state where Mary Jo Kopechne died. Massachusetts is the state that sent Barney Frank to Congress, and then, after it was revealed that he had let his roommate operate a house of prostitution out of his townhouse, sent him back in a landslide. Emboldened by this, Frank went out and wrote a book called *Speaking Frankly: What's Wrong with the Democrats and How to Fix It.* I don't blame Frank for his writing, Kennedy for his driving, or Studds for his socializing. But the whole time we were in Massachusetts, my wife and I never let the kids out of our sight. Sure, Gord's only five and Bridget's only eight—but *you can never be too careful.*

We arrived in Manchester, the state's largest city, on a Thursday evening about three weeks after the New Hampshire primary. I had booked the suite Patrick Buchanan had occupied in the Holiday Inn a few weeks earlier because I wanted to bask in his evanescent aura of near-greatness, to warm the cockles of my heart in the fading embers from the penumbra of the outer recesses of the nether cheeks of the last onion ring of borderline celebrity that Buchanan had enjoyed during his glory days in New Hampshire. As I sat, in the same chair Buchanan had so recently sat in, gazing out at the bargain-basement skyline, I felt a wave of powerful emotions sweep over me. I felt proud to be an American. I felt at one with my neighbors to the north. I felt that their fight was my fight, that their dreams were my dreams. And I felt that, hey, maybe the Nazis had gotten a bad rap all these years, that maybe they'd only killed five million Jews . . .

Just then, the phone rang.

"Bob?"

"No, this isn't Bob."

"Is this Room 1102?"

"Yes, but it isn't Bob."

"Well, what's your name?"

"Joe."

"Joe? That's a nice name. What are you doing?"

"I'm listening to some music."

"Are you enjoying your music?"

"Yes. Who's Bob?"

"He's a friend of mine. He comes into town once every six months or so."

"What do you do for a living?"

"I'm a . . . legal secretary."

"Right."

"What do you do?"

"I'm a writer. I'm writing a book about politics. Did you vote for Pat Buchanan?"

"Yes. But I'm not for Buchanan. I'm really tired of all the bureaucracy and things in this country . . ."

"What's Bob look like?"

"He's about six-one, well-built. He dresses very conservatively, with long black sox and tassel loafers and a dressy shirt. What are you wearing right now?"

"Jockey shorts and a sweatshirt."

"Are you married?"

"Yes."

"For how long?"

"Sixteen years."

"That's a long time."

"It sure is. Is Bob married?"

"Bob is not married."

"What does he do?"

"He's in investments."

"Does he drive a Mercedes?"

"I don't know."

"Would you vote for Quayle in '96?"

"Are you serious?"

"Yeah, would you vote for Quayle in '96?"

"Well, I don't know too many people who would vote for Quayle. Look, I called a room where I thought I was going to talk to a man who was going to get me all excited . . ."

"You don't find talking about Dan Quayle exciting?"

Click.

Leslie the legal secretary called back on Friday night and Saturday night, still looking for Bob, or, if Bob was not available, me. But I had promises to keep. And miles to go before I . . . slept. Legal secretary. Good dresser. Code name Bob.

Made you think.

———

Manchester, like its foreboding English counterpart, is one of those unbelievably gray cities God seems to have created as a prop for smarmy politicians radiating false camaraderie with people they secretly despise. It is filled with badly dressed, badly groomed young men with Meatloaf hair and Allman Brothers sideburns who look like they were placed on this earth just so they could sit next to some millionaire's son for five minutes every four years and say:

"I'm fed up and I ain't gonna take it."

"I want to send Washington a message."

"You politicians just don't get it."

"I don't want no more sweet talk."

I walked into a diner on a side street the second day of my visit, and tried to strike up a conversation with a waiter. I explained that I was a journalist, the vanguard of the rest of the 1996 media legions, if you will.

"I'm here to cover the 1996 primaries," I explained. "Kind of early,

I'll grant you, but I'm here to check the pulse of the people, see if this recession is hitting them where they live. So I'll be coming in here mighty regular. Gosh, can you imagine how many cups of coffee I'll be drinking in here over the next four years?"

"No," he replied.

They're a sullen, unflappable lot, these New Hampshireans, not given to much small talk. I could see right off the bat that the news I bore—that media coverage of the 1996 primaries would be getting started almost four years in advance—left the personnel at Steve's Restaurant nonplussed, to say the least.

"I've come up early for the 1996 election to see how Dan Quayle's going to do," I explained to my waitress. "I'm the advance guard for the rest of the press. For the next four years, I'll be coming in here at least five times a day to ask your wizened, haggard patrons: 'Is this recession hitting you where you live? Are you ready to send Washington a message? Are you tired of sweet talk? Are you fed up with all these guys down in Congress who *just don't get it?*' "

She looked at me long and hard.

"Do you want to see a menu?"

———

Wandering around the highways and byways of this no-frills commonwealth, I came away with mixed feelings about Quayle's future. Folks I talked to in cafés, taverns, barber shops, and convenience stores pretty much gave me the same answer over and over again when I asked how they felt about Quayle in '96: "I hadn't really thought about it."

But I definitely got the feeling that the sun had set on Pat Buchanan's presidential aspirations, that his just-plain-folks candidacy wasn't fooling anyone. "He snapped his fingers at me twice when he wanted his check," said a friendly waitress at the Holiday Inn. "I'm a mother of two, a widow at age thirty, and I'm making $2.13 an hour. I don't need Pat Buchanan snapping his fingers at me."

A lot of people made similar comments; even those who had voted for Buchanan did so less because they liked him than because they wanted to stick it to George Bush. I had to feel that further down the road, the sunny, congenial Dan Quayle was going to be more to their liking. He didn't look like a finger-snapper. Marilyn, on the other hand . . .

Of course, the day of reckoning was still four years off. And if there was a groundswell of support for the vice president, it was a very tiny swell coming from very deep in the ground. The closest I could get to a ringing endorsement was from a gnarled man wearing a Merrimac Valley Security gimme hat: "At first people up here didn't like him, but now they think he's pretty good."

Then one afternoon I had an experience that made me change my mind. I was rummaging through an antique shop in Manchester when I happened to notice an attractive young woman in her late twenties modeling a funny hat.

"It makes me look like Minnie Pearl, doesn't it?" she asked, as our eyes met.

"Yes," I agreed, "but Minnie Pearl had a very successful career."

Eventually we started talking about the primary that had so recently ended. The woman expressed pique with the national media who "deliberately go out to parts of the state where the people are the products of incest, and have teeth coming out their eyes, and ask them if the recession is hurting them." Of course the recession is hurting those people, but these are people who still think Coolidge is in office. Then we got talking about the 1996 election. I told her I was working on a book about Dan Quayle, and thought he had a good chance of being president. I asked her if she would vote for him. She said she didn't know.

A few minutes later, I got into a bit of an argument with a couple of artsy-craftsy types who expressed that generic, wide-eyed terror at the thought of a Quayle candidacy that they learn from watching too many reruns of *The Parallax View*. While they were quaking in horror, the woman with the Minnie Pearl hat nudged past me and said, "Don't you think a lot of the things you read about him are exaggerated?" I said yes, they were, because the press hated him, and the press are a bunch of misshapen scoundrels and pricks. But I also said that it didn't help Quayle that he was one of the worst public speakers ever to occupy his office. She nodded. Then I asked her what she did for a living and she said, "I'm a graphic designer."

Coming from New York, I had never met a young Republican graphic designer before. Coming from New York, I had never met a young Republican before. So the information was a shock. But then I realized why New Hampshire is such a bellwether state. In New York and Los Angeles and Chicago and Philadelphia, everyone who works in the graphic arts is a Democrat, if not a communist. But out in the hinterland, there are all kinds of unusual Republicans: Republican painters, Republican ecologists, Republican graphic designers. And they didn't necessarily hate Dan Quayle. It wasn't the Rebas and Garths and Jebs that were the swing votes; it was the moderate Republican graphic designers. If you could lock up that moderate Republican graphic designer vote—which put you in the same ball-park as the moderate Republican day-care center manager vote—you had a shot. And I could see from the look in her eyes that given a choice between a Buchanan or a Bennett, or, further down the road, a Clinton or a Harkin or a Jerry Brown, Quayle had a shot at her vote.

———

After four days, we headed back to New York through Vermont, wanting to put as much distance between us and Teddy Kennedy and Barney Frank and Gerry Studds as possible. On the way, I couldn't help thinking of Lewis Lapham's remark that "a political system decays when large numbers of reasonable and high-minded people come to the conclusion that politics is beneath them." And I couldn't help thinking of Walter Russell Mead's comment: "For most of its history, the United States has not had outstanding leadership in its govern-ment, yet this lack did not prevent America's rise to power." I also started thinking about the separation of church and state. And, dog-gone it, for some reason I couldn't help thinking of John Adams's comment: "While all other sciences have advanced, government is at a stand; little better practiced now than three or four thousand years ago."

I don't know why, but that got me thinking about Republicans. As Mead points out in *Mortal Splendor*, except for flukes, Republicans have controlled the White House for 132 years. Between 1860 and 1912, the Democrats won just two elections, both by Grover Cleveland, the most conservative Democrat until Jimmy Carter. Special circum-stances—the collapse of Western civilization—brought FDR and Tru-man to power—but throughout the rest of that period, Democratic victories have been anomalies. Wilson won in 1912 because Teddy Roosevelt split the Republican vote; he was reelected because the world was at war. Carter won because of Watergate. Johnson won because of the reaction to Kennedy's assassination, and because he was running against an exceptionally pitiful Republican candidate.

As Mead notes, in normal, peacetime circumstances the Democrats have won only three elections on their own steam: Cleveland in 1888, Truman in 1948, and JFK in 1960. Truman had run against a guy with a silly mustache, and Kennedy's victory was tainted by all those ballot boxes that showed up at midnight in downstate Illinois. Basically, Republicans have a lock on the office, having held it since Lincoln. They can do what they want with it. And one of the things they can do with it is to select any vice president they damn well please. The best the Democrats can do is to cajole or trick or shame them into picking a manageable, tolerable sort like Rockefeller or Bush, rather than a liberal's nightmare like Nixon or Agnew or Quayle.

There is a silver lining in all this, though. Bad presidents, even really bad ones, can only do so much damage to the nation. For the most part, American history has not been written by politicians, but by inventors, businessmen, activists, artists, and religious leaders. A list of the most important Americans of the twentieth century would probably include such names as Henry Ford, Jonas Salk, Thomas Watson, Jackson Pollock, Muhammad Ali, Duke Ellington, George Gershwin, Martin Luther King, and maybe even Rosa Parks, but it would not include such names as William Howard Taft, Warren Harding, Herbert Hoover, Gerald Ford, or Jimmy Carter. Moreover, the nation has always been privileged to have at its beck and call dozens of great politicians who did not become president: Benjamin Franklin, Alexander Hamilton, John Jay, Daniel Webster, Henry Clay, John C. Calhoun, William Jennings Bryan, Robert LaFollette, Sam Rayburn, Everett Dirksen, and Hubert Humphrey.

"American democracy has always managed to find great leaders in times of great crisis," wrote the historians Allan Nevins and Henry Steele Commager. But in times of not-so-great crisis, we get guys like Bush, and, on more than one occasion, guys like Quayle. Sadly, the public's misconceptions about the history of the presidency is largely the fault of journalists. The journalism profession is dominated by people in their forties, people who grew up in the 1960s and who mistakenly assume that the sixties were a typical period in American history. But this is not true. The sixties were an uncharacteristically festive and uproarious decade. All kinds of things happened, and all kinds of people died, though, unfortunately, Neil Diamond was not one of them.

But most of American history hasn't been uproarious. Americans have gone out of their way to have as little history as possible; a creature arriving from another planet might even mistake this place for Canada. Nothing happened in America between the Age of Jackson and the Age of Lincoln; things just festered. There are no interesting presidents between Abraham Lincoln and Teddy Roosevelt. Nothing happened in America during the 1950s; Americans wanted it that way. So if Quayle should become president, it would not be out of character with American history. He would just be another forgettable chief executive in another era when the rest of us simply got on with our business, which is, for the most part, business.

Thinking these thoughts, I also came around to the view that Dan Quayle was dying for other people's sins. After all, one of his greatest assets to the Republican party is to serve as the point man, the flak-catcher, the lightning rod, the sitting duck who diverts attention away from all the other hopelessly unintelligent, underqualified people in the administration. Every single day of his life, Treasury Secretary Nicholas Brady must leap out of bed, fall to his knees, and thank his merciful saviour for having named Quayle the Designated Bozo. If Quayle wasn't the official punching bag, the Washington press corps would have to scurry around and look for another target, and Brady— never confused with Cardinal Richelieu—might be it.

Driving down Route 22 in New York, we spotted some deer at the side of the road up ahead. When the headlights of our van shone into their eyes, they *did* have that Dan-Quayle-trapped-in-the-headlights expression on their faces. But it was just that kind of sentiment that underscored the vice president's extraordinary value to his party. Think of all the numbskulls from whom his foibles divert attention. How about the Ayn Rand protégé who once dated Barbara Walters and who now runs the Federal Reserve? Or the Secretary of Education who hails from a state that for all intents and purposes doesn't have an educational system? Or the Secretary of the Interior who is an out-and-out moron? Or . . . well, never mind.

Bad as these characters are, Americans really ought to stop pretending that all this horrible stuff that happens in Washington is somebody else's fault. Americans have shown progressively less and less interest in education and the arts, so it is not entirely inappropriate that we have a badly educated, culturally marooned vice president. Conservatives can even argue that Quayle is Bork's revenge: *You don't care for our intelligent standard-bearers? Try Danny Quayle for a spell.* Indeed, Quayle's triumph over academic adversity sends a powerful message to the youth of America: It's okay if you screw up in school, because you can always get credit for life studies. In this sense, the vice presidency has become merely the latest makeup exam in the continuing education of Dan Quayle.

As we drove back to New York across Vermont, deliberately avoiding the state where Teddy Kennedy left a young girl and the presidency in a pond, I started thinking about his brothers. In the foreword to the Pulitzer Prize–winning book *Profiles in Courage*, which John Kennedy had somebody write for him, Bobby Kennedy had a few memorable words to say about his brother's thoughts on the Cuban missile crisis of 1962. The words written by Bobby—or by whoever was doing the writing for him—on December 18, 1963, less than a month after Jack's assassination, were:

> The one matter which really was of concern to him and truly had meaning and made that time much more fearful than it would otherwise have been was the specter of the death of the children of this country and around the world—the young people who had no part and knew nothing of the confrontation, but whose lives would be snuffed out like everyone else's. They would never have been given a chance to make a decision, to vote in an election, to run for office, to lead a revolution, to determine their own destinies.

Every American child alive during the 1962 Cuban missile crisis had long since come of voting age on the first Tuesday in November 1988. By a margin of roughly 55 percent to 45 percent, they voted against a liberal from Massachusetts and his oil-o-crat running mate from Texas, twenty-eight years after their parents had voted *for* a liberal from Massachusetts and an oil-o-crat from Texas. They voted for George

Bush and they voted for Dan Quayle. They had a chance to determine their own destinies, and they did. You can blame that one on Lee Atwater and Willie Horton, or you can blame it on Mike Dukakis and the tank photograph and the Democratic party, or you can blame it on the 50 percent of the electorate that doesn't bother to vote. But one person you can't blame it on is J. Danforth Quayle.